THE
POLAR
BEARS

FROM NORMANDY TO THE RELIEF OF HOLLAND WITH THE 49TH DIVISION

PATRICK DELAFORCE

CHANCELLOR
PRESS

First published in 1995 by Alan Sutton Publishing Ltd, an imprint of
Sutton Publishing Limited
Phoenix Mill · Thrupp · Stroud · Gloucestershire

This 1999 edition published by Chancellor Press,
an imprint of Bounty Books, a division of the
Octopus Publishing Group Ltd., 2–4 Heron Quays, London, E14 4JP

British Library Cataloguing in Publication Data
A catalogue record for this book is available from the British Library.

ISBN 0 75370 265 7

Typeset in 10/12 Plantin Light.
Typesetting and origination by
Sutton Publishing Limited.
Printed and bound in Great Britain by
Redwood Books Limited,
Trowbridge, Wiltshire.

CONTENTS

Acknowledgements

Dozens of veteran Polar Bears have been of great help in the production of this book. Brig. T. Hart Dyke DSO has permitted the use of extracts from his fine personal history of the Hallamshires, *Normandy to Arnhem*, Brig. Paul Crook CBE, DSO, once brigade major of 147th Brigade, has permitted the use of extracts from his memoirs, as has Lt.-Col. Godfrey Barker Harland MC extracts from his book, *Battlefield Tour*, and from a short history of the 1/4th KOYLI. Several people's journals have also helped to bring a very personal touch: Rex Flower's *An Infantryman's Saga*, Ken West's *An' it's called a Tam-o'-Shanter*, Bob Sheldrake's *The Uphill Road!* and John Lappin's personal diary.

Thank you to:

Edwin Anderson, Jack Bailey, Ken Baker, J. Barker, Maj. Edgar Bowring MC, Henk Bredewolf (Roosendaal), Thiery Chion, T.H. (Nobby) Clark, Harry Conn (Polar Bears' Association), Harry Cooke, Gordon Cowie, Bob Day, Stanley Dickinson, Maj. Ronald Dinnin, Islwyn Edmunds, Stan Faulconbridge, Bob Faxon, H. Fensome, R. Gough, Arthur Green, Percy Habershon, Roger Hardy, Fred Hoseason, Bill Hudson, Lt.-Col. Robert Hudson, Jack Lindley, John R. Longfield, Brian Lott, Arthur McMillan, George Marsden, John Mercer (*Mike Target*), R.A. (Dick) Newsum, H.J. Nicholls, Jack Oakley, Charles R. Pell (*Tigers Never Sleep*), Jim Preston, Graham Roe, Eric Rolls, John Russell, H. (Monty) Satchell, Tommy Short, Jack Snook, Geoffrey Steer, Les Sturmey, Harry Teale, T. Van Renterghem (Amsterdam), Tom Weller, George Wilkinson.

A special thank you to George Barker, who has so generously allowed me access to his distinguished father's diary and correspondence. Maj.-Gen. 'Bubbles' Barker DSO, MC (as he was then) has given the reader a very real look behind the scenes at the problems of 'managing' a great fighting division. Additionally thank you to Col. F.K. Hughes RAEC who has very kindly allowed me to quote from and use the excellent maps from his book, *A Short History of the 49th West Riding and Midland Infantry Division*.

Last, but certainly not least, thank you to Bill Ashby, for his dedicated research into the operations in Normandy where his father fought and was killed. His maps of Operation Martlet indicate so clearly the progress of that savage battle.

Photographs have come from many sources, including the Imperial War Museum, and delightful sketches by Michael Bayley.

Introduction

With its roots in the West Riding of Yorkshire, the British 49th Infantry Division were a territorial unit formed originally in 1907. They fought with distinction throughout the First World War, earning three Victoria Crosses. From 1940 to 1942 they took part in the ill-fated campaign in Norway and garrisoned Iceland for two years, which earned them the title and divisional insignia of the Polar Bear. During the north-West Europe campaign – from Normandy via Le Havre to the relief of Holland – the Polar Bears acted as Monty's left flank, often under the command of the Canadian Army. During their eleven months in combat they suffered 11,000 casualties and earned a fine Victoria Cross. Indeed, after the ferocious battles at Cristot, Fontenay and Rauray, the infamous Lord Haw-Haw christened the division the Polar Bear Butchers. By now they were a completely British division with units including the Durhams, the King's Own Yorkshire Light Infantry, the Lincolns, the Royal Scots Fusiliers, the Tyneside Scottish, the Kent Yeomanry, the Loyal Suffolk Hussars, 89th LAA (the Buffs) and the Royal Leicesters. In August 1944 the Polar Bears were joined by the South Wales Borderers, Gloucesters and Essex Regiment. For twenty months they were led by Maj.-Gen. Evelyn (Bubbles) Barker KCB, KBE, DSO, MC until 30 November 1944, when he was promoted to corps commander.

After the battle for Normandy the Polar Bears took a major role in the capture of Le Havre, campaigned vigorously in Belgium and Holland, and garrisoned the Island between Arnhem and Nijmegen during the winter of 1944. They captured Arnhem and advanced into north-west Holland to relieve Utrecht and Hilversum. The Recce Regiment pushed its armoured cars – first – into Amsterdam. In the last weeks of the war the Polar Bears brought food supplies into starving Holland. All of which amounts to a fine record.

This is the story of one of Monty's best infantry divisions told by the soldiers – privates, NCOs, junior officers and battalion commanders. Fortunately, Maj.-Gen. 'Bubbles' Barker's own views and comments on the campaign have also been included. This book is dedicated to the 1,500 or so young Polar Bears who were killed in action, in that traumatic and dangerous year, to free France, Belgium and, particularly, Holland from the Nazi terror.

If there are errors of name, rank, date or place they are mine alone.

CHAPTER ONE

Outbreak of War

Norwegian Campaign

The division was commanded in 1939 by Maj.-Gen. P.J. Mackesy CB, DSO, MC, whose divisional HQ was at Bedales. The 146th Brigade HQ was at Husthwaite, 147th Brigade HQ at Catterick and 148th Brigade HQ at Barnard Castle.

The divisional order of battle was as follows:
146th Brigade (HQ at Doncaster)
4th Lincolns (Lincoln, Spalding, Grantham, Boston and Stamford)
4th King's Own Yorkshire Light Infantry (Wakefield, Normanton, Dewsbury and Batley)
Hallamshire Battalion York and Lancaster Regiment (Sheffield)
69th Field Regiment RA (Leeds and Ilkley)
231st Field Company RE (Sheffield)
146th Field Ambulance (Leeds)

147th Brigade (HQ at Brighouse)
1/5th West Yorkshire Regiment (York, Harrogate, Tadcaster and Selby)
1/6th Duke of Wellingtons Regiment (Skipton, Barnoldswick, Bingley and Keighly)
1/7th Duke of Wellingtons Regiment (Milnsbridge, Upper Mill, Springhead, Slaithwaite and Mossley)
70th Field Regiment RA (Bradford, Halifax and Otley)
230th Field Company RE (Sheffield)
147th Field Ambulance (Sheffield)

148th Brigade (HQ at Nottingham)
1/5th Foresters (Derby, Ilkeston, Ripley and Church Gresley)
8th Foresters (Newark, Arnold, Mansfield and Worksop)
1/5th Leicesters (Loughborough, Ashby, Melton Mowbray, Leicester and Coalville)
71st Field Regiment RA (Sheffield)
229th Field Company RE (Sheffield)
137th Field Ambulance (Derby)

In December the 2nd South Wales Borderers joined the division and took the place of the 1/5th Foresters at Barnard Castle. Early in 1940 it was planned for the division to be sent to Finland via Norway as part of Avon Force. However, the Finns, vastly outnumbered, surrendered to the Russian armies on 12 March.

It has not been possible, because of lack of space, to do justice to the many naval battles which added fame and glory to the Senior Service in the subsequent campaign. This story is centred mainly on the six Polar Bear battalions which saw active service on the snow-clad Norwegian coasts and fjords.

Winston Churchill, First Lord of the Admiralty in overall charge of the naval operations, wrote before the ill-fated campaign started, as the expedition prepared to set sail for the Arctic Circle: 'They lacked aircraft, anti-aircraft guns, anti-tank guns, tanks, transport and training. The whole of Northern Norway was covered with snow to a depth which none of our soldiers had ever seen, felt or imagined. There were neither snowshoes nor skis – still less skiers. We must do our best.'

Thus began this 'ramshackle campaign'. A key policy agreed by all was 'no landings against defended locations'.

In the spring of 1940 Hitler overran Denmark and launched a savage attack on Norway. Winston Churchill, First Sea Lord, wrote:

> Surprise, ruthlessness and precision were the characteristics of the onslaught upon innocent and naked Norway. Nowhere did the initial landing forces exceed two thousand men. Seven army divisions were employed – three were used in the assault phase and four supported them through Oslo and Trondheim. 800 operational aircraft and 300 transport planes were the salient and vital feature of the design. Within 48 hours all the main ports of Norway were in the German grip.

German forces descended on Kristiansand, Stavanger and, to the north, on Bergen and Trondheim. Ten German destroyers, each carrying two hundred soldiers, supported by the *Scharnhorst* and *Gneisenau*, reached Narvik on 9 April. Oslo was taken despite gallant Norwegian defence by troop-carrying planes and by landings in the fjord. Churchill was determined to retake the northern ports. He wrote: 'We must seal up Bergen with a watchful minefield and concentrate on Narvik, for which long and severe fighting will be required.' The British Cabinet approved all possible measures (with the French government) for the rescue and defence of Narvik and Trondheim. Maj.-Gen. Mackesy was to command the expedition, and the first convoy sailed for Narvik on 12 April. For the major attack on Trondheim, Mauriceforce would attack from the north (Namsos) and Sickleforce from the south (Aandalsnes)

Two brigades of the 49th Division were involved: the 146th Brigade would land the 1/4th Lincolns and the 1/4th KOYLI at Bergen and the Hallamshires at Trondheim; the 148th Brigade would raid Stavanger and then join up with the 146th Brigade. The third brigade – 24th Guards Brigade – included the 2nd South Wales Borderers, part of the Polar Bear Division, and would land at Narvik. Each of the operations had a codename – Namsos was Operation Henry, Aalesund was Operation Primrose and

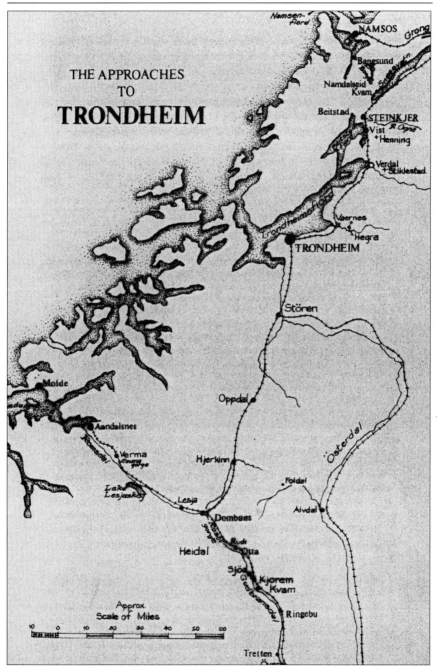

The Trondheim area.

The Narvik area, 14 April to 8 June 1940.

Namsos for Trondheim was Operation Maurice. It was a chaotic campaign with everyone on different wavelengths. The aggressive naval commander, Lord Cork, and the less forceful Gen. Mackesy had been issued with different and contradictory instructions. The 146th Brigade, bound for Namsos in the *Empress of Australia*, only had maps of Narvik, and the men of 148th Brigade were equipped with maps of Namsos, but were to land at Aandalsnes . . .

The Narvik Operation

The 2nd Battalion South Wales Borderers, commanded by Lt.-Col. P. Gottwaltz MC, sailed in the *Reina del Pacifico* on 12 April from Scapa Flow. The GOC with the 1st Scots Guards had sailed already in the cruiser *Southampton*. Gen. Mackesy intended to land his force – initially the 24th Guards Brigade – at Harstad on the Island of Hinnoy in the Lofotens. There, at a distance of 35 miles west of Narvik, he would reassemble his troops and equipment, and make a plan to recapture Narvik, now firmly in German hands. The first sea battle in the Narvik fjord took place on 10 April and the second battle three days later. In ferocious fighting the Royal Navy sank or beached ten enemy destroyers and many merchantmen.

The South Wales Borderers landed at Harstad on 15 April and occupied a large, very smelly, ramshackle fishmeal factory, which was standing on stilts above snow level. Then the GOC moved them to Ballangen, 18 miles south-west of Narvik, and the Irish Guards to Bogen, 10 miles north-west of Narvik. Ballangen was held by 750 fighting troops of 139th Carinthian Mountain Regiment, who had plenty of machine-guns, mortars, four mountain guns and 75 mm guns. Lord Cork now put pressure on Gen. Mackesy's troops to mount an immediate attack on Narvik, preceded by a bombardment from HMS *Warspite*, three cruisers and eight destroyers. This bombardment, on 24 April, had little effect, and a direct attack on the town was called off.

The South Wales Borderers moved 12 miles closer to Narvik on 29 April, to Skjomnes, 4 miles from Ankenes village. Their front extended along the mountains overlooking Narvik from the south-west. 'D' Company was fiercely attacked on 30 April, and Brig. Fraser, who was visiting the Borderers, was wounded. PSM R.F. Richards was awarded the DCM for rescuing the wounded men under heavy fire. The following day another strong attack came in on 'D' Company, whose CO, Capt. Charles Cox, called down point blank fire from HMS *Aurora*. He wrote: 'an amazing sight to see – a ship firing 4-inch shells at single Germans from point blank range. Among the enemy dead, wounded and prisoners, not a single officer or NCO was found.' The next day – 2 May – a German plane dropped fourteen HE bombs which caused eight casualties. CQMS Tom Flower wrote: 'We buried six of our dead and some German bodies in a communal grave about three feet deep in the frozen ground.' On 15 May the Polish Highland Brigade relieved the Borderers, who returned by boat to Harstad and then sailed in HMS *Effingham* 160 miles south to Bodo. Only 12 miles away from Bodo the cruiser struck a shoal at 23 knots and sank. There was no panic and there were no casualties, as their journey resumed on HMS *Echo* and then on the cruiser *Coventry*. However, the ten Bren gun carriers were lost, as were the field ambulance, other vehicles and ammunition.

On 13 May Lt.-Gen. C.J.E. Auchinleck replaced Gen. Mackesy, and the new brigadier reckoned that with reinforcements he could hold Bodo against 4,000 Germans advancing north from the Mo-Mosjean area. For a week the Borderers guarded Bodo Airport despite very heavy bombing on 27 May, which razed the wooden town and destroyed the Red Cross hospital. Soon, orders were given for Stockforce, commanded by Lt.-Col. Stockwell, to withdraw as part of Bodoforce, under the command of Brig. Gubbins. Evacuation from Bodo started on 29 May and the 1st Scots Guards and the Borderers remained as rear guards. In the Borderers' war diary, 31 May was described as 'probably the longest day most of us have experienced'. Maj. I.T. Evans commanded 'C' Company, and for two brave actions PSM 'Jarvie' Johnson was awarded the DCM. With the Scots Guards they were the last troops to be evacuated by destroyer, then by SS *Franconia* to the Harstad base on 31 May.

Namsos and Mauriceforce

The 146th Brigade – 2166 strong – was commanded by Brig. C.G. Phillips DSO, MC. The Hallamshires were commanded by Lt.-Col. C.G. Robins, the 1/4th KOYLI by Lt.-Col. W.S. Hibbert and the 1/4th Royal Lincolns by Lt.-Col. R.W. Newton, together with a section of the 55th Field Company, RE. Maj.-Gen. Carton de Wiart VC commanded Mauriceforce, which consisted of 6,000 men including three battalions of French Chasseurs Alpins. There was no artillery or air support, and little motor transport: no snowshoes or skis for the thick-lying snow.

On 16 and 17 April the 146th Brigade arrived at Namsos via Lillesjona, courtesy of the Royal Navy. Three days later they had marched to Grong, 20 miles east, and via Kvam to Steinkjer, a further 50 miles south-west, to link up with the Norwegians. The allied forces now numbered 4,000 French, 2,200 British and 2,000 Norwegians, and were destined to fight 5,000 Germans (Austrian mountain troops) – well trained, well armed and with air support – who were advancing north-eastwards from Trondheim. Behind the lines, Namsos was literally destroyed by air attack on the 20th, and in Steinkjer the brigade HQ was heavily bombed. The 4th Lincolns were heavily engaged at Vist and had to withdraw up the main road towards Steinkjer. Capt. Dick Newsum recalled:

> We travelled by train to Steinkjer at the head of the Trondheim fjord. On arrival we discovered how short of equipment we were, as much of it had been left behind in the UK due to our rather hurried and mismanaged departure. We had mortars and bombs but no sights, telephones but no exchanges, and absolutely no transport, not the best way to start a war.

Also the 1/4th KOYLI, who were on the Vist–Verdalsora road, had to fall back to Sparbu and Maere, and again, on the 22nd, to Fikness. As Maj. Godfrey Harland related:

> Hard pressed by the ruthlessly efficient and then victorious *Wehrmacht*, the Bn under Lt.-Col. Hibbert on receiving orders to withdraw broke off action and led his men through days and nights of hard marching through the snow to Namsos. Casualties had been very light [49 including 44 missing], the Bn embarked on troopships and despite the *Luftwaffe* arrived back in England having been away only a fortnight.

On the 22nd the Lincolns, under Lt.-Col. Newton, were engaged by *Luftwaffe* machine-guns on the fjord near Sparbu, by enemy destroyer fire from the fjord and enemy infantry in front. The last men out of Steinkjer had to swim the river, and all of the Lincolns' kit was left behind as the brigade extracted themselves to reform north of Beitstradfjord and Snaasavatn. The Lincolns suffered 72 casualties and 52 missing.

By 23 April – a black day for Gen. de Wiart's forces around Steinkjer – the extremely mobile German force, supported by dive bombers, light artillery and naval gunfire, had expelled the British from the Trondheimfjord area. Mauriceforce was now on the defensive, with 19

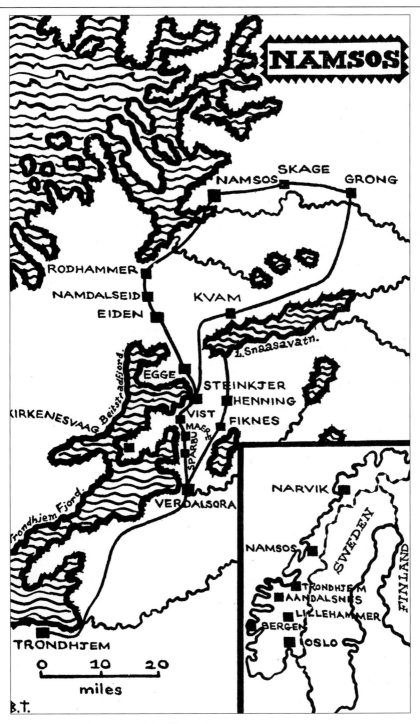

The Norwegian Campaign. (Brian Thexton)

killed, 42 wounded and 96 missing or captured. The Hallamshires were in reserve at Namdalseid and were relieved by the 13th Chasseurs. Before that, when they were in action at Beitstad, CMS Howden had won the MM. Then eventually evacuation orders were received on the 28th. The Lincolns and the Hallams embarked on HMS *Afridi* and the convoy disembarked in the Clyde on 8 May to re-form at Hawick. On the way home the *Afridi* was bombed and 93 men were killed, including 13 Hallams: the survivors transhipped to the destroyers *Griffin* and *Imperial*.

Aandalsnes and Sickleforce

The 148th Brigade, renamed Sickleforce under Brig. H. de R. Morgan, were to land in the Aandalsnes area 120 miles south-west of Trondheim, then take Dombas, 60 miles inland. Their orders from Gen. Ironsides were: 'When you have secured Dombas [key railway junction], you are to prevent the Germans from using the railway to reinforce Trondheim. . . . Make touch with the Norwegian GHQ in the Lillehammer area.' Their main objective, however, was Trondheim.

The 148th Brigade consisted of the 1/5th Royal Leicesters under Lt.-Col. C.T. German, the 1/8th Sherwood Foresters under Lt.-Col. T.A. Ford, the 168th LAA Battery and the 55th Field Company RE. After much muddle and confusion they sailed on 17 April from Rosyth in the cruisers *Curacao*, *Carlisle*, *Galatea* and *Arethusa*, and arrived safely on the 19th at Aandalsnes. Lt.-Col. F.K. Hughes' short history of the division noted: 'As a result of the confusion of loading, the change of plans and enemy bombing, Sickleforce landed with one lorry, three motor bicycles, four Bofors guns (with ships carpenters sights) and a dozen 'Shell Tourisme' motor maps (scale 16 miles to one inch!).'

The War Office orders were quite explicit. They said that from Dombas they were to: 'demonstrate northwards and take offensive action against the Germans in the Trondheim area.' However, the 2nd Norwegian Division commander, Gen. Ruge, stressed: 'concentrate every available man on the decisive front below Lillehammer [50 miles south-east of Dombas and 70 miles north of Oslo] until British reinforcements could redress the inferiority in numbers . . . Trondheim could wait for the major British assault by sea.'

Brig. Morgan's brigade was dependent on the Norwegians for transport communications, artillery support and maps, as well as rations, but he hoped to boost their dwindling morale. Accordingly, Morgan linked up with the Norwegians around Lillehammer on 20 April. A Norwegian colonel recalled: 'These were not regular troops, armed only with rifles and light machine guns. No A/A guns, no heavy A/Tk guns, no artillery, no vehicles . . .'.

The next three days brought unmitigated disaster. On 21 April, three German battalions under Gen. Pellengahr, supported by heavy mortars, tanks

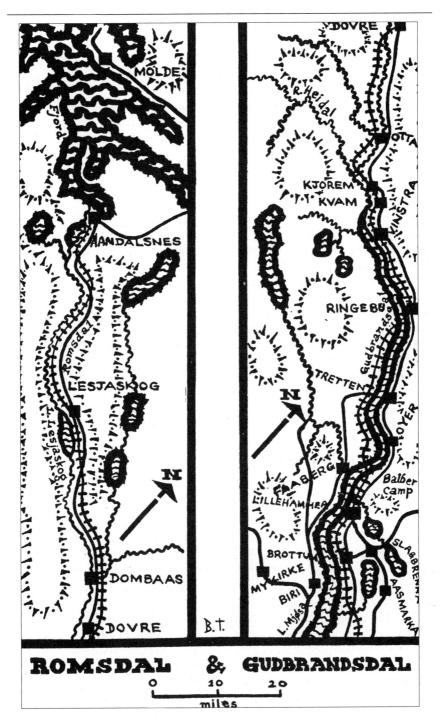

The Norwegian Campaign. (Brian Thexton)

and dive bombers, struck west and east of Lake Mjosa, and both the Leicesters and the Foresters suffered very heavy casualties at Asmarka and Lunderhogda. On foot (the Leicesters marched 14 miles through freezing night) or in open trucks the survivors regrouped at Balbergkamp, north of Lillehammer. More than a hundred men were captured and many LMGs and anti-tank weapons were lost. On 23 April the combined survivors, including Norwegian Dragoons and two companies of Leicesters who had just arrived, made a stand at Tolstad and Tretten, 19 miles north of Lillehammer. They were annihilated, captured or put to flight. It was a desperate battle, and the remains of 148th Brigade – 9 officers and 300 men – were evacuated by bus towards Kvam and Heidal. Despite the arrival at Aandalsnes of 15th Infantry Brigade (Green Howards, 1st KOYLI and 1st York and Lancaster) from France, 148th Brigade were back in Dombas by 26 April.

Gen. Paget's regular 15th Brigade put up a good fight and repulsed German assaults on Kvam, Kjorem and Otta. Walter Hingston in *Never Give Up* wrote:

> About 1 p.m. German tanks came into action in support of their infantry held up by 'B' and 'C' Companies of the York and Lancaster Regt, in front of the village. Corporal Stokes was in command of the third gun beside the road at the back of the village. With his first shot Stokes stopped the tank. His second burned it up and left it on the side of the road. There was a slight pause and then up from the dip waddled another tank. Stokes waited until it was alongside the first and 'killed' it with two shots in exactly the same way as the first. Round the bend came an armoured car and drove rapidly towards the destroyed tanks. Stokes waited until the car was just between the two tanks and then neatly knocked it out with one shot. That blocked the road completely.

Soldiers of the 2nd Bn, the South Wales Borderers, disembarking from SS *Franconia* at Greenock on 10 June following the final evacuation from Northern Norway.

In two days of fighting before Kvam, the Germans lost more than 50 men, 5 tanks and 3 armoured cars. Withdrawn to Kjorem, then Otta, the Germans again suffered heavy losses and the 15th Brigade held Dombas until 30 April. They suffered heavy casualties in 6 days – 30 officers and 850 other ranks. Now the *Luftwaffe* bombed Aandalesnes heavily almost around the clock, as well as Molde and Kristiansvad, and King Haakon VII and his government were evacuated on the cruiser *Glasgow*.

The whole of Sickleforce was evacuated on 30 April and 1 May. They had lost 1,402 men, and 148th Infantry Brigade never saw active service again. There were countless acts of heroism. The CO of the Leicesters' Mortar Platoon, PSM L. Sheppard, was awarded the DCM, and Lt.-Col. German, who was taken prisoner, received the DSO.

So ended what Winston Churchill described as a 'muddy waddle, backwards and forwards'. Adolf Hitler noted: 'The whole history of warfare teaches that carefully prepared operations usually succeed with relatively insignificant losses.' Lt.-Col. Hingston, who fought with the KOYLI at Namsos, wrote:

> The retreat of 146 Infantry Brigade to Namdalseidet is not a bright story in the history of the British Army. Indeed it is doubtful whether British troops have ever been forced to retire with so little effort on the part of the enemy. On the other hand it is also doubtful if a British force have ever before been asked to do so much with so little.

CHAPTER TWO

The Cold War

Occupation of Iceland – Alabaster Force

On 28 April 1940 Winston Churchill wrote: 'It seems indispensable that we have a base in Iceland for our flying boats and for oiling the ships on the Northern Patrol. Let a case be prepared for submission to the Foreign Office. The sooner we let the Icelanders know that this is what we require, the better.'

The 49th Division were now entrusted with the defence of Iceland. There were seven defended ports, and a naval base had to be established: later the mounting of coastal defence guns without cranes would prove an immense task.

Royal Marines landed initially on 10 May 1940, and the 147th Brigade, instead of sailing to reinforce the disastrous Norwegian expeditions, set off from Glasgow on 14 May. Brig. G. Lammie MC commanded the 1/6th and 1/7th Duke of Wellingtons and the 1/5th West Yorkshires, known collectively as Alabaster Force. Reykjavik, the capital of Iceland, was screened off by the 1/6th Duke of Wellingtons, the area south-west and south around Kaldadarnes, Sandskeid and Hafnafjordur by the 1/7th Duke of Wellingtons, and the area north-west of Reykjavik, Akranes and Brauterholt, by the 1/5th West Yorkshires.

Iceland is a large volcanic island of 40,000 square miles, with a population of 200,000. Glacier fields and ice-covered plateaux make it an inhospitable military base. The historian of the 294th Field Company RE wrote:

> We soon found ourselves in Greenock on board a ship bound for Iceland. We got there to find ourselves the only field company in an island bigger than Ireland, so immediately one platoon (or section as it was called then) was sent off to Seydisfordur on the east coast and another to Akureyri in the north, while the rest remained in Reykjavik. We erected camps, built pill-boxes along the coast, cleared away lava for airstrips, kept the roads (really only tracks) open for traffic and did the 1001 tasks that are always found for sappers as well as a certain amount of winter warfare and mountain training.

On 26 May the divisional HQ under the new GOC, Maj.-Gen. H.O. Curtis, arrived on the island with the 146th Brigade from Hawick. The 1/4th KOYLI sailed from Glasgow in HMS *Andes* on 23 June. They disembarked in two fjords, 50 miles apart, on the north coast near Akureyri and prepared defences against an unlikely German invasion. The battalion historian described the wild and fantastic scenery:

Apart from a small wooded area of stunted ten-foot high birch there are no trees on the island. Barren mountains, the highest covered in perpetual snow, tower over deep valleys and gorges. Flat pebbly plains, moors covered in heather, glaciers and vast fields of lava, almost impossible to cross even by a man on foot, make for a country that in the main is useless to man. There are geysers spouting boiling water at regular intervals and streams of running water, bright yellow in colour with sulphur and too hot to touch.

Rex Flower was a young reinforcement who soon joined the 1/4th KOYLI. He sailed on the 26,000 ton liner *Georgic*. He wrote: 'It was a luxury cruise, magnificent food, cabins and some boat drill. After the Clyde estuary the ship zig-zagged to avoid U-Boats.' Most of the 146th Brigade was on board. The Hallams and the 4th Lincolns were dropped off at Akureyri, the 1/4th KOYLI at Seydisfjordur, Reydarfiord and Eskifiordur. Flower arrived on 1 August, and it was still light at 2300 hours. The view was disheartening, with many wooden buildings having corrugated iron roofs. Posted to the 1/4th KOYLI, he underwent fatigues, training, more fatigues and lectures about frost bite. (It was 40 degrees below freezing point at Christmas.) The battalion trained its own specialists – storemen, sanitary men, a tailor, a cobbler – so Flower learned how to cook. Rats were the main enemy, and during the night they would eat everything faintly appealing. Flower was caught in a blizzard when eight men died, did guard duty on a lighthouse and persuaded the local fishermen to sell him their finest plaice.

In August the division newspaper, *The Midnight Sun*, appeared in print, as did the new divisional sign. The famous white polar bear was reproduced in his natural attitude – face lowered to look into a hole in the ice, preparing to grasp his next fishy meal. In October, Brig. Kirkup, who was commanding the 70th Brigade, which now replaced the 148th Brigade,

Budurerie, Iceland, 1941. (Rex Flower)

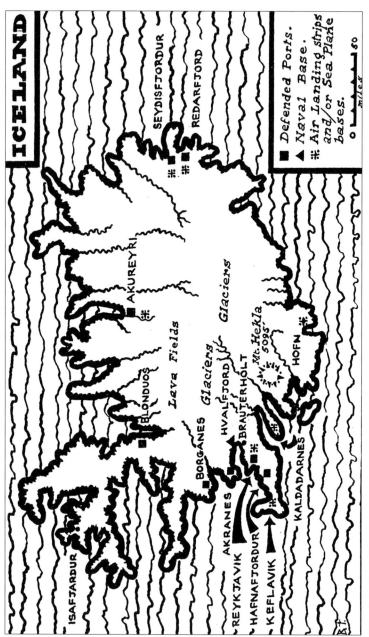

ICELAND

ISAFJARDUR

AKUREYRI ✳

BLONDUOS ■

Lava Fields

BORGANES ■

Glaciers

SEYDISFJORDUR ■ ✳
REDARFJORD ■ ✳

Glaciers

HVALFJORD

Glaciers

Mt. Hekla
5095'

BRAUTERHOLT

HOFN ✳

AKRANES

REYKJAVIK

HAFNAFJORDUR ✳

KEFLAVIK ✳

KALDADARNES ■

■	Defended Ports.
▲	Naval Base.
✳	Air Landing strips and/or Sea Plane bases.

0   *miles*   50

'The Cold War.' (Brian Thexton)

arrived with the 1st Tyneside Scots (originally the 12th Battalion Durham Light Infantry), and the 10th and 11th Battalions of the Durham Light Infantry backed by the 143rd Field Regiment RA, with their 25-pdr guns. Maj. E.R.H. Bowring wrote: '386 Bty remained near Reykjavik in support of 70 Bde. 388 Bty to the NW sector, Borganes, Blondos and Reykjaskoli. The third Bty 507 was formed in 1941. After 18 months of vigil we handed over to the Americans and returned to England in April 1942.'

Ronald Dinnin wrote:

I was commissioned into the 10th Bn DLI in July 1940 and soon found myself in Iceland. I was instructed by my CO (Lt-Col David Marley) to take a detachment of 50 troops to take up a Defence at the head of the Fjord in the NW area. We were then 100 miles from my company and 200 miles from my CO's HQ. Rather daunting for a newly commissioned 2nd lieutenant! Within a few weeks I received a visit from Field Marshal Lord Gort and spent an hour with him discussing the situation. Once we withstood a 10 day snow blizzard which left us with snowdrifts 80–100 feet high. Our cookhouse was lost and our electricity shut down, water supplies frozen solid. Those wonderful Icelandic ponies were out in the wilds all through the storm without any food.

Capt. A.P. Whitehead's history of the Tyneside Scottish is equally interesting:

The first night at anchor off Reykjavik is unforgettable – the starry brilliance of the northern sky, the countless lights of the capital [no blackout!]. When daylight dawned we saw utilitarian buildings of corrugated iron, the harbour works of massive construction, served by lighters. With a disconcertingly stony gaze the natives appeared to ignore our presence altogether. There were excellent modern shops and magnificent great shining American saloon taxis. Our camp at Baldurshagi was a primitive affair of Nissen huts on the banks of a fast flowing river offering the finest salmon fishing in Europe. Ambrose Walton and his Coy guarded the wireless station on the heights of Vatnsendi. Radio was of course the key to Icelandic communications. A platoon guarded the most important and biggest bridge at Selfoss and gave close support to the RAF airfield at Kjadadarnes, 25 miles distant. Our main disposition was as Iceland Force reserve with a mobile counter attack role in a practically roadless country.

Lt.-Col. Oxley, the CO, made Baldurshagi camp smart and 'redded up' by the immaculate TSM Williams, and roads were built by Ken Calderwood's team. As OC Roads, he remarked: 'The Romans never built a road like this!' The GOC next ordered the Tyneside Scottish to:

show the flag in the capital, with every available kilt fluttering in the keen Icelandic breeze. The pipes and drums immediately became the talk of the town. A set-piece brigade exercise took place in a snowbound valley about 15 miles away called Kleifarvatn, where an attack was carried out with field firing and full artillery support. The rumble of the guns was awe-inspiring in that desolate cleft in the hills. The crump of mortars and the whoosh and crack of 25-pdrs became as familiar to the troops as the feel of their own rifles. Vickers medium machine guns took part in all exercises. The infantrymen of the Polar Bears were accustomed to being 'shot over' long before battle schools became the fashion in the UK.

Robert Hudson, who commanded the 274th Battery, 69th Field Regiment RA, took five days after several unscheduled stops to take a vital piece of gunnery equipment (Apparatus Pulling Back) from Akureyri in the north to Reydarfjordur on the east coast – a distance of 200 miles. In October 1940, mountains of snow blocked his return route. He wrote:

We persuaded a Fleet Air Arm Walrus to drop us off in Seydis on a routine patrol and pick us up on their way back to Reydar. They were late back, the night was dark, the wind had changed and the fjord was very narrow with very steep cliffs. The two Petty Officer pilots made it at the third attempt. In the harbour at Reydar was a banana boat, home to a fortress unit of Royal Marines commanded by Col. Barclay-Grant which had mounted its last coast defence gun and was returning home in ballast via Akureyri, so we (my driver, my MT officer, four Driver/Mechs, one 8 cwt and two 15 cwt trucks) got a lift home – by sea.

Capt. Dick Newsum wrote:

The 4 Lincolns were sent to Iceland three weeks after our return from Norway, equipped with a load of mosquito nets. We lived in tents in the north of the island at Akureryi and later were supplied with 'do it yourself' kits of Nissen huts and built ourselves hutted camps for the winter. With only four hours of daylight, the first winter was boring with little time for training. Later on the troops took to ski-ing and winter conditions and became a very efficient mountain battalion. The Icelanders were sharply divided. Some were delighted to see us. Others were pro-German and couldn't stand the sight of us. In the spring of '42 we moved to Seydisfjord on the east coast used by the Navy for assembling Russian convoys. We built up a happy relationship with the RN.

At Christmas the Alabaster Force pantomime, *Snow White*, was put on with brilliant success in an old fish shed in Reykjavik. Bill Angus represented the Tyneside Scottish and George Paton was the impresario in the battalion concert party. Maj. Packard ran the Brigade Tactical School on real staff college lines, with lectures and TEWTs.

In the spring of 1941 the Tyneside Scottish exchanged with the 6th Dukes and moved into the town of Reykjavik. There were some amenities: Borg Hotel with its professional dance band for the officers; and the YMCA, NAAFI, TocH, a few civilian cafés and a couple of cinemas for the men. The Borg Hotel bandleader was an Englishman from Sunderland and his rendering of 'Blaydon Races' every evening persuaded many Icelanders that it was the

Budurerie, Iceland, 1941. (Rex Flower)

Intake platoon, Seydisfjordur, 1940. (Rex Flower)

Budurerie, Iceland, 1940. Front row, far left, Pete Bancroft; far right, Pte. Smith. Both were killed in action. (Rex Flower)

English National Anthem. Soon, 21 days' leave back to the UK was possible, with the roster fairly organized by ballot. Not a single leave party was disturbed by enemy action. The *Royal Ulsterman* and her sister ship bore charmed lives. In fact the only enemy action noted was a Heinkel that attacked the Tynesiders at Selfoss, inflicting two casualties on a platoon marching to Sunday church parade. A long-range Focke Wulff, also flying high on a Sunday morning, incurred every form of anti-aircraft fire, including an anti-tank rife.

Company route marches were organised to Thingvellir, near the shores of a vast inland sea, 36 miles away. Troops lived under canvas for a few days and 'engaged' in various schemes. Maj. McGregor and Capt. Chudleigh led their companies 'home' in a single day – an extraordinary feat over the non-existent Icelandic 'roads'. Many visitors were made welcome, including the new Prime Minister, Winston Churchill, on his way home from visiting President Roosevelt. Churchill suggested that the Polar Bears should train as a mountain division, and also as an Arctic division. Winter warfare training intensified during 1941 at the mountain and snow warfare school at Akureyri. Rex Flower of the 1/4th KOYLI remembered:

> Each company had a ski platoon training under Norwegian instructors. We had proper equipment, trousers, 'parkas' in white and drab, rucksacks, string vests, special boots, and snowshoes with a small ski attached. Everyone had to take part in the training. We had survival training in two man tents. We had to stay in them for 2 days with weapons, rations and a small stove.

Eventually the US government agreed to take over the garrisoning of the island. The US Marine Brigade of 4,000 men arrived in July. During December, the 70th Brigade left for Scotland; the 147th Brigade left in April 1942 and finally the 146th Brigade left in August 1942. As Capt. A.P. Whitehead wrote: 'Iceland had given us so much. More than anything it had forged a firm and abiding link between all who wore the Polar Bear.'

CHAPTER THREE

Waiting for the Balloon to Go Up

Arctic, Mountain or Assault Division?

On their return from Iceland the division spent much of 1942/3 in South Wales and on the Welsh border. The 146th Brigade, under Brig. N.P. Proctor MC, were in Hereford and Ross, the 147th Brigade were under Brig. E.R. Mahoney in Chepstow and Monmouthshire and the 70th Brigade were under Brig. P. Paulet King in Carmarthenshire.

Capt. A.P. Whitehead of the Tyneside Scottish wrote:

> Llanelly was the Battalion's 'second home'. We arrived there tired and dishevelled after an all-night journey from Gourock, the port of disembarkation, on Christmas morning 1941. The friendly citizens of 'Slash' [perhaps the Welsh double LL] took us to their hearts right away and practically every man enjoyed a splendid Christmas dinner in a Llanelly home that day. In due course there were many Tyneside Scottish–Llanelly matrimonial unions.

After three months the battalion moved to Crickhowell to train as mountain troops, and spent the spring of 1942 at Penrhyndeudraeth, high up in Snowdon country. Whitehead wrote:

> We enjoyed magnificent weather and climbed all over the North Wales mountains with the aid (or burden) of mules and pack-horses. It was not unusual to see a 'Jock' pulling a beast out of a bog while the Indian muleteer stood idly by, lost in contemplation of the infinite. The 2 i/c Major R.H.C. Drummond-Wolff was Master of the Horse and George Paton, ex Scots Greys, the riding instructor.

The Tynesiders then moved to Pembroke, and summer camp at Kington, Herefordshire, where Brig. Phil Kirkup left to be succeeded by Brig. P. Paulet King of the Gloucesters. The autumn was so cold and wet that bell tents were erected *inside* store tents. Whitehead again: 'With no heating and no light to speak of, life was rather miserable all round.' In November there was a move north to Barrow-in-Furness, and on New Year's Day 1943 they went back to Llanelly.

At the beginning of the war the Suffolk Yeomanry (founded in 1792) were based in Bury St Edmunds and Lowestoft. They trained and trained for four years as the anti-tank regiment of the Polar Bears. They had four batteries – 217th, 218th, 219th and 220th – each with three troops, 'A'–'C',

'D'–'F', 'G'–'I' and 'J'–'L', and were commanded by Lt.-Col. E.C. Bacon. Each battery had a troop equipped with towed 17-pdr guns, another with SP guns and the third with more modest 6-pdr guns. Each troop had about 32 men and was commanded by a junior officer with a troop sergeant as his second in command. R.D. Sheldrake was the troop sergeant of 'A' Troop in the 217th Battery. He wrote:

> Our four 17-pdrs retained a muzzle velocity of nearly 3000 ft per second right up to the moment of impact at say 800 yds. With its barrel over 20 ft long it was avoided by tanks whenever possible: just by being there we did our job in protecting the infantry from tank attack. In action the troop would be attached to a Bn, sometimes even down to an infantry company.

Under Lt.-Col. W.H.J. Montgomerie-Cunninghame, the 11th Battalion of the Royal Scots Fusiliers left the 76th Infantry Division to join the Polar Bears in Pennypont at Llandrindon in Wales on 7 September 1942. Then in the winter of the same year they moved to Chepstow, where cadres were formed for mountain training. Later, in 1943, the battalion went with other units to the west of Scotland in their 'beach assault' role, embarking and disembarking over the bows of landing craft at Rothesay and Inverary. Other towns and villages known to them were Lowesmuir, Watson, Irvine, Maybole, Drumclog, Stewarton and Saltcoats, and they visited Leith to practise street-fighting.

Maj. Godfrey Harland MC described the KOYLI's years of waiting and training:

> Back in England again the Bn was stationed at Ross-on-Wye and quickly began to 'catch up' with the latest methods of military training. Battle schools and all manner of courses for officers and NCOs gradually brought the Bn up to the standard of efficiency which was to be required of the soldiers who were to invade the 'Fortress of Europe'. The Arctic and Mountain roles were eventually abandoned and Lt.-Col. Walker devoted all his time and energy to training up the Bn which he was destined to lead later in the Normandy Bocage.

In the spring of 1943, Exercise Spartan, an Army exercise involving all of the Polar Bear units, lasted a fortnight and was intended to be a severe test. Ironically the 'enemy' was Gen. Macnaughton's Canadian Army, under which the Polar Bears later fought many of their battles in north-west Europe. Fitness was at a high level. Maj. W.L. McGregor marched his HQ company, the Tyneside Scottish, 50 miles around Llanelly in under 24 hours, which included a 3 hour halt at Dynevor Castle for a meal and a rest.

Brig.-Maj. Paul Crook, a talented swing musician and cricketer, wrote:

> I knew all about mules and malaria and they were expert in snow ploughs and frost bite. Once again I was to live in a tent in mid-Wales in a wet September [1943]. The Division, 49 West Riding was mainly composed of sturdy territorial soldiers from Yorkshire and as yet was very little changed after spending 18 months together in Iceland. My Brigade, 147 Infantry Brigade was made up of a Bn of the West Yorkshire Reg and two Bns of the Duke of Wellingtons Regt. I had friends in the artillery (143 Field Regt Kent Yeomanry) based on Maidstone, which is a great asset for an infantry brigade major. The Brigadier was a charming Irish Guardsman, Edmund Mahoney, an excellent infantry soldier with little interest in the capabilities of other units (anti-tank artillery, engineers, etc). The Staff Captain was John Driver of the DWR and the Signal Officer, Gus Wolff. The wretched Brigade Major endeavoured to communicate with Divison and the units in the group by

dashing from one wireless set to another – in the backs of vehicles parked around muddy farmyards or fields.

The new 49th Recce Regiment was formed up in Porthcawl under Lt.-Col. G.B. King, and in September 1942 the 5th West Yorkshire left the 147th Brigade and were replaced by the 11th Battalion Royal Scots Fusiliers. In the spring of 1943 the Polar Bears became part of the 1st Corps and were earmarked as an assault division for the invasion of Europe, and Maj.-Gen. E.H. Barker CBE, DSO, MC took over as GOC from Maj.-Gen. Curtis, who left to command Salisbury Plain District. A new GSO1 arrived, Lt.-Col. R.W. Jelf, to take over from Lt.-Col. A.E. Snow, who left to command the 115th Brigade.

The new GOC was a highly decorated First World War veteran with the DSO, MC and two mentions in dispatches, who fought with the KRRCs. He also served at Salonica, and like 'Bolo' Whistler, GOC of 3rd Division, in South Russia. His father was also a major-general, and in his obituary [*The Times* 25 November 1983] his nickname of 'Bubbles' aptly expressed his effervescent spirit and puckish sense of humour. When commanding a division he had a habit of doubling about at a speed which his staff found extremely trying to their legs and mind. In action the sight of his stocky, sturdy figure, often seen in the foremost positions, lifted the spirits of his troops. Before taking command of the 49th Division he had commanded a brigade in the withdrawal to Dunkirk, and then for two years led the 54th East Anglian Division in England.

Capt. Ken Baker of the 49th Recce Regiment recalled that:

General Barker came to the Division looking and speaking very much like Monty and determined that we should be thoroughly trained and fit to play a full part in the invasion of Europe. The GOC described the divisional emblem as 'a droopy timid-looking bear just like that one on those [Fox's] mints. I wanted a ferocious animal, with a snarl on its face.' This typified his own aggressive attitude, which he succeeded in instilling into all [sic] ranks of his command. He made full use of his recce regiment, more so than many other divisional commanders, employed in a wide variety of tasks.

Brig. Paul Crook's verdict was that Major-General Curtis along with a number of very worthy territorial officers was deemed to be a bit too elderly and nice to cope with the pace of active warfare. He was replaced by Major-General 'Bubbles' Barker, a very vigorous and efficient general who rapidly smartened us up considerably. A fire-eater, he was in some respects not unlike General Montgomery and so we were able to cope when Monty took over command of 21 Army Group and came to inspect us. For an awful period the Division was trained in snow-and-mountain warfare role amidst the Highlands of Scotland, but happily was changed to follow-up division for the invasion. Monty decreed that any CO over 40 should be replaced, so we lost two CO's in the Dukes.

Polar Bears hunt fish with their heads down to see and claw back their prey; they also lower their heads before charging. The GOC, 'Bubbles' Barker, evidently felt that the lowered head indicated a lack of martial intent. He wrote: 'That Bear is too submissive. I want a defiant sign for my division, lift its head up and make it roar.' So 16,000 soldiers, each with two battledresses and four divisional signs, were issued with new 'aggressive' signs.

'Nick' Nicholls of the 89th LAA Regiment (The Buffs) recalled: 'Our Battery tailor got fed up to the teeth with the sight of a Polar Bear. [And] our new CO, Lt-Col Bob Cory, ex Royal Horse Artillery, startled everyone

The unsatisfactory 'timid-looking' polar bear.

by introducing a daily 'stables hour' for vehicles and gun maintenance. You can imagine the ribald comments this caused.'

Maj. E.R.H. Bowring MC of the 143rd Field Regiment RA remembered: 'On our return from Iceland we spent the next fifteen months in or near Pontypridd in S. Wales, a town for which the regiment will always have a lasting affection and 386 Bty left and a new one, 190th was formed.'

Every Polar Bear had a 'home' town. The historian of the 294th Field Company RE wrote:

> We left Iceland and went to Wales. Our wanderings around Britain started then, more camps to be built, more exercises to take part in, more training bridges to be built until we arrived in Stourbridge. Training went on there too. The mention of the name Stourbridge will immediately recall pleasant memories to those who were there.

The Duke of Wellingtons moved initially into winter quarters at Chepstow racecourse, then in April 1943 to a hutted camp at Darvel in Ayrshire and finally to Ludham in Norfolk. The 1/6th were commanded by Lt.-Col. R.K. Exham MC and the 1/7th by Lt.-Col. Bishop, and by Lt.-Col. J.H.O. Wilsey for the invasion.

Scotland

To enable the Polar Bears to become an assault division, training in combined operations was essential, so in July 1943, with the 3rd British and

The new 'aggressive' polar bear.

the 50th Tyne Tees Divisions, they moved north to Scotland, mainly to Inverness and Rothesay.

Capt. A.P. Whitehead of the Tyneside Scottish wrote:

General Barker, soon to be known as 'Bubbles', was a demon for physical fitness and field training. Under his command the whole Division rapidly became a battle school. We entrained for Hamilton Park racecourse, Lanarkshire, where life became a busy round of special training and exercises – the 'real thing' for mock landing craft and loading tables figured prominently in the curriculum, not to mention co-operation with tanks. For the whole month of October [1943] we moved to Rothesay, Isle of Bute, where we did our 'wet bob' course with real LCAs and LCIs – a full scale programme, with live ammunition and explosives.

The Tynesiders had three COs in a year. Lt.-Col. Oxley left after three years to command a Durham Light Infantry battalion. Then Lt.-Col. 'Jim' Cassels, who had been Gen. Ritchie's chief staff officer in the 52nd Division, became the CO. Whitehead wrote: 'He brought the Bn up to absolute concert pitch, but he was whisked away after six months by General Ritchie, as Brigadier-General staff of 12 Corps. So Lt.-Col. R.W.M. de Winton, a Gordon Highlander, took command.'

The 1/4th KOYLI were based on Crief until December for their combined ops training, and the 143rd Field Regiment RA went to Newmilms, where they were converted from towed 25-pdrs to American 105 mms (Priests). Of course, a few months later they were reconverted and re-equipped with 25-pdrs. One of the first things the 294th Field Company RE had to do was to build mock-ups on a blasted heath near Muthill in Perthshire: replicas in wood and canvas of the German defences expected on the English Channel coast assault. Their historian wrote: 'At Rothesay we really did get wet getting out of real landing craft where we "landed on the Continent" under a hail of artillery and mortar fire where sections of sappers stormed canvas pill-boxes with platoons of infantry and where everybody went to bed at night completely worn out.'

Lt. 'Nick' Nicholls of the 89th LAA Regiment, who was BHQ subaltern, remembered that 'in Loch Lomond we carried out our vehicle waterproofing training'. Rex Flower recalled that the 1/4th KOYLI and the Hallams were camped on a racecourse near Blantyr and the 4th Lincolns were billeted in a huge hydro with its own grounds.

Lt.-Col. T. Hart Dyke joined his Hallamshire battalion at Inverary. He wrote: 'In almost continuous rain we learnt how to embark and disembark ourselves and our transport in landing craft and ships until we felt more like sailors than soldiers.' Company, battalion and brigade exercises followed. He recalled:

> Beaches had been skilfully made to resemble those on the northern coast of Europe with wire and blockhouses to be breached and blown with Bangalore Torpedo and Beehive charges. . . . Field firing inland of the beaches of Loch Fyne enabled us to carry out most realistic training . . . like other units we had our toll of accidents . . . when we went [later] into battle we were not unduly perturbed by the noise and danger of war. The beaches at Tignabruaich were most ingeniously constructed with mines, sea-walls, scaffolding and masses of barbed wire [the divisional sappers hard at work as usual]. We got to know our affiliated 444 Bty of the 69th Field Reg. RA under Harold Sykes, and our affiliated Engineer Platoon under the 'Wizard of 69th Field Coy'.

East Anglia

In January 1944 the division moved south to East Anglia with divisional HQ at Norwich, and now it joined the 30th Corps. Brig. A. Dunlop DSO of the Argyle and Sutherland Highlanders took over command of the 146th Brigade from Brig. Proctor, and Brig. E.C. Cooke-Collis of the Green Howards was the new CO of the 70th Brigade in place of Brig. King.

On their way south the Hallamshires, as senior Territorial Battalion of the York and Lancaster Regiment, took part in the Freedom of the City of Sheffield and had the proud privilege of marching through the city with fixed bayonets. Shortly afterwards they arrived at Hopton Camp near Great Yarmouth.

Having trained to be an arctic, then a mountain division, and then, more recently, an assault division skilled in combined operations, it was perhaps inevitable that this role would change. Monty wanted his old regular division

Sapper Bill Hudson, 757
Field Co. Royal Engineers,
1943.

– the 3rd British – and one of his favourite North African divisions – the
50th Tyne Tees/Northumbrian Division – to make the two crucial beach
assaults. Rex Flower expressed a typical view: 'Monty chose 50 Tyne Tees
to assault Gold Beach, 49th to our chagrin relegated to backup role.
Everybody was disappointed. We had been training for it for a year.' As Lt.-
Col. Hart Dyke wrote:

> The 49th were to follow up after the initial landings. Intensive training for our new role of
> 'Follow Up' division was carried out after Christmas [1943]. This included Field Firing with
> Tanks and Artillery, River Crossing Exercise, Road Movement and Night Operations. The
> Brigade Commanders arranged Brigade camps for the Signals, Snipers and Pioneers which
> paid handsome dividends later. During the last two months the MsT drivers were constantly
> practised in water-proofing vehicles and driving them through deep water.

Ronald Dinnin was Motor Transport Officer for 10th Durham Light
Infantry. He remembered how on one huge exercise the Durham Light
Infantry played its part as the 'enemy'. Lt.-Col. Peter Jeffrys, the CO,

> stole a march by literally marching the Bn through the night for 25 miles in 12 hours (7pm to
> 7am). The 'attacking' force just couldn't believe where the 'enemy' had disappeared to! The
> exercise lasted for three days and covered areas the size of Sicily. It gave the Canadian Army a first
> class example of tackling a large Army Force – their first experience of what war could be like.

49 Divisional HQ Staff. Back row, left to right: Vic Oliver (REME), Peter Piper (RAPC), Leslie Troupe (Defence Platoon), ? (RASC), ? (LO), Robson (REME), Pippin Cox (CAMP), Sidebotham (Signals), Germain (Padre), Bob Latham (RAOC), ?. Centre row: Bill Cramplin (G–3), Michael Jerome (G–3), Guy Whitcombe (Padre), Hugh Morgan (APM), ? (REME), David Patterson (DADMS), Nigel Parker (DAAG), Tom Coate (DAQMG), Arnold Woodcock (G–3 (I)), Dick Carrick (G–3 (L)), Marson (EDM), Englisant (IO), Frank Smart (SC (Q)). Front row: John Harrison (Umpire), Michael Barnes (ADOS), ? (CRASC), Pop Walker (ADMS), Geoffrey Brennan (A/Q), Dick Jelf (G–1), GOC, Buggins Brinker (CRA), Conway Gordon (Div Sigs), Ronnie Foster (CRE), Warhurst (GL), Scotty (G–2), J. Hall (ADC). (George Barker)

Two famous generals: 'Bubbles' Barker and Monty. (George Barker)

The Durham Light Infantry took their vehicle waterproofing very seriously. Dinnin recalled:

A special 60-foot-long drive-in Tank/Bath was constructed (open ended) with a ramp at both ends. All Divisional vehicles were involved and were compelled to make three consecutive runs. 10 DLI scored 99.9% successful points and later were asked to supply a team of Instructors to be loaned to other Divisional units who hadn't been successful and required more instruction.

Rex Flower noticed:

Our infantry organization changed. A new 'S' Company support [the 1/4th KOYLI] with mortars, anti-tank guns, carriers and assault pioneer platoons. Also we had a new 'battle drill' for defence and attack, the changes being necessary, gained from experience in the North African campaign. Our mortars now had a different base plate, a stronger barrel. The 10lb bomb now had a more powerful propellant with a range up to 2 miles. The mortar was now carried at the rear of an adapted Bren carrier, the engine down centre with space for three gunners to sit. In front sat the driver and Sgt. i/c. We carried 66 HE and smoke bombs as well as rifles, PIAT and its ammo.

Gen. Montgomery visited the Polar Bears in East Anglia. Lt.-Col. Hart Dyke recalled:

He took COs into his confidence and told us the general plan for the invasion of Europe. Gen. Barker then had a large scale model made of our area of operations and the various roles we might undertake were all thoroughly discussed at a Divisional Study Period at Norwich.

The 756th Field Company RE spent many months at Taverham near Drayton, and their historian recalled:

One Sunday morning General Barker gave us an address in the Odeon cinema along with the rest of 147 Brigade. He was both serious and humorous in his speech. We were going 'over there' to prove ourselves against the enemy. He was confident we would make a good show as we were a really efficient and reliable Division, having made quite a name for ourselves on the many exercises we had completed during our training period . . .. He warned us of Boche tricks and told us to make the Hun come to us and never go to him, when he was surrendering.

On a lighter note, he remembered: 'Who will easily forget the "Round Well" or the "Red Lion" where we repaired in the evenings of the hot days of May 1944 while England waited like an armed camp in the sultry haze with an air of hushed expectancy?"

Lt.-Col. Peter Barclay, the CO of the 4th Lincolns, had a sharp brush with Gen. Montgomery just before D-Day. Monty was inspecting the regiment and, as was his custom, ordered the battalion to break ranks and cluster round his jeep. Lt.-Col. Barclay refused to allow his ranks to be turned round to observe Monty at close quarters. He told the general that it was against the Lincolnshire tradition to face each other and was branded 'a very obstinate young man'. Much later Monty asked Barclay to write a pamphlet on the maintenance of morale, a request which he refused. Perhaps that was why this very able, brave soldier did not become a brigadier until several years after the war.

CHAPTER FOUR

Countdown and Channel Crossing

'Vengeance of the Gods'

The waiting was nearly over, as Maj. Godfrey Harland of the 1/4th KOYLI wrote:

> At last the days, the weeks, the months, the years of waiting were to end. All the training and the preparations were completed. The vehicles were waterproofed, the drill of the actual landing 'on the other side' was known backwards. Everything was ready. Every soldier sensed the dramatic significance of the enterprise in which he was about to take part. Like the men before Agincourt, like the men before Waterloo, like the men before Minden – the British infantry soldier was again about to make history.

In Lowestoft, Rex Flower recalled:

> We had a party in the Fighting Cocks public house with wives. We drank and sang songs and sandwiches were consumed. On the surface everyone was bright and jolly. The undercurrent was there alright. Heartbreak was only just around the corner for some. Sadly the carrier platoon [the 1/4 KOYLI] suffered heavy losses in the event. We had no illusions about being the infantry. [On 4 June] We travelled all night and as dawn broke we halted on Hampstead Heath for a while and had our rations. The whole army seemed to be converging on London. We arrived at a cleared bomb site in East Ham behind barbed wire. We were not allowed out!

Flower was No. 3 in the 3rd Detachment Mortar Platoon and was also the PIAT man.

On 2/3 June the 4th Lincolnshires moved from Kessingland in Suffolk, where they had been based for six months, south to a marshalling area near Lewes in Sussex. Their rifle companies had trained with bicycles to give greater mobility in the early stages of the 'follow-up' after the initial landing of the assault division [the 3rd British and the 50th Tyne/Tees]. Two rifle companies sailed from Newhaven in LSIs, and Capt. Dick Newsum of 'S' Company of the carrier platoon recalled: 'the tremendous generosity of the East Enders, wherever our convoy stopped people came out of their houses to give the troops tea and sandwiches as if rationing did not exist'.

This generosity was not, however, shared by the civilian London dockers, who 'at 5 p.m. with loading not finished packed up to go home. Fortunately the Merchant Navy took a different view and with their derricks loaded the vehicles much quicker than when the dockers were doing it.' That night Tommy Trinder was the star of the ENSA show that entertained many of the Polar Bears. Capt. Dick Newsum remembered: 'As the follow up Division we were scheduled to land on D+1 and the carrier and the mortar platoons were to make a dash for Villers Bocage where they were to relieve units of 7th Armoured Division.'

The Tyneside Scottish left Lowestoft for Thetford, where they were inspected by King George VI. Capt. A.P. Whitehead wrote: 'We were also chosen to co-operate in the first practical demonstration with the new 'top secret' armoured invasion weapons, 'flail' tanks [and many of Hobart's splendid 'Funnies'] watched by General Eisenhower and the CIGS, Lord Alanbrooke.'

Early on 7 June, marching troops went to Newhaven and the transport column to the West India Docks, London. Practically the whole of the enormous invasion force remarked on the efficiency of the transit camps, 'with excellent canteen facilities, entertainment, good feeding and good weather as well'. Lt.-Col. Hart Dyke wrote:

> these camps were very well organised and we were kept occupied with cinemas and singsongs and with the final administrative arrangements. The camp was very strictly 'sealed' with pickets. All the soldiers were briefed as to the place of landing and their role. Maps were issued and everyone received 200 French Francs (£1). Special ration packs, sea sickness tablets and bags were issued. At a memorable church parade our padre blessed our home-made Regimental Flag with a black background. Finally the stirring personal message from Monty our C-in-C was read out to all men.

Ken West was a gunner with the 274th Battery of the 185th Field Regiment RA, stationed in Sheringham. His troop commander, Capt. Thompson, briefed them shortly after D-Day:

> Well chaps, this is it! We are due to land on D+7, four days from now. We will go to the docks this afternoon and get on board our troop ships. When we get to France we will be taken ashore on Rhinos – large flat bottomed landing craft, like huge rafts. Our objective is to get as far forward as possible and take over from the assault troops of the 50th Division. The aim of 21st Army Group is to reach Mount Pincon – here it is on the map, some twenty miles inland. That is what we are heading for. That's about it. We've trained for a long time for this and now it has come!

West later noticed:

> in Plaistow the crowds of cheering East Enders. Flags flew in many windows, bunting was draped across bombed buildings, banners were stretched over the road bearing such messages as: 'Good luck – Tommy'; 'Down with Hitler'; 'Give them what they gave us'; 'God save the King'; 'God bless our lads'.

The 2nd Kensingtons (Princess Louise's), under their CO Lt.-Col. D.V.G. Brock, finally arrived at the East London Dock area. Jack Oakley, a stretcher-bearer, wrote:

> On 7th June we were granted 5 hours evening leave and I met my wife in the George at Wanstead. Next day we all marched out with full kit to the Victoria and Albert Dock. Our ship, an American liberty ship 'Fort Poplar', eventually anchored off Southend and joined a convoy near the Isle of Wight.

Lt. 'Nick' Nicholls of the 89th LAA, in their concentration area at Grays in Essex, said they saw: 'our first V1 (Doodlebug Buzz bomb) on its way to London. [Later] We were in a convoy of 22 ships in two lines astern, escorted by 4 destroyers and an MTB.'

Some of the 147th Brigade, including the 756th Field Company RE, the 2nd Kensingtons and the 55th Anti-tank Regiment RA, travelled on the SS *Fort Macpherson*. The sapper historian noted: 'Fortunately despite a few 'thick heads' as a result of the previous evening's festivities, there were no absentees. The ship was packed to the limit, however the cooks under Corporal Tom Phelps soon had the inevitable 'char' on the go and we sampled the 'compo' which was to be our staple diet for so long.'

When George Wilkinson, a Geordie with 'A' Company of the 11th Battalion Royal Scots Fusiliers, left the home base at Great Yarmouth bound for Southampton docks to board the troopship *Cheshire*, he recalled:

It was an unbelievable sight. I had a pick stuck in my web belt whilst others had spades in their small packs and some carried aluminium ladders and rolls of chicken wire. We were like a DIY gang going to a building site. We reckoned our landing would be during the night on to a possibly defended beach so we blackened our faces with burnt cork, but with the long delay we got down the scrambling nets on to the LCA in broad daylight looking like the Kentucky Minstrels.

For most of the Polar Bears the crossing was long, dreary, uneventful and even boring. In his book, *Mike Target*, Gunner Ken West recalled: 'During the next day or two we all sunbathed and read or played cards and smoked incessantly. We talked and grumbled and longed to get ashore and get on with the war. D+7 lengthened into D+9 and still we anchored offshore.' West read George Orwell's *Burmese Days*: 'Every night the *Luftwaffe* returned and we suffered the din and the nagging worry that a bomb might get us. Tempers became frayed.'

Sgt. R.D. Sheldrake of the 55th Suffolk Yeomanry Anti-tank Regiment described his 'team'. George Savage drove 'Flo' the ammunition truck portee. Lt. O. Martin was his troop commander, a 20-year-old Cornishman with a respectable sandy moustache, known as 'the Guvnor'. 'Wilco' Adams with his long, white face was the wireless set operator. Jimmy Todd was the short, tough reliable carrier driver. Bert Ennis was the 'Guvnor's' batman. The anti-aircraft gun was manned by 'Math', whose ginger hair in the quad roof hole showed he was the No. 1. The other three sergeants were Les Bulman, Norman Asher and Jas King.

On board their huge LVT ship *Derrycunihy*, wrote Bob Sheldrake:

there were 250 of us in the hold, one complete muddle of men, in hammocks and on the deck, reading and playing the fool, playing cards and Crown & Anchor. We fed in groups of 14, each with a 'compo' pack every 24 hours. This pack was a wood and cardboard box about 2ft x 1ft x 1ft containing everything 14 men could need for 24 hrs from tinned sausages and fruit to cigarettes, boiled sweets, even toilet paper – the army form blank, inevitably khaki in colour. The compo tea, a mixture of tea, sugar and dried milk, and the selfheating soup practically saved our lives. At 4 am June 15th Dave and I were landed on the beach at Arromanches: towing our gun we dashed up the beach with no time to marvel that we were in France.

Fusilier George Wilkinson (aged 18), 11 RSF, 49th Division, 1943. (George Wilkinson)

At 0300 hrs on 11 June a radio-controlled glider bomb struck the SS 'Fort Macpherson' in the starboard after cabin, wrecked a lifeboat and finally ended in the coal bunker, fortunately without exploding. Capt. Burdett and Corp. Jackson (who were later awarded the GM) rendered the fuse safe. The bomb was lifted up with a derrick and finally heaved overboard. The steering gear was damaged and the ship crippled, but eventually it anchored safely off the beach at Courseulles. It was possible that a 'slave' labourer in a Ruhr bomb factory had 'doctored' the fuse.

Lt. John Lappin of 'D' Company of the 7th Battalion Duke of Wellingtons wrote:

> Our little ship LCI had quite a record – took part in Anzio landing and took the Airborne boys over to this show on D+1 [presumably back-up and support troops]. On the return journey 'she' shot down a Junkers 88. We had all our rations on board for this trip and boy – what an orgy. It would have made any housewife green with envy. By the end of the trip we were giving away tins of salmon salad in mayonnaise, fruit pudding, canned beef and soup. The soup tins were ingenious. You applied a cigarette end to the special top and in five minutes – hey presto – a tin of hot soup.

The 7th Battalion with most of the 147th Brigade and its 333 light bicycles embarked on SS *Cheshire* at Southampton Docks on 10 June. They left Waterloo station from platform 14. On platform 15 a special race train was taking race-goers to Ascot.

The Tyneside Scottish arrived off the French coast between Le Hamel and La Rivière. Capt. A.P. Whitehead wrote:

> quite suddenly the sea seemed to teem with vessels of every description. All the various types of assault craft that we had seen at Rothesay were there, tugs towing over portions of 'Mulberry', freighters sunk offshore in lines to form a breakwater, Rhino ferries, tramps, warships, steamers, launches – hundreds of ships and boats covering the bay with the sandy, sun-bathed Normandy coast and lazy countryside rising mistily beyond . . .. Arriving about mid-day, at about 1500 hrs the craft nosed slowly into the beaches and the order came to disembark. The majority landed dry-shod but a few were unlucky and had to wade ashore through water up to the neck.

The Tynesiders and indeed most of the Polar Bear Division were safely ashore on the beaches of Normandy.

Jack Snook drove a 3 ton truck with HQ Platoon of the 118th Company RASC. He wrote:

> The SS *William Carson* nosed on to the beach, her ramp came down with a rattle of chains and within seconds the first Bedford was down the ramp and into the sea. My turn came and with the sea up to the windscreen I put my foot down and away I went, following the truck in front. We just went like crazy: the engines roaring their heads off, what a thrilling feeling, pulling out of the sea and up that beach. I shall never forget it. We joined a stream of vehicles pouring inland, trucks, guns, jeeps and motor cycles all under a cloud of red dust. There was barbed wire with *ACHTUNG MINEN* signs of Skull and Cross Bones all around us.

The landing craft with the 4th Lincolnshires aboard forced its way up the beach with terrific bumps over the sandbanks. Their CO, Lt.-Col. Barclay, congratulated the craft commander but did not stop to hear the latter's murmured reply: 'And now I've got to get the bloody thing off again.'

Rex Flower noticed: 'There were ships, ships everywhere. I had never seen so many gathered together in one place . . . mostly transports but interspersed among them were ships of the Royal Navy. Battleships, destroyers, cruisers all firing away at the enemy most of the time. It was a mighty, moving spectacle. Talk about the 'Vengeance of the Gods'.'

The General wrote home to his wife:

> 2 June. I have a first class party to go with – I am satisfied that my chaps are in as good, if not better shape, than any others. . .. It will be a grim business but what fun when we see the Boche start to crack. After all these years of waiting I wouldn't miss this for anything. 6 June. We have been two nights on board, now anchored off Southend. There is a mass of ships, its really a great sight. The Captain has very kindly handed over his cabin to me, and Buggins (the CRA) and Dick Jelf (GSO1) share the bed and I sleep on the couch under the window . . .. it is very boring being so far away from it all. 7 June. Our convoy of some 28 ships mixed American and Canadian Liberty ships – ours is Canadian built. News so far seems decidedly good especially that John Crocker's chaps are fighting in Caen. Some of the coastal villages have not been cleared up to late yesterday p.m. The Boche seems to have re-acted slower than I expected but his two Panzer Divs appear to be on the move. As I write a destroyer is putting down a smokescreen to screen us from the Boche gunners on the French coast. Its quite impossible to realise that we are going into battle.

CHAPTER FIVE

Arrival and First Action

'We'd Got Our First Blood'

The 1/4th KOYLI under Lt.-Col. 'Johnny' Walker was the first unit of the Polar Bears to go ashore, and it concentrated in Coulombes, seven miles inland from La Rivière. This was on the edge of the Normandy bocage country, which almost literally engulfed attacking infantry and armour. Each stone-built farmhouse and barn was a natural defensive position. The small fields and orchards were surrounded by thick hedgerows on earth banks three or four feet high with ditches on either side. For the sniper and anti-tank gun the bocage was ideal country. Undulating hills, steep-sided valleys, woods, thickets, occasional streams and open cornfields meant that every yard had to be fought for. The Germans had had four years to prepare their defences and the countryside now largely protected them from the allies' overwhelming strength in tanks and planes.

The 7th Battalion Duke of Wellingtons landed with folding bicycles from LCTs and LCMs. They wore battledress denim trousers, gym shoes and 'Mae Wests' with boots strung round the neck. Carrying full arms and equipment, and a 24 hour ration pack, by 1345 hours on 11 June they were ashore in shallow water on Jig-Green Beach, just west of Arromanches. They plodded inland on marked infantry tracks – sometimes cycling, most often pushing. Maj. Barry Kavanagh's 'D' Company was attacked by a lone enemy plane at hedge height. By 1600 hours, having travelled via Crepon and Creully, they were digging in at St Gabriel. On the way they were guided by French gendarmes and saw the RAF using fighter 'strips'. Capt. Pyrah's MT team of vehicles arrived without a single loss, due to efficient waterproofing. The Polar Bear divisional sign and '62', the 7th Duke's sign, were duly erected.

As divisional troops the 2nd Kensingtons rarely fought as a regiment. 'A' machine gun Company was allocated to the 146th Brigade, 'B' Company to the 147th Brigade and 'C' Company to the 70th Brigade. In the heavy mortar 'D' Company, the platoons – 12th, 13th, 14th and 15th – were spread across the divisional front facing the appropriate targets. Jack Oakley described the landing of 'A' Company HQ:

June 12th. Unloading began in earnest, the vehicles being winched up from below and deposited into the landing barge. First the cook's truck, then the water carrier followed by their personnel over the side in scrambling nets. Taffy Shaw, the cook, froze possibly due to vertigo, then it was my turn together with Chang Ling to join the water truck followed by Lurgy Smith, Harry Lonsdale, Dick Parker, all stretcher-bearers. It was disconcerting to see a wrecked DUKW on the beach, some British helmets scattered about and a German sign by the roadside 'Achtung Minen' in Gothic print, all of which deflated our former euphoria. Eventually we arrived at Cancagny and spent the night in a ditch. The next day we moved to Ducy Ste. Marguerite and I suspected 49 Div was being prepared for its first action.

The Hallams had problems. Their CO, Lt.-Col. Hart Dyke, had been told that a dry landing had been organized. He wrote: 'I was the first to go ashore and as I plunged (in battle dress) up to my waist in water, I cursed my gullibility! We then marched three miles inland to Rucqueville and shared a large field with the KOYLI and Lincolns. Meanwhile 'D' Coy under Major Peter Newton had been landed on the wrong beach.' Despite the pleasure of finding 3,000 eggs in a farm ready for despatch to Germany, worse was to come. All of the battalion transport had been delayed by the shortage of landing craft.

Hart Dyke wrote: 'The weighbills had now been lost and no one on the beach knew which craft our vehicles were in. Our support officers, John Brinton, Arthur Cowell and Leslie Gill and the MTO Colin Mackillop located and landed the vehicles quickly.'

Owing to bad weather, troops were still landing on Le Hamel beach on 12 June and divisional HQ was not ashore until the 14th. The division concentrated at Rucqueville in a bend of the River Seulles, south-west of Creully. When Lt. John Lappin landed at the end of the month to join the 7th Duke of Wellingtons, he noted:

Hundreds of balloons floating above the landings – a huge crowd of ships of all descriptions. The landing craft close in with the marines in their square nosed little LCMs running a taxi service back and forwards. The French coast looked quite English in character – flat beaches running up to meet low hills just inland [La Rivière]. Plenty of signs of battle here. Blasted buildings, a number of discarded Jerry respirators, a dud Bangalor torpedo and all the signs of an old fight [Ver-sur-Mer]. The people seem pretty grubby on the whole, but quite pleasant. I bid everyone '*Bon Soir*' and shout to a little girl '*Ici-chocolat*'.

On 12 and 13 June the Desert Rats – the 7th Armoured Division – made a determined dash for Villers-Bocage and received a bloody nose. Lt.-Gen. Bucknall, the corps commander, noted:

The two brigades of 49 Div could not prepare in time to be sent to Villers-Bocage to affect the fight there. [They were committed to the 50th Division sector north-east of Tilly-sur-Seulles on the night of 13 June.] They were destined in the Army plan in any event for the Fontenay front on the east flank of the Corps. Moreoover 49 was a young Div with no recent battle experience and it was important to launch them nicely into their first fighting in a properly co-ordinated battle and not bundle them down helter-skelter into hot armoured scrapping like that around V-B and Amaye.

So the 146th Brigade, now ready for action, relieved the 69th Brigade of the 50th Tyne Tees Division. The 1/4th KOYLI relieved the 7th Green Howards at Bronay (or Brolay) and quickly sent out two fighting patrols. The Polar Bears made their first kill 3½ miles north-east of Tilly. Rex Flower wrote:

We took over the mortar pits of the outgoing Green Howards – another famous Yorkshire Regt – got our mortars set up, ammo off and settled down. The countryside was beautiful, the sniping was not! Next day we fired our mortars for the first time 'in anger' at an enemy party spotted 'digging in'. We soon dispersed them and caused some casualties. We had got our first blood! It was here that the Bn took its first prisoners. A patrol led by Lt. N.L. Wilson captured two prisoners and killed and wounded others. The two sergeants involved were awarded the MM. They also won the two prizes promised from the Div GOC General Barker for the first German to be killed and for the first prisoners. Sadly Lt. later Capt. Wilson, 2 i/c 'C' Coy (awarded the MC) was mortally wounded later at 'Tessel Wood'.

John Longfield's 1/4th KOYLI platoon went on reconnaisance towards Le Hamel, crossed the railway bridge in single file and very soon came under Spandau fire. With his Bren gun, and aided by a Kensington's Vickers MM in a carrier, Longfield remembered:

we created enough havoc against the enemy to enable our platoon to get back out of the hot spot. Of course I did not see any Germans – just spotted the area where their fire was coming from. The general rule was that anyone who was seen – unless he was moving fast – was killed or wounded. A battlefield, large or small, generally looks pretty empty of men, except perhaps in a set piece attack – and then one does not see much of the defenders until one is right on top of them.

By Tuesday 13 June, on a fine and clear day, the 4th Lincolns were dug in around Coulombs, up to strength in manpower and with most of their vehicles. The following night they relieved the 6th East Yorkshires of the 50th Division at Tilly-sur-Seulles and St Pierre. Vigorous night patrolling took place around the hamlet of Les Hauts Vents and into Le Parc de Boislande, where Lt. H.D. Gaunt, second in command of the Anti-tank Platoon, was killed. Capt. Dick Newsum, who was in command of the carrier platoon, recalled:

We soon settled down in the wood, dug our slit trenches and made ourselves as comfortable as possible. . .. Apart from fairly regular shelling and mortaring life was a bit tedious. The worst thing was the dusk and dawn stand to. With the very short nights, dusk stand down was about 2300 hrs and dawn stand to at about 0200 hrs which meant very little sleep. Our CO liked to keep the officers on the go and shortage of sleep was my worst enemy. Fortunately the MO had a large supply of wakey wakey pills. Later, when I was wounded my first reaction was 'thank heaven, now I can get a decent kip!'

On 14 June the 70th Brigade, who were in reserve, were ready for action. The Durham Light Infantry historian wrote: 'The absence of any enemy activity was surprising. Indeed when on the 12th both battalions waded ashore armed like the complete tourist with Michelin guide books, francs and tins of boiled sweets, the war seemed far away.'

The march inland for about 6 miles was along narrow, dusty roads in blazing sunshine, and vehicles of all kinds from DUKWs to Air Force lorries streamed along them from the beaches. Ron Dinnin, the battalion transport officer, who had supervised closely the vehicle loading in a large cargo ship, was proud to report to the CO, Lt.-Col. 'Jumbo' Sanders: 'All present and correct, Sir!'

The Tyneside Scottish assembled at Esquay-sur-Seulles and moved inland on the 15th to Ducy-Ste-Marguerite, where in the battalion HQ, a charming old-time mill, 'war seemed very remote with Normandy Calvados and cider to sample, Camembert cheese to buy and letters to write home reporting safe arrival', wrote Capt. A.P. Whitehead.

Brig.-Maj. Paul Crook of the 147th Brigade recalled:

We hung around in the bridgehead for a bit and were subjected to a little bombing at night which I hated. I did not mind too much being shot at or shelled but hated bombing. The Intelligence Officer at 147 Brigade HQ was an important member of the team I had selected. He was very neat, painstaking and marked a map beautifully and played a 'boogy-woogy' piano superbly. Finally he was ostensibly more frightened then I was which was good for morale, mine if not his.

Gnr. Stanley Dickinson of the 274th Field Battery of the 185th Field Regiment was in HQ troop on D+10 and, he remembered, he was:

'occupied all morning digging and delivering 25 pdr ammunition to the gun positions. My little entrenching tool merely scratched at the stony soil as I tried to dig my slit trench. A loud bang overhead and I felt a violent blow on the inside of my left thigh. Charlie Stone and others gathered around when another overhead explosion came and a very sharp pain in my right shin with it. Now that one did hurt! I was carried out of that orchard on a stretcher and out of the Battle for Europe.'

Sgt. R.D. Sheldrake of the 55th Anti-tank Regiment had various adventures:

We had trouble with a French farmer who was determined to mow his meadow in the middle of which, neatly camouflaged, was Norman Asher's [17-pdr anti-tank] gun. Jimmy Todd was very keen to speak to the first Frenchman we had seen. After carefully learning to say 'Bonjour Monsieur' he tried it out. Overwhelmed at finding at last someone who could speak his language, the Frenchman flung his arms round Jimmy and began to talk at a furious rate, to the latter's embarassment and the amusement of everyone else – interrupted by enemy shelling the woods half a mile away.

However, five days later they watched the destruction of an RAF Spitfire. Sheldrake recalled: 'Hours afterwards the six of us Guv, Dave, Wilco, Bert, Jimmy and myself admitted that the experience had gone down deep.' The Suffolk Yeomanry's first shelling, the careful ranging by the German gunners, he continued:

the first 400 yards to the front and to the left of our wood, the next 100 yards closer and in a direct line – slit trenches had always been a nuisance inflicted on tired troops by officers – we watched the shells like giant footsteps marching diagonally across the fields towards us. When it was all over, we were a bit shaken but years wiser.

CHAPTER SIX

The Hallams' Action at Audrieu

Canadian Massacre

On 14 June Lt.-Col. Hart Dyke wrote: 'The first offensive role given to the battalion was the clearing of the enemy from the village of Audrieu [south-east of Ducy Ste-Marguerite], which ran north and south and stretched for about a mile along the future axis of the division.'

The woods to the east of the village were occupied by the enemy, so two companies plus the carrier platoon crossed the Bayeux–Caen railway line and later, after some initial deployment confusion, occupied Audrieu without a shot being fired. Frank Telt, an excellent platoon commander, although blind in one eye, was shot and killed by a sniper in the woods to the east of the village. This was their objective for the next day – the 15th – plus the wood clearance to the south of Audrieu and its château.

Despite the inability of brigade HQ (Brigadier Dunlop) to provide the essential artillery support 'Harold Sykes, our Gunner Battery [the 444th Battery of the 69th Field Regiment] succeeded in getting his CO 'Mimi' Crawford to make his Regiment available at 1930 hrs, which would just give us time for the task,' continued Hart Dyke. Patrols had assessed that the woods to the east and south were each defended by an enemy company.

Initially, 'A' Company, under Maj. Ivor Slater, would attack the château and clear the woods around, and then lend fire support to 'D' Company under Maj. Peter Newton, who would be tackling the eastern woods. With coordinated HE, smoke and artillery fire backed by Hallam mortars, both attacks went well. The enemy companies were lacking in strength and retreated, and the Hallams left standing patrols on both objectives, having themselves suffered few casualties: a Canloan officer, Lt. Noiseux, Capt. Dick Sandford and some other ranks killed or wounded. Hart Dyke continued:

I was very fully satisfied with the day's work. Both companies had shown excellent manoeuvrability, the plan proved flexible and the artillery and mortar support were first class. To dislodge the enemy's two weak companies from the orchard, banks and woods would otherwise have been no easy task. [The following day] I came across the bodies of fourteen soldiers of the Regina Rifles lying in a row in front of a hedge. They had obviously been stood up against the hedge of the château orchard and murdered. All had two or three shot holes in the forehead. They had been dead some days and I arranged for our Padre Thomas to bury them. The Canadian regiment had been stationed near my home in the Isle of Wight and I felt very bitter about this callous act. Local civilians reported that Russian soldiers in the German Army had done the deed. The château itself had been the scene of a desperate fight earlier on as dead bodies littered the stairs.

Cpl. Graham Roe, a signaller, of 'C' Company of the Hallamshires recalled:

the beach with its battered barb wire entanglements at Ver-sur-Mer, multiple jagged iron pieces with mines attached, pill-boxes, half destroyed vehicles, tanks, landing craft and DUKWS. We moved inland and saw several Sherman tanks being blown to pieces – until I saw them emerge from the smoke and flying bits, untouched. They had been blowing the waterproofing material off them with explosive charges already in position . . .. I had to go out into No Man's Land and repair cables cut by enemy mortar or shell fire. I used to lie on my back and repair the cable across my chest to present the smallest target to snipers. One sunny day, I found myself looking up into the muzzle of a rifle and saw the silhouette of two burly soldiers in field grey. The words of psalm 46 'God is my refuge and strength and a very present help in trouble' came into my thoughts. They were two Russians inducted into the *Wehrmacht,* who handed over a safe passage leaflet and then surrendered. Plucking up courage, I said '*Bleiben sie da*' and finished joining the cable. Then I marched them back into our lines.

CHAPTER SEVEN

Lincolns' Skirmish at St Pierre

Capt. Dick Newsum, OC of the carrier platoon, recalled how the London dockers were extremely difficult: 'Overtime was not part of their contract and off they went.' He found the same situation on arrival on the Normandy beaches: 'Gangs of Pioneer Corps came on board to do the unloading. We found to our cost that they were civilian dockers dressed in battledress and were no more helpful then their counterparts had been in the London docks.'

Once installed near some French farms short of electricity, Newsum arranged a barter of Army paraffin for Camembert cheese and wine: 'Officers attended the CO's 'O' Groups all armed with boxes of well ripened Camembert and teaspoons.' The main 'tea wallah' of the carrier platoon was a Thames bargee who 'possessed that profession's flowery language which he used when handing out the tea.' One early morning the CO arrived wanting a mug of tea and 'insisted in standing in the queue to get his own and also [unwittingly received] the usual flow of bargee comments!'.

During the morning of the 15th, Lt.-Col. Peter Barclay, CO of the 4th Lincolns, was ordered to reconnoitre the village of St Pierre, 2,000 yards south-east of Cristot and to the east of the Tilly–Fontenay road. If the enemy were not in occupation, they were to seize and hold the village until further orders. So a rifle company under Capt. J.O. Flint was ordered to carry out the recce with a carrier mortar group. Just before noon the village was entered and the main street was found to be blocked by a damaged British tank. So the carrier platoon divided into two groups, as Capt. Dick Newsum related:

After about a week in our wood we had our first taste of action. We were due to go on an armed reconnaissance near to the village of St Pierre and the carriers were ordered to provide a screen on their left. The operation got off to a bad start because my 2 i/c [Lt. Morley] in charge of the leading section took a wrong turn and motored into St Pierre which was held by the Germans, and promptly got put in the bag. The second carrier seeing what had happened tried to make a rapid about-turn whilst going over a bridge but went over the parapet into the river. The crew were OK but the carrier was wrecked. When I arrived we found the right turning and set ourselves to cover the left flank of D Coy. Quite soon I spotted German tanks in a wood about half a mile away. The next thing was a shell which exploded immediately above my carrier and it promptly 'brewed up' killing my driver and wounding my platoon sergeant. They then set about shooting at the other carriers so I decided to move away and jumped on the back of the gunners' carrier, collected the rest of the carriers and went to a safer place from where I radioed the Battalion and asked for the

RAF to send some Typhoons to deal with the tanks and they wasted no time in doing this. One of my men was missing for two days, returned, said he had been at the receiving end of the Typhoon attack. He was a cockney and had been through the Blitz on London but swore that nothing in the blitz was anything like as bad as that Typhoon attack.

Sgt. Hutchinson, Corp. Britten and Pte. Fish of 'A' Company brought back two of the damaged carriers, and later Capt. Newsum had to go back to the beach head to collect replacement carriers.

Just south of St Pierre on 17 June, Pte. Panter of the 11th Platoon of the Kensingtons celebrated his twenty-first birthday. In the morning he took part in a harassing shoot in support of the 10th Durham Light Infantry. On returning to the platoon area he found that the platoon cook had prepared a special tea in honour of the event and spread on a neatly laid table in a barn, but the birthday party was rudely interrupted by a nasty spell of *Nebelwerfer* mortaring.

It was now clear that St Pierre, although not held by the enemy in strength, was dominated by stronger forces in the large village of Fontenay, 2,000 yards to the east. The next day, the 16th, 'B' Company of the 4th Lincolns occupied Les Hauts Vents, halfway between Cristot and St Pierre, and patrols of the 10th Durham Light Infantry moved into St Pierre and occupied it on the 17th and 18th. Spr. Bill Hudson was a platoon wireless operator with the 757th Field Company RE and his CO was Lt. Little. He wrote:

We followed up and cleared the hamlet of St Pierre of mines and booby traps. Two medics came back to the halftrack. They wanted to move a wounded infantryman to the dressing station but he was lying close to a wounded German. They thought he was booby-trapped. The German was crying out '*Mutter, Mutter*' for his mother. His arm was sticking out and a wire was attached to his wrist. I quickly stood on his wired arm and kicked him in the mouth with my other foot. Army boots can make an awful mess. An 'S' mine, we called them 'Jack in the Box', was buried behind him – a pretty lethal weapon. He was a Hitler *Jugend* from the SS Panzer Lehr Division and was wired by a comrade as a martyr to the Fatherland.

The Polar Bears were finding out about the brutal aspects of war.

CHAPTER EIGHT

Infantry and Tank Cooperation

Despite many training exercises in the UK before Operation Overlord, infantry and tank cooperation in the field was, to put it politely, inconsistent.

Most infantrymen disliked the sight of their large 'friends'. They were noisy, smelly, tin-can monsters which nearly always attracted incoming fire, not only on themselves but also on the nearby infantry. The PBI (poor bloody infantry) made no bones about the fact that they would not have a 'tanky's' job for anything, and the reverse was also true.

At dusk, when inevitably the tanks withdrew to 'laager' a mile or two behind the sharp end, the infantry felt a sense of abandonment, but the tank crews need to refuel, re-arm, rest and have meals was paramount. Also they had to stretch their legs after being cooped up from dawn to dusk in their Sherman, Cromwell or Churchill. At night, tanks are blind and vulnerable, and more or less sitting targets for prowling Panzer Grenadiers equipped with Panzerfaust or hand grenades.

The three Armoured Divisions – the 11th (the Black Bull), the 7th (Desert Rats) and the Guards – with their own armoured and infantry brigades had formed close relationships in working together, and as a consequence they were formidable professional units. Very few infantry divisions in the British Army had permanent armoured support.

Martin Lindsay's history of the Sherwood Rangers recounted:

On the next day we were suddenly switched to the command of 49 Division. This was the horror of belonging to an independent armoured brigade: one changed hands from day to day like a library book. The Regiment would be flung into a battle at a moment's notice with infantry who had never had experience of co-operating with tanks. Then, as soon as the infantry had been taught to work with us and everyone was beginning to enjoy the benefit, we would be moved off to support a different, strange formation. This day's attack [15 June] was greeted by shelling which sent the infantry to ground: when they re-emerged they made no effort to contact the tanks again. It was all very disheartening and drove one officer to remark that 'all infantry brigadiers look the same: middle aged, rather grim, slow thinkers and without any sense of humour'.

There were also many first-hand accounts of the inability of infantry platoons or company commanders to contact their closed-down tank support. There was little they could do apart from clambering up on the monster and beating on it hard and noisily (usually during an incoming stonk). It often took a lot of time and effort to persuade the tank commander to open up and communicate. Of course, depending on the character of the commanders, good, sometimes excellent, interdependant relationships were formed.

Maj. Godfrey Harland, a company commander and historian of 1/4th KOYLI, wrote: 'No infantrymen could have wished for better tank support than that which was provided for us in the early Normandy battles by the skilled, courageous and dashing cavalrymen of the 24th Lancers in their Sherman tanks.'

Brig.-Maj. Paul Crook recalled: 'We had very good support from the tanks and their crews of the Sherwood Ranger Yeomanry who did their best but were no match for the German Tiger tanks, and infantry tank co-operation was not as good as it should have been in this difficult country.'

CHAPTER NINE

The KOYLI's Battle for Cristot

'World Seemed to End'

The little village of Cristot lies south-east of Audrieu with its château. A Hallams patrol had by mistake entered Cristot. Lt-Col Hart Dyke wrote: 'The patrol leader being ashamed of losing his way, never reported this fact to me. Consequently the 1/4th KOYLI were ordered to capture this village with naval fire support and that of the whole Divisional Artillery.'

The waging of war is always untidy and occasionally comical. To capture the village of Audrieu (discovered to be empty), the Hallams were officially denied artillery support. To capture Cristot, a village 'known' to be empty, a huge artillery plan was sanctioned.

The 1/4th KOYLI in Bronay had been relieved by the 11th Royal Scots Fusiliers and had moved to La Motte. John Longfield wrote:

As the days passed casualties mounted from small arms fire, mortars and artillery. Reinforcements came in to replace those who had left. Quite a few expressed the view 'I could not kill anyone'. When it came to the crunch I hope they changed their view. Even a fraction of a second's hesitation in deciding to pull the trigger can be fatal. Our first platoon officer disappeared after our first really hot action. Later on we had a Canadian platoon officer. He gave us a good morale raising pep talk but later on he vanished. The platoon was often commanded by a sergeant . . ... The day before the attack on Cristot an isolated shell landed smack on 'D' Company's position, killing and wounding several more – possibly one of our own.

Maj. Godfrey Harland, OC HQ Company, recounted:

After Bronay, my CO Johnnie Walker asked me to accompany him to meet Brigadier Andrew Dunlop at a grid reference in a little wood. This brilliant young commander who had won a DSO in the desert now looked pale and anxious. 'The Divisional Commander wants me to attack Cristot to-morrow. It's over there.' He pointed. 'I want your Bn [the 1/4th KOYLI] to do it.' The Bn attack on Cristot was successful thanks to massive artillery support and the matchless co-operation of 24 Lancers. A few days later Brigadier Dunlop was invalided home 'sick' and never returned. A sad loss. A great tragedy.

L/Cpl. Geoff Steer of 'B' Company recalled:

the village of Cristot had been bombed and shelled for two days prior to our attack. The sunken road from the start line to the village was littered with rotting horses and cows killed by our shelling. The church was used by the Germans as an OP and snipers were using it as well. Our officer told me to go in at the front of the church whilst he went in at the back. As we went in a burst of fire rang out in the vestry. He had shot the sniper. The first dead German killed since the landing. Cristot was a unhealthy place as the German gunners had got the range . . .. the support from the 24 Lancers was first class, their tanks were always at the forefront of the attack.

On 16 June, 'A' Company, under Maj. A.R. Keeping, on the right and 'B' Company, under Maj. A.B. Little, on the left led the assault, closely supported by Sherman tanks of 'B' Squadron of the 24th Lancers and the 55th Anti-tank Regiment guns. This first set-piece attack was backed by an immense fireplan of seven field and four medium regiments of artillery, while RAF fighters and fighter-bombers plus Royal Navy heavy guns attacked the village.

Capt. Lewis Keeble recalled:

I was 2 i/c of 'B' Coy. Tony Little [the Company CO] and I couldn't match the start line on the map with the ground. Walker, the CO, came up and was rather scornful about this, but he couldn't match them either. 'Oh well' he said, 'it's too late now.' And it was. Down it [the huge barrage] all came, a lot of it on the start line we had taken up. Tony had set off at H hour with the leading platoons but within a minute he had the Company doubling back. I wondered whether he would get them going again, but of course he did. The battalion were almost all quite new to battle. We were raw, if very thoroughly trained troops. Apart from the initial debacle, it was not a difficult attack but infantry-tank co-operation was a bit of a shambles.

'We took our position on a start line marked by white tape at about mid-day and the attack was made through a waist high corn field,' recalled John Longfield. His 'D' Company and 'C' Company were following up. He continued: 'I well remember passing an enormous unexploded naval gun shell. We were happy to get through the cornfield into the village.

Rex Flower of the mortar platoon wrote:

Before the attack we were told that 400 enemy infantry of 12 Panzer Division supported by SP guns, the usual mortars and some tanks were defending Cristot. Our officer detailed us (No. 3 detachment) to accompany 'A' Coy and advance behind a 'creeping' barrage. It was very close country, high hedges between the fields, small narrow lanes. The Padre was there and led us in a short prayer as we paused there in the sunshine. Nobody said much! It was a day for life, not death, I thought. It was about noon. Suddenly with a terrific crash and roar our guns opened up! I had never heard or seen anything like it. In front where the shells were bursting, nothing could be seen but a huge wall where the world seemed to end. 'A' Coy and the tanks moved off and a few seconds later it was our turn to go into what looked like bloody hell. Talk about Dante's Inferno. There were some casualties already. I could see rifles, stuck into the ground among the waist high corn to indicate a wounded man. [Later] I came face to face with the CO Colonel 'Johnny' Walker and another officer. I could hardly believe my eyes. What the hell was he doing here. He must have gone in with the foremost line. 'Who are you?' he barked. I came to attention. 'Mortars, sir, doing link with the carrier.' The CO said no more. Suddenly with a stupefying crash, enemy mortar bombs began exploding all over the field. Crash! one dropped nearby and the air hummed with splinters . . .. The stonk went on for about 15 minutes.

Leonard Willis, the historian of the 24th Lancers, recalled:

The plan was for the infantry 1/4 KOYLI of 146 Brigade to attack the area Cristot–Bouets, thought to contain some 400 enemy infantry, some SP guns with six tanks in the vicinity. The KOYLI advanced from Le Haut d'Audrieu on a front of 500 yards with two companies up. One troop of tanks of 'C' Sqn led each company with one troop behind the barrage with the tanks firing their machine-guns into all the hedges in front and to the flanks. Apart from a few snipers no opposition was met until about 500 yards short of Cristot, when some heavy mortar fire opened from the direction of the village. Observation was extremely difficult owing to smoke from our own barrage. 'C' Sqn fired HE into the village, and the church tower thought to contain an Observation Post. After 15 minutes the enemy mortar fire ceased and the infantry got into the western edge of the village. Two troops of tanks managed to cross a difficult anti-tank obstacle. The remaining tanks worked their way round the left flank. The wrecks of two SPs, one armoured car and two halftracks were found in the village. Close country with sunken roads and deep ditches made it difficult in getting tanks into good fire positions. At 1600 the KOYLI moved forward SE over a front of several hundred yards beyond the village. They then sent forward patrols to the high ground in front but no opposition was met.

Maj. Godfrey Harland recounted:

The village was a shambles after the barrage . . . the nightmarish crossroads which the Germans shelled so accurately and so repeatedly . . . the shattering sound and spectacle of the artillery bombardment as the soldiers of the two leading companies moved through the standing corn behind the creeping barrage supported by the tanks of the matchless 24th Lancers is an indelible memory in my own mind. In the village itself the consolidation phase was carried out successfully despite the inevitable shelling and mortaring by the Germans. By nightfall the Bn was re-organised and firm in its positions after its first major victory in the Normandy campaign.

Cristot was taken, with the mortars helping to break up the usual determined enemy counter-attack, for the loss of only three dead and 29 wounded. Then the KOYLI exploited as far as Le Hamel, a mile or so to the south, and at dusk on the 17th they were relieved by the 7th Duke of Wellingtons. In their first five days in action the KOYLI had suffered 66 casualties.

CHAPTER TEN

The Dukes Attack Le Parc de Boislande

Lt.-Col. R.K. Exham MC was now to lead the 6th Battalion Duke of Wellingtons into a disastrous two-day battle. The objective was Le Parc de Boislande, a thick wood 500 yards across west to east and 750 yards north to south, halfway between Cristot and Fontenay. There was a château in the centre, standing on the ridge overlooking Fontenay. Little was known of the enemy strength except that tanks had been reported in the park. The attack was to be supported by 'B' Squadron Shermans of the 24th Lancers, two troops of the 234th Anti-tank Battery, and 'C' Company of the Kensingtons with heavy mortars and machine-guns. A section of the 160th Field Ambulance was attached for this action. A fire plan was tied up with the divisional artillery and Lt.-Col. Exham met the 24th Lancers' squadron leader at the forming-up line in Les Haut Vents.

The countryside was very enclosed and visibility was limited. At dawn on 17 June a patrol of the Dukes under Lt. D.C. Smith was sent out into the park to contact the enemy. In spite of being deterred by a large number of enemy snipers they discovered a deep ditch about 300 yards from the start line, which an officer of the 24th Lancers decided was not an obstacle for his tanks.

The attack started at 1300 hours on the 17th, with 'A' Company on the right and 'B' Company on the left, each having a tank troop in support, and 'C' and 'D' in support on the right and left respectively. The remaining tanks were to move centrally and immediately to the rear of the forward companies. The artillery barrage, fired by four field regiments, was lifting 100 yards every three minutes, but in the bocage country the leading companies 'lost' the barrage and became separated from 'their' tanks.

Defensive fire by the enemy soon began to take its toll, and a number of snipers who had hidden until the tanks had passed began to open fire at short range. Very early on the radio link to companies had broken down, and the CO could only get information – and not much at that – from his tank support. Casualties were mounting and three of the carriers on the left flank were blown up on mines. Then suddenly, two hours after the start of the advance, 'A' Company's wireless came to life with the welcome news that they had reached their objective, and by 1600 hours the wood had been cleared of Germans and the Dukes were consolidating their position. About

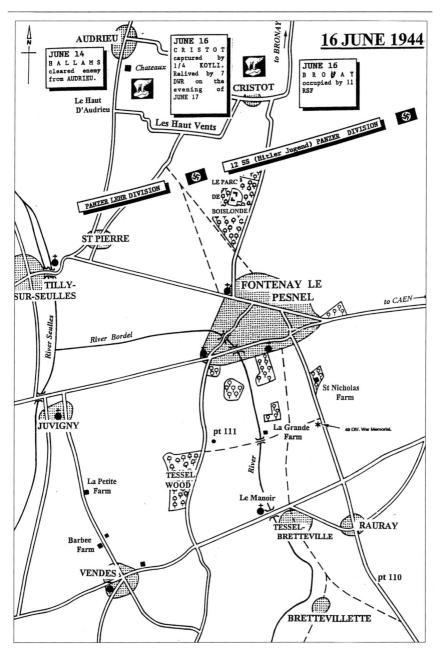

Fontenay Le Pesnel, 16 June 1944. (Bill Ashby)

30 men of the crack 12th Waffen SS Hitler *Jugend* Company had been captured and many more had been killed or wounded, but the Dukes had also suffered heavy casualties in the attack. Maj. K.W. McHarg, Lt. G.V. Parrier and some 50 other ranks had been killed, and Capt. J.G. Beckwith, Capt. G. Newsholme, Lt. J. Green, Lt. D.A. Gledhill, Lt. R. Henshall, Lt. J.K. Steele, Lt. H. Thompson and approximately 100 other ranks had been wounded.

Leonard Willis recounted how 'B' Squadron of the 24th Lancers fared:

> This wood [Le Parc de Boislande] which harboured tanks and infantry had caused us much trouble. At 2 pm the start line was crossed with two troops up and the attack went well except that Roy Bennett, the Squadron Leader, said that neither he nor the 2 i/c Ian Kerr, could see their own men and finished up leading the attack themselves. Not according to the book! Little opposition was met until reaching the actual objective when pockets of stiff enemy resistance were met. The tanks shot up well over 50 enemy infantry in a hedgerow. The left hand troops worked round to the forward edge of the objective, took up fire positions and fired HE at the enemy retreating over the skyline. On the right resistance was stiffer and the DOW had a heavy task in clearing the enemy out. At 4 pm in position by the château facing east two of our tanks were shot up by 88-mm guns. Trooper Ronald Quinn was killed, but Trooper Dansie was rescued by Corporal Carmoodie, commander of a nearby tank. At about 6 pm, five Tigers were reported on the right flank. Lt. Frank Fuller hit and brewed one up at 100 yards. Three more were shot up by our SP 17-pdrs. At 6.45 pm seven Tigers were reported on the left flank. Our own A/Tk guns had difficulty getting into position and two of our tanks were shot up with HE and Sgt. Sidney Norton was killed. By skilful manoeuvring of our tanks the enemy were prevented from entering the position. At last telescope light, 10 pm, 'C' Squadron arrived to take over and by 2 am 'B' Squadron were back at the rest camp at Hervieu. The next day 'C' Squadron were relieved by the Sherwood Rangers Yeomanry.

Although the position had been occupied there was little respite for the front line companies as continuous artillery and mortar fire deluged the area. A number of enemy snipers came to life in the thickest part of the woods and had to be eliminated. The only track to the rear was heavily mined and casualties took a long time getting back to the RAP. And the evening meal did not arrive punctually. At dusk the supporting tanks and anti-tank guns withdrew, but fortunately no counter-attack came in during the night. 'C' Squadron of the 24th Lancers now appeared to replace 'B' Squadron.

Inevitably the counter-attack did come in and the area was blanketed and saturated with heavy fire for four hours between 1000 and 1400 hours on the 18th. It was a prelude to a very heavy counter-attack of infantry supported by tanks. Lt.-Col. F.K. Hughes wrote in his short history of the 49th Division: 'The Dukes had dug in insufficiently during the night and were without adequate overhead cover. Many casualties were thus suffered from shells bursting in the tree-tops and then the enemy followed up with a quick raid on the foremost positions.'

Gradually, fighting every yard, the Dukes were forced back. A platoon of 'C' Company was isolated, then surrounded, but they fought their way out, although their officer was killed. A section of carriers who were dug in between the support companies did excellent work in holding up the enemy advance; they continued to resist when completely surrounded and perished to the last man. An officer with two sections of anti-tank guns hung on to the right flank and caused great destruction before running out of ammunition and having to retire. A private of the anti-tank detachment seized a PIAT, went forward alone and shot up a machine-gun nest, which was causing a lot of casualties. When he returned he remarked laconically to his officer: 'That's capped 'em.'

The two front companies had put up a most gallant resistance but had been overrun almost to a man. It must be said that the survivors, demoralized by the ferocity of the Hitler *Jugend* counter-attack, fell back in some disorder. Maj. R. Helme, Lt. D.C. Smith and 30 other ranks were killed, and Maj. M. Curran, Capt. K.E. Wright, Lt. D. Fraser and 30 other ranks were wounded. In two days of savage fighting, 16 officers and approximately 220 men had become casualties in their first major battle, and four tanks from the 24th Lancers had been destroyed and some of the crews killed.

The Dukes' regimental history noted rather sadly: 'There were almost more non-Dukes than Dukes left in the unit. Certain well-known regimental figures still remained – Captains Allan, Horsfall, Chadwick and Manning, Lieuts Turner and Parr, RQMS Fitter, CSMs Jackson, Miller and Forest, CQMS Calvert, Sgts Deaking and Ancill, and Cpls Kendrick and Spikings.'

There were losses too among the Sherwood Rangers Yeomanry. Their historian, Martin Lindsay, had little to say about the day's fighting:

> 49 Division were in action for the first time. On the 18th 'A' Squadron supported an infantry battalion [the 6th Duke of Wellingtons Regiment] in Le Parc de Boislande, north of Fontenay. The enemy greeted us with shelling and mortaring and the infantry abandoned the wood at top speed, leaving their transport and equipment behind. In the shelling Sgt. Bartle, a stalwart of the Recce troop, was killed and Lts Denis Elmore, John Bethel-Fox and Sergeants Rush and Harding were wounded. Sgt. Dring was spotting targets for the gunners. Major Peter Seleri came up on the wireless 'Surely you're wrong about the target – surely it is a cow? Over.' The reply was 'I've never seen a cow with a turret on it before. Off.

Lt.-Col. Hart Dyke, CO of the Hallams, was waiting north-west of Les Haut Vents to participate in the second phase – the advance on Fontenay. He wrote:

> Meanwhile things were not going well with the 6th Dukes. They had lost many men during their attack and the Boch then counter-attacked and drove all but one company out of the wood. Large numbers came through my battalion rather shaken from this terrible ordeal in their first action. I was very sorry for Roy Exham and his 2 i/c, both very good chaps and was glad to be able to offer them a nip of whisky, a cigarette and a snack before they reported back to their Brigadier [Mahoney]. Many of their men joined the 7th Dukes, who avenged this reverse the same evening and restored the position. I felt very relieved that we had never been launched to the attack on Fontenay. Norbert, one of our French Canadian officers, had discovered from civilians that Fontenay was strongly defended.

Gnr. John Mercer's book, *Mike Target*, recalled how their first regimental Mike target (the regiment's twenty-four 25-pdrs) in support of the Dukes was under 2,000 yards, and the range of the next had fallen to

1,500 yards. Soon, as the German counter-attack developed on the 18th, the order came:

'800 yards – open sights' . . .. Our gun crews prepared to fire their limited supplies of armour-piercing shells directly at enemy tanks as soon as they appeared. Some of our infantrymen ran through the orchard looking fearfully behind them. [But the enemy advance was halted and later] news came from the OP that what had happened earlier that day had been a heavy mortar bombardment by the Germans on the newly deployed Duke of Wellington's Regiment. The company that 'A' troop was attached to had been badly shaken by the accuracy and severity of the mortar fire and had suffered many casualties. When tanks and accompanying infantry of the Panzer Lehr Division moved forward behind the mortar attack many of the British infantry fled. Capt. Thomson and his carrier crew remained in position and brought down the fire of the Mike Targets until the attack was halted by our shell fire, our tanks and dug in anti-tank guns.

Another gunner regiment, the 143rd Field Regiment RA, fired many barrages to support the Dukes, and both of their observation post parties in Le Parc de Boislande were blown up on mines within a few minutes of each other.

George Marsden joined the 6th Dukes as a reinforcement. He recalled:

I joined the queue of 'A' Coy for a hot meal when a lone German spotter plane flew over. Shortly after there was tremendous and incessant shell and mortar fire that went on non-stop . . .. [Later] The enemy attacked and overran our positions. I finished up in an old bomb crater. The Dukes put up a terrific battle. Afterwards it looked like a World War One scene with bodies all over and trees and hedges blasted by the shelling. Immediately after the battle I was in a slit trench in a field with only about 20 men and one officer. He had to calm those who were shellshocked and were prone to jump out of their slits every time the spasmodic mortaring dropped close by. After two nights four of us were sent across to join 'A' Coy 7th Dukes for the attack on Fontenay. I was unlucky in most of my service, although I still enjoyed being soldier.

Later, in Holland, Marsden was wounded and captured. He said: 'Although I was badly treated by a few Germans, I had great respect for their brave men in the front line.'

The Kensingtons supported the Dukes, and Cpl. Calland with the 8th platoon recalled:

As soon as the mortaring stopped we could hear shouts and see movement in the field and then they came on, some yelling, some weaving quietly like Indians through the corn. I fired through battle sights, swinging traverse and saw them fall and it was a queer feeling because this was the first time I had seen Germans and it all seemed unreal. We pulled them up in front of us but they got by on either side and the infantry were running back. Grenades were bursting all round us and bullets whistling through the branches and the Section Commander told us to take out the [gun] locks and fall back. We made our way back through the woods. We lost 9 casualties and much equipment lost or destroyed. But later a burial party found 40 dead Germans in the field opposite 8 platoon.

Calland was awarded the MM. Maj. Brian Gooch was second in command of the 55th Suffolk Yeomanry Anti-tank Regiment and in his history wrote:

On this fine morning in June, at 1100 hrs the Germans put in a short attack preceded by a most severe mortar bombardment. At about 1345 hrs Lt. Woods, troop commander of 'M' troop supporting the Dukes appeared at RHQ – badly shaken – to report that one of his 17 pdrs had received a direct hit and only 11 of his troop [of 32] could be accounted for.

Two patrols were sent out into the eerie and sinister woods of Le Parc de Boislande. Capt. Barton retrieved one of the four guns, but the other three were knocked out. The 20 casualties included 8 killed in action, buried by Padre Evans, and 6 men taken prisoner.

So the 6th Dukes were withdrawn to Le Haut d'Andrieu to reorganize. Much equipment had been lost or destroyed and many vehicles burnt with all they contained. Reinforcements for the 230 casualties – the heart of the regiment – had to be assimilated, equipment had to be drawn and issued, and a general reorganization was necessary before the battalion could again become an efficient fighting unit. All of the company commanders were casualties, and scores of the 'virgin' young leaders, platoon officers and sergeants were also casualties. The 6th Battalion were withdrawn to Brouay into brigade reserve.

Brig.-Maj. Paul Crook wrote:

> Our first attack by the Scots Fusiliers on Cristot was successful, but the next one by 6th Dukes, less so and they suffered severe casualties particularly among officers. This Bn was singularly unfortunate and suffered casualties wherever it went, even during a pay parade which was hit by shelling when they were in reserve. In two weeks they lost 23 officers including the CO, Ken Exham, and all the company commanders and 350 ORs. They were subjected to a particularly vicious and efficient counter-attack by 12 Panzer SS Division which resulted in an unplanned withdrawal. By the end of June their morale was at rock bottom.

Their MO, Capt. Griffiths, who later joined the Hallams, was awarded an immediate MC for his gallantry during the two-day battle.

Maj. Godfrey Harland of the 1/4th KOYLI recounted:

> This attack affected us in two ways. 6 DWR had severe casualties and lost not only many officers but also had many of their radio sets knocked out. Our CO Johnny Walker was asked by Brigade HQ to send an officer immediately to 6 DWR with as many radio sets as we could spare since we were at this time in reserve. Major Bruno Brown, our 2 i/c set off for Le Parc de Boislande in a bren carrier loaded with 18 sets.

He was wounded and subsequently lost an arm. Harry Ward was one of a number of the 1/4th KOYLI stretcher-bearers sent to help and rescue the 6th Duke of Wellington Regiment's wounded, and for his selfless work he was awarded the MM.

The 7th Battalion were honour bound to retake Le Parc de Boislande. They too had not yet been in action and had scrapped their 333 bicycles after landing. They were stationed at St Gabriel on 12–13 June, and on 15–16 June they were at St Croix whilst the 11th Royal Scots Fusiliers were around Brouay. On 18 June, Waterloo Day, the CO of the 7th, Lt.-Col. J.H.O. Wilsey, received several sets of orders as the battle raged in Le Parc de Boislande. The situation in front and on the right flank was confused. Lt.-Col. Hart Dyke, CO of the Hallamshires, wrote:

Once the 6th Duke of Wellington's had evicted the enemy from Le Parc de Boislande we were to advance from NW of Les Hauts Vents and advance on Fontenay and Tessel Wood . . . . [But later] Felix Wilsey, CO of the 7th Dukes and an old pal of mine at Sandhurst and later at the Staff College, came up in his carrier. He said he had been ordered to form up in the same place as my battalion and that he was shortly to advance through the 6th Dukes. There had obviously been no tie-up between Brigades. I ordered the Hallamshires to stand up, right turn and move 400 yards to the right. This worked like a dream and made Felix happy.

At 1330 hours their tank 'friends' were ordered up to support the 6th Battalion, whose desperate situation was reported by their RQMS and some other 6th Battalion men who arrived in 7th Duke of Wellingtons Regiment area. At 1440 hours final orders were received from brigade HQ that the initial attack on Point 102 and the northern edge of the Parc would go in at 1515 hours. With 'A' Company on the left, 'B' Company on the right, and 'C' and 'D' in reserve, the attack went in supported by artillery concentrations. From the start line to the objective was about 1,000 yards slightly uphill through cornfields and hedges. The assault companies went forward without a check and disappeared into a curtain of smoke and dust. Enemy positions were quickly overrun and all objectives were captured. The battle lasted only 25 minutes, and the inevitable counter-attack by infantry and tanks was broken up by the divisional artillery.

No contact was made at all with the 6th Battalion Dukes. but now there was a change of tactics. The CO decided not to occupy forward positions in the Parc salient but to hold a reverse-slope position and to dominate the Parc by patrols. Lt. Bezalt and Lt. Evans were sent forward on patrol with a troop of tanks, each with gunner FOO parties, but the gains made earlier by the unfortunate 6th Battalion were not recaptured.

In 1942 at Porthcawl, on his twenty-first birthday, Monty Satchell was promoted to the rank of sergeant. That evening, having duly celebrated the double event, he was accosted by a CMP patrol and later reprimanded by his CO. The redcaps were not his favourite unit of the British Army. Two years later he was taking his armoured car ('B' Squadron of the 49th Recce Regiment) up through a badly damaged village to join the 7th Dukes, who were expecting a counter-attack, to give them some extra fire power. He was skilfully guided – under 88 mm airburst – through the wrecked village, past a minefield and two burning German tanks by a lone CMP on point duty, his motorcycle parked in a ditch. After that his views of redcaps changed, as he saw them at river crossings, roadblocks, mined verges and guiding traffic at crossroads – always taking risks.

In their first day in action the 7th Battalion suffered heavily. Capt. F.C. Scholes of 'A' Company and four other ranks were killed in action, Lt. Duncan, Lt. Delaney, Lt. Rogers, Lt. Bennet and 60 other ranks were wounded, and 18 other men were missing – a total of 88. Pte. Peach was awarded the MM. The 7th Battalion stayed near Point 102 until 22 June, when they were relieved by the 11th Durham Light Infantry of the 70th Brigade.

CHAPTER ELEVEN

Build-up to Operation Epsom

'A Sombre and Depressing Scene'

On 19 June the GOC decided to change his 'management' and replaced Brig. Dunlop of the 146th Brigade with Lt.-Col. 'Johnny' Walker, the CO of the 1/4th KOYLI. This coincided with some good news – and some bad. The 8th Armoured Brigade consisting of the 4/7th Royal Dragoon Guards, the 24th Lancers, and the Nottinghamshire Yeomanry backed by the 12th Battalion KRRC, their armoured infantry regiment, now officially came under command. Their Sherman tanks had already been supporting the Polar Bears, and by midnight on 17 June they were helping to hold the line from St Pierre to the west, Le Haut d'Audrieu and Les Hauts Vents on the high ground overlooking Fontenay in the centre, to Hill 102 and Le Parc de Boislande on the east flank – a front of 2,500 yards.

The bad news was that from 19 to 22 June, storms in the Channel had wrecked one Mulberry harbour and severely damaged the second. As a result, supplies of reinforcements, vehicles and ammunition were considerably delayed. The allied build-up was lessened and the 8th Corps were late arriving, so Field Marshal Rommel had a few extra days to bring up reinforcements on the Caen sector (not, however, from the possible invasion zone in the Pas de Calais). It was the worst June gale for nearly half a century: dozens of vessels were sunk at sea and almost 800 were wrecked on the Normandy shores. Nearly 25,000 tons of supplies were landed on the 18th, but a mere 4,500 on the 20th. Monty's major offensive to envelop Caen was postponed until 25 June. Lt.-Col. Hart Dyke, CO of the Hallams, wrote:

> Our Bn HQ was shelled and we lost most of our signal equipment and both medical 15 cwt trucks were knocked out by shells landing on the Medical Post (RAP). This taught us never to leave our unarmoured vehicles in the forward area and to dump and dig our stores. Rough seas had delayed the arrival of ammunition but the strength of the enemy defences at Fontenay and Tessel Wood was confirmed. The next few days were spent in conferences and reconnaissances for the big attack.

The Lincolns patrolled vigorously into the German line from Tilly, a small hillside town, to Fontenay-le-Pesnil, a village whose church was an excellent observation point. However, they lost the whole of their carrier platoon from shell fire due to their moving in error across a forward slope. Traffic signing, which had been drummed into everyone in the years of training in the UK, was rather neglected. The Hallams' patrols, in particular, under Maj. Tony Nicholson and Mike Lonsdale-Cooper, dominated No Man's Land and brought back useful information.

Maj. Ed Wardleworth MC assumed temporary command of the 1/4th KOYLI until Lt.-Col. C.D. Barlow OBE of the KSLI took over command on 28 June. The KOYLI were in reserve of the 146th Brigade until the 25th. The 70th Brigade were also still in reserve, but the unfortunate 1/6th Duke of Wellingtons, reforming and recovering at Brouay after their heavy casualties in Le Parc de Boislande, were again in trouble.

It was a sunny afternoon on 20 June, as the regimental historian wrote:

> A more peaceful background it would have been difficult to imagine. The woods, fields and parkland, the courtyards and the barns of the farms were like a piece of Sussex. There was no noise, no distant rumble of gunfire. Groups of men were busy at various jobs: a meal was cooking under the trees. Reinforcements, many from the 10th Bn Dukes, just arrived were standing about eating their food and chatting.

An enemy fighter plane came over and machine-gunned the Dukes with no damage done, but it had obviously reported back: 'There came a screaming whistling followed by an alarming loud bang. The shelling went on for half an hour: a carrier was hit and its ammunition exploded.' Many of the men had no slit trenches or tools with which to dig them. The shelling caused 20 casualties. Worse was to come.

Brig. Mahoney had arranged to inspect the 1/6th Dukes at 1445 hours that same afternoon. The regimental historian continued: 'It was decided to hold the parade in a clearing in a wood to avoid another concentration in the open. At 1430 hrs the Bn groups began moving into the wood and at 1440 hrs the wood was suddenly and violently shelled – a disturbing co-incidence.' HQ Company was caught in the open and received a direct hit, which caused 20 casualties, and another 12 were hit in the wood. The CO, Lt.-Col. Exham, now left to take over command of another battalion.

Meanwhile, Lt.-Col. A. Warhurst took over, pending the arrival of Lt.-Col. A.J.D. Turner MC of the Suffolk, from England. On the night of the 22nd the unlucky Dukes moved to Ste Croix-Grande Tonne, and the 7th Battalion held the northern sector of Le Parc de Boislande until the same day, when they were relieved by the 11th Battalion Durham Light Infantry.

The divisional gunner regiments were in action every day with harassing DF tasks and occasionally full-scale barrages supporting not only the Polar Bears but also neighbouring divisions. With a range of over 13,000 yards they could cover a wide front. John Mercer was a gunner with 'A' troop of the 185th Field Regiment RA, whose CO was known as 'Charlie Handlebars' on account of his magnificent moustache. Much of the time the

185th Field Regiment supported the Duke of Wellingtons, but more usually they supported the three battalions of the 70th Brigade. He wrote:

George Newson (the gun artificer), Dennis Bould (the Lance-bombardier driver and co-radio operator) and I decided upon a common dug out. Between times of duty on gun maintenance and manning the radio we dug a neat trench behind the gun position and covered it with branches, earth and a ground sheet. The command post was four foot deep and six foot square. Lt. Cannell, the GPO, was six foot two inches tall. Over the next few days he made us dig deeper . . .. On the third day a big programme of fire was laid down to support an attack. Two hours before dawn the guns began a creeping barrage behind which the infantry with supporting tanks moved forwards. Round after round was fired, the night sky illuminated by constant flashes of gunfire and the countryside filled with the heavy roll of the bombardment. As dawn broke the guns ceased and there was a strange silence. Acrid cordite smoke assaulted the nostrils and drifted through the orchard. It had been an Uncle Target, that is to say a divisional target embracing three regiments of 25-pdrs and a regiment of 5.5 inch [medium] guns. The silence did not last long. Sustained mortar fire could be heard like the thumping of a table by a hundred hands and the rattle of machine-guns audible in the distance. First the 'rat-a-tat-tat' of the Bren gun used by our infantry, then the 'pop-pop-br-br-br' of the German Spandau in reply.

Sgt Monty Satchell, with his heavy armoured car crew 49 Recce in Normandy, 1944. (Monty Satchell)

For the first five weeks of the campaign the 49th Recce Regiment was employed in a purely infantry role, for the majority of the time protecting the left flank of the Polar Bears and covering the gap between the 49th Division and the 1st and 12th Corps on the left. In June they were based on Le Hamel, and they covered and patrolled the long, open cornfields that stretched southwards for 3–4 kilometres.

David Rissik, the historian of the 11th Battalion Durham Light Infantry, described the scene they inherited from the Dukes between Cristot and the notorious Parc de Boislande:

> Here shellfire had denuded most of the trees of their foliage and the rich pasture was scored with the marks of tank tracks and pockmarked with mortar bombs. The enemy was close at hand. Over everything hung the overpowering stench of dead cattle whose bloated corpses, lying with their feet in the air, dotted the open fields round about. It was a sombre and depressing scene . . . the eeriness of Le Parc de Boislande. The undergrowth was unusually thick making silent movement [for the night patrols] impossible and the trees creaked in the wind in ghostly fashion. No wonder patrols sometimes returned to the Command Post wreathed in perspiration.

Cpl. Woodhead was taken prisoner on a patrol, escaped and made his way back bootless to his lines, and Capt. Jack Pearson in his slit-trench received an invitation to play cricket for the Army against the RAF – in a distant country.

The GOC, Maj.-Gen. Barker, recorded in his diary and letters some of the key events that took place in the first two weeks of the campaign:

> *12 June.* The last two or three days have been v. sticky as the Boche has had time to deploy his initial Panzer Divisions. Bobby [Erskine, GOC of the 7th Armoured Division] and his chaps are getting going again and made splendid progress. The whole thing is to keep this battle fluid and not allow it to crystallise. My guns were in action this pm firing their first shots in anger. The Boche are fighting well [some 3000 captured and the same number killed] but with little support from guns and their air is simply non existent. The country here is frightfully enclosed – typically English country with thick hedges and ditches and their infantry are taking every advantage of it. They are lobbing grenades into the tank turrets and putting sticky bombs on, which Bobbie [Erskine] found most disconcerting. I am having breakfast with Monty tomorrow. Altogether things have gone really splendidly and everyone is in great heart.
> *13 June.* Monty showed me his two caravans with great pride. They are lovely. One belonged to the Italian General 'Electric Whiskers' and the other to Messe. The latter has a bath and bedroom complete. News is v.g. I hear Bobbie [Erskine] is doing extremely well on the right flank and gone cracking on.
> *14 June.* Had breakfast with [Brig.] Andrew Dunlop and hatched future plots. The Boche have dug in in front of him and are going to be difficult to move. They lie doggo in the ditches and then appear in the rear shooting everyone up. Bobby [Erskine] finished up last night having retained nearly all the ground [Villers-Bocage] he made during the pm . . .. I am just off to Corps to tell Gerry [Bucknall] what I'm doing.
> *18 June.* My second attack went in yesterday and was successful. Knocked out two Tigers and one Panther. Unfortunately the Boche put in a pretty strong c/attack this pm and partly regained his previous posn. They are fighting quite excellently, with the greatest skill. Everyone is getting well blooded. 'Bimbo' Dempsey has been up to see me.
> *20 June.* The Boche is quite fanatical in front of us – they belong to the crack Panzer Divs, but we have given them a hell of a pounding. Their 6 barrelled mortars are the worst b—y things . . .. I usually go to bed about mid-night and then if planning an operation up about 5 am, if not 6 am, which gives me plenty of sleep.

22 June. I have had a lot of worry about one of my senior Commanders [Brig. Andrew Dunlop] who I eventually sent home. He had completely broken down and gone off his head. It's very tragic as he had a fine war record and got one of the best DSOs of the war. Luckily I have a splendid chap [Lt.-Col. 'Johnny' Walker] to replace him.

23 June. I went round my RASC units and REME workshops – all excellent. The former have had a really hard time dumping quantities of gun ammunition. At 6 pm went to a conference at Monty's HQ. All Div. Commanders there and photo taken after. Monty analysed our achievements so far – and our prospects – all v. good. Everyone in great form. My chaps have been doing some excellent patrolling. We had a little party yesterday killing 25 Boche and capturing 3.

25 June. I have just been round all my gunners. They are shooting magnificently. We are moving [divisional HQ] from the orchards into the local chateau. Dick Oxley's lot are with me – my old Bn. Went round my Medical units yesterday . . . All v.g. Saw my Jocks [the Royal Scots Fusiliers] after dinner last night – in grand form looking so fit.

CHAPTER TWELVE

Operation Martlet

Stage I – Blind Man's Buff

Monty wrote:

> Eventually 30 Corps attack was fixed for 25th June with the 8 Corps thrust commencing 24 hours later. 30 Corps started its thrust on 25th June with the object of occupying a commanding feature in the Rauray area. The attack by 49 Division with 8 Armoured Brigade under command began in darkness and thick mist at 0415 hrs.

The object of Operation Martlet was to secure Fontenay and the higher ground to the south. Then 8th Corps, newly landed, with the 11th Armoured Division (in which the author served), the 15th Scottish Division and the 43rd Wessex Wyverns would encircle Caen from the south-west, cross the River Odon and the River Orne, and take the vital heights of Hill 112 during Operation Epsom.

Bill Ashby, whose father fought with the Hallams, has designed a series of Operation Martlet maps. They show not only the three divisional objectives of Barracuda, Walrus and Albacore, but also the initial front lines held by the Panzer Lehr Division and 26 SS (Hitler *Jugend*) Panzer Grenadier Regiment. Barracuda was the Juvigny–Fontenay–Caen main road, Walrus was 1,000 yards further south between the north end of Tessel Wood, Point 111 and east to La Grande Ferme, and Albacore was another 1,000 yards south to the Vendes–Tessel–Bretteville road.

The divisional plan was for an advance on a two-brigade front: the 146th Brigade on the right (west) and the 147th Brigade on the left (east). Supported by a barrage of 250 army and naval guns – one gun to less than ten yards of front – plus the invaluable Sherman tanks of the 8th Armoured Brigade, it looked like one of Monty's classic well-supported frontal attacks.

The 4th Lincolns – 'Bright Red Scarf, Inspired . . .'

Led by Lt.-Col. Peter Barclay DSO, MC, the objective for the 4th Lincolns was the capture of Bas de Fontenay. From the start line it was a little under a mile, two thirds of the distance being down a gently falling slope and through wheatfields, and the remainder was typical bocage country, or orchards and woods intersected by thick double hedges set on banks. Captain J.O. Flints of 'A'

Company led on the left, and 'D' Company under Major B.H.T. Barlow-Poole were on the right. 'C' Company under Major J.M. Staniland, backed by 'A' Squadron of the 24th Lancers, was responsible for protecting the exposed right flank – although the 50th Tyne Tees had reportedly cleared Tilly-sur-Seulles, 1000 yards to the left. 'B' Company under Maj. W.E. Pattin was in reserve. A sand model of the operation had been closely studied on 22 June and a thorough briefing given to all ranks in forming up for a night attack. Shortly after midnight on the 24th, the battalion Intelligence Officer, Lt. D.F. Cooke, and his taping parties left for the brigade RV. It was a fine, though dark, night. The move to the start line was carried out perfectly, with the artillery softening-up barrage drowning the noise of tanks and carriers moving up. The carrier platoons' job was to act as armoured transport to ferry ammunition up to the rifle companies. Capt. Dick Newsum recalled:

We were parked on the start line behind a high hedge, which screened us from the enemy. Just after the attack started an ambulance turned up and parked in one of the gaps in the hedge. I told the driver to get to hell out of it, but it was too late. In a few minutes we were at the receiving end of heavy mortar fire. A bomb dropped near me wounding my leg. After the wound was dressed in the RAP, the ambulance driver who had caused the trouble came up to me and said 'You will be needing me now Sir, won't you?' [Dick's language was unprintable.] Thus ended my brief and not particularly glorious time in Normandy.

Within 24 hours of being wounded he was in a Basingstoke hospital.

The attack went in at 0415 hours in thick mist, to which the Germans quickly added smoke. The valley mist made it difficult to distinguish one group of men from another, and it was difficult for commanders to retain control by shouting. 'A' Company's radio was destroyed by mortar fire and 'D' Company's was screened by close country. There was some brisk mortaring, and enemy machine-gun Spandaus opened up from all directions. A 24th Lancer troop leader recalled:

We left harbour at 0230 and reached the forming up point at 0330. We hoped to see the Lincolns carrying out the first phase of the attack. All we could hear was the constant noise of the tremendous barrage our artillery were putting down. At first periscope light we moved forward down the forward slope hoping to move down to the sunken road. We were enveloped in a fog so thick that the commanders could not see the end of their 75-mm guns.

Visibility improved a little as the leading companies neared their objectives, but 'A' Company had suffered casualties and became slightly disorientated, so the CO sent up his reserve, 'B' Company. With his bright red scarf, heavy walking stick and map board, he was inspiring in his determination. On the right flank, 'C' Company overcame two enemy posts and 'D' Company reached its objective. Maj. Barlow-Poole led a patrol which captured a halftrack with its occupants, and Lt. Stainton led his patrol into a spirited hand-to-hand fracas. Pte. G.H. Sneesby engaged two more halftrack crews, 'brewed' them both up and was later awarded the DCM. The Lincolns reached the Juvigny–Fontenay road and quickly dug in before the German DF fire started – particularly on 'C' Company's area, who suffered badly. Maj.

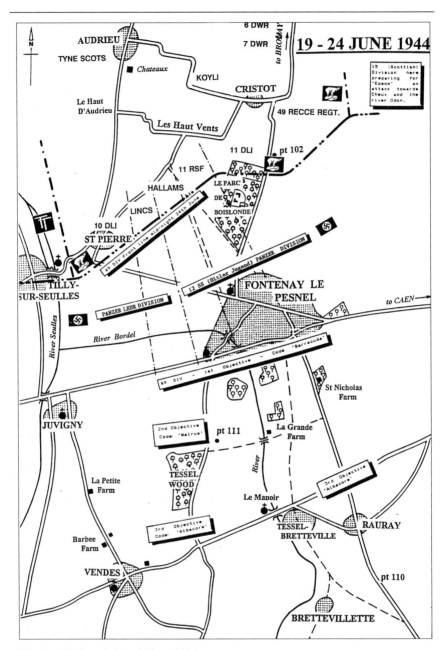

Fontenay Le Pesnel, 19 to 24 June 1944.

Richardson of the 185th Field Regiment, 'their' FOO, brought down enough fire to deter the usual counter-attack, and by noon the 1/4th KOYLI, on schedule, passed through the Lincolns in the second phase. This was the first major action for the Lincolns, who suffered 11 men dead 64 wounded, but they had taken 53 prisoners and killed another 50 enemy. The 24th Lancers managed to destroy – in the fog of war – a Mk III tank and several halftracks.

The Hallams – 'The Situation was Somewhat Unorthodox'

The CO, Lt.-Col. Hart Dyke, decided that 'B' Company, under David Lockwood, and 'C' Company, who had not been in action at Audrieu, should

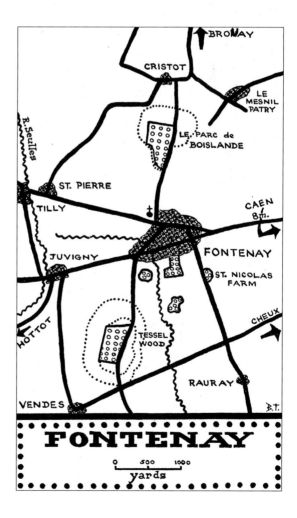

Fontenay. (Brian Thexton)

lead the advance with 'A' Company and 'D' Company in reserve. The second in command, Maj. Johnnie Mott, was in charge of the reserve ammunition, anti-tank guns, signals, medical stores and the mortar platoon. Jerry Bedward, the IO, had white-taped the axis of advance. Hart Dyke wrote:

> Every man in the Bn had had the whole scheme explained to him on a cloth model prepared in a barn. The Divisional Commander came up the evening before the attack and made us feel it was a dead cert and too easy: he inspired us all with great confidence. This was the Division's first big attack and we were going to succeed.

Visibility was restricted to five yards. Hart Dyke continued: 'I could get no information out of either [lead] company until both at last reported that they were lost in the mist and had lost touch with all their platoons.' Their objective was a stream, so now the two reserve companies were committed to take both objectives, the second being the far hedges of the orchards beyond the Fontenay–Juvigny road. Sgt. Bennett, the intelligence sergeant, used his compass and took bearings every five yards. Hart Dyke said: 'It was a slow and eerie business. En route we ran into two carriers and at least a platoon of the Royal Scots Fusiliers, moving painfully across our front. I gave them the compass bearing [left and parallel to the Hallams] to their own sector.'

The CO with battalion command post, the dismounted carrier platoon, the pioneer platoon and some Royal Engineers had crossed the main road and were on their main objective, and then,

> we had hardly halted when machine-guns and tank fire seemed to open up on us from all directions. We dug scrapes rapidly and I thought hard. I was out of touch with all the companies who were actually behind us. The situation was somewhat unorthodox . . . I ordered the Engineers to fix bayonets and Wizard, looking rather surprised and pained, started to lead his men off to clear the houses to the west of the road junction while the Pioneers began to move.

Fortunately Peter Newton with 'D' Company turned up and Gnr. FOO Peter Hewitt emerged from the mist. Cpl. Graham Roe of 'C' Company remembered:

> We were advancing through a cornfield with ripening corn heads about waist high. The enemy was firing at us with their Spandaus and Schmeisser machine-guns even though they could not see us. I saw the corn heads dropping all around us and began to wonder how long it would be before I became a cornhead . . . . [Later] looking for my O.C. Major Lonsdale-Cooper in the dark and dense fog created by the smoke, cordite and dust from the massive barrage, I heard very clearly the C.O. talking to the Adj. or IO, 'I think we're lost but it will sort itself out in due course'. I soon recognised Pte. Roy Simon and his mate Pte. Peddle and knew I was with the rest of 'C' Coy.

By 0900 hours visibility was up to 60 yards and the Hallams' advance speeded up. Peter Newton's 'D' Company soon occupied 'Queen', the code sign for the River Bordel line, and was pushing south to 'King', the main Juvigny–Fontenay road, when Capt. Bill Ashby turned up with a platoon of 'B' Company. Hart Dyke wrote:

I ordered him to work eastwards down the south side of the road as far as the bridge and contact the Royal Scots Fusiliers. I found Peter Newton had disposed 'D' Coy and dug in on their objective. My carrier arrived and I toured down the road to the right and contacted the Lincolns. There were a lot of Boche dead about, the result of our artillery fire. Our anti-tank guns were now in action under Arthur Cowell who was in his element. So I got onto the Brigadier and told him it was OK for the KOYLI to get cracking with their attack on Tessel Wood. I told him I had only about four mixed platoons on the objective, but I felt sure I could hold it.

So the Hallams were firmly ensconced in the western sector of Fontenay – or were they? Three German tanks arrived on the scene from Fontenay and began shelling the Hallams. Hart Dyke wrote: 'Retribution was swift.' Sgt. Williams' anti-tank gun, firing new sabot ammunition, knocked out the leading tank. The second tank then knocked out the Hallams' anti-tank gun. Hart Dyke again: 'Sgt. Williams, who was wounded, dragged up another gun and dealt with the second tank. They were the first Panther tanks to be met and knocked out during the campaign and earned the £5 prize offered by the GOC.' Sgt. Williams was awarded the MM for his gallantry.

Lt. Bob Hart of 'A' Squadron of the 24th Lancers recalled: 'My troop was sitting astride the Fontenay–Juvigny road facing east. The CO of the Hallams asked me to deal with a Panther holding up his advance . . . .. At that moment two more Panthers appeared just south of the road. I knocked one out and the other withdrew.'

Lt.-Col. Hart Dyke wrote:

Brigadier Johnnie Walker got on to me and said it was the Divisional Commander's personal order that I must contact the RSF on our left, at all costs and join up with them. So with a mixed bag of cooks, storemen and battalion HQ staff, with great caution we pushed eastwards . . . .. I could see no sign of any of the RSF as we pushed further into their sector.

Luckily they met Lt.-Col. Montgomerie-Cunninghame, CO of the Royal Scots Fusiliers, at the Calvary in Fontenay 'only half way to their first objective,' continued Hart Dyke. 'He said he had only 40 men left and they were digging in. I reassured him by saying that a large number of his men were in my sector and as far west as the Lincolns. He was a grand chap. He was killed at this spot by a shell two days later and was buried at the Calvary with many of his men.'

The Hitler *Jugend* now reacted predictably by shelling and mortaring the Hallams. Most of the mortar platoon carriers under Capt. Abbott were knocked out before they had dug in. Hart Dyke wrote:

It was sad to see and hear their carriers, ammunition and mortars going up. A bomb killed CSM Morton and wounded Lt. Brinton, a South African officer. All day our doctor Gregory-Dean worked like a trojan under fire while so many ambulances were knocked out working between Les Haut Vents and Fontenay that evacuation was no longer possible.

Sgt. Goodliffe and his stretcher-bearers were heroic. L/Cpl. Penn rescued 32 men, 11 of whom he saved under close small arms fire. Hart Dyke: 'Recommended for the Victoria Cross, he received the DCM and later had a leg amputated. The bravery and devotion to duty of the Hallamshires during the long summer's day was beyond praise.' They suffered 123 casualties, which included three company commanders. Bill Ashby now took command of 'B' Company, Maj. Tony Nicholson (awarded an MC for his bravery) took over 'A' Company and Leslie Gill took charge of Support Company.

Lt.-Col. A.W.H.J. Montgomerie-Cunninghame DSO, known as 'Big Monty', assembled his Royal Scots Fusiliers near Le Parc de Boislande and, with the Hallams and Lincolns, set off at H-Hour 0400 hours in thick mist and almost zero visibility. They had the toughest objective of all – the capture of Fontenay-Pesnil. Under command they had 'B' Squadron of the Sherwood Rangers Yeomanry, two platoons each of the 2nd Kensingtons Mortar and MMG platoons, and three troops of the Anti-tank Regiment. Codeword 'Barracuda' was given for the capture of Fontenay. From the start line the advance of 2,000 yards would be by the western side of the thick woods of Le Parc de Boislande, down the valley across a crossroads junction known as 'Hell's Lane' and into the northern sector of Fontenay. 'B' Company and 'D' Company were to lead, with 'C' Company and 'A' Company in reserve. Maj. H. Macpherson was OC of 'B' Company. He wrote:

> We were right forward Coy and formed up for the attack at 0345 hrs, and crossed the start line at 0415 hrs in a fairly compact bunch of units. The barrage was tremendous, distance behind it was kept very well, as was direction. The men stood up to and kept behind the barrage like veterans. Just after the platoons had opened out a cloud of combined mist, smoke and dust started to rise. The fog rose so quickly that runners and platoons were lost. Enemy MGs on either flank opened up. Visibility was down to five yards. 18 set communication had gone. 12 platoon on the left was completely adrift.

Some from 'B' Company reached the Calvary next to the two incoming roads in the north-west of Fontenay, and cleared several buildings. The rest of 'B' Company linked up and formed 'composite' companies with 'C' Company and 'A' Company in the thick fog of war. Their losses were heavy: 6 dead, 25 wounded and 13 missing.

Maj. W.F. Mackay, OC of 'D' Company, said:

> We were left forward Coy and proceeded at the rate of 100x [yards] in 4 minutes [the barrage rate] for the first 600x when a ground mist came down. After a further 100x visibility was only about 3 yds. I lost touch with 17 pl, visibility came worse, the rate of advance slowed down resulting in the loss of the barrage. All platoon comd. had the compass bearing to the first objective. 17 pl was subjected to intense mortar fire, obviously an enemy DF task. I was by this time completely out of touch with everyone even by 38 set [except for Lt. Irvine and 15 other ranks] when we reached Hell's Lane.

Eventually part of 'D' Company linked up with the defensive position around the Calvary, but when 'A' Company in reserve started to pass through, he continued: 'we were caught in our own arty and MMG fire out in the open.'

Later Maj. Mackay made his way back to the CO, made his report and was ordered to take command of a composite company of stragglers who had lost their direction in the mist. The extremely muddled and disorganized battle in the thick mist went on for several hours throughout the day, until at 2030 hours the 7th Dukes came through the battered Fusiliers.

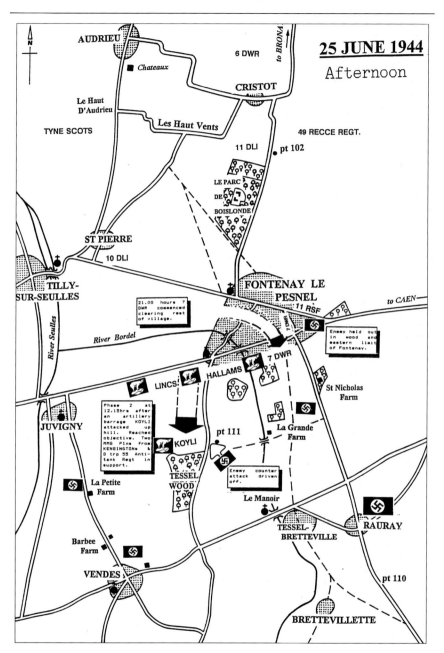

25 JUNE 1944

Afternoon

Fontenay Le Pesnel, 25 June 1944. (Bill Ashby)

Capt. Macaulay, OC of 'A' Company', recounted: 'Half an hour after Zero through the 2 i/c Major Liddell we were ordered to move down to the start line, together with 'C' Coy.' The supporting tanks had chewed up the track-marking tapes, so the Fusiliers followed the tank tracks in such terrible visibility that, Macaulay continued: 'I closed the Coy up into a single "snake", ordered the men to hold on to the equipment of the man in front.'

Again under heavy enemy DF fire, the 'Blind Man's Buff' went on for several hours with platoons getting lost and sometimes linking up with other companies. When the sun came out at 0630 hours, heavy sniping around the Calvary caused a steady stream of casualties. A Sherwood Ranger tank was 'brewed up', another got bogged down, and a third went up on a mine and lost a track. By the end of the day, Capt. Macaulay's 'A' Company had lost 11 killed in action and suffered 34 wounded.

Bitter hand-to-hand fighting took place around the Calvary, several counter-attacks were beaten off, mortaring was intense and a heavy toll of casualties was caused by the house-to-house clearance. All the time the Panzer Grenadier defenders fought bitterly and skilfully, and by the end of 25 June the Royal Scots had suffered 201 casualties, including 7 officers and 194 other ranks.

CHAPTER THIRTEEN

The KOYLI's Attack on Tessel Wood

'It was the Hell of a Day'

'Walrus' was the name of the second phase of Operation Martlet. The reserve battalion of the 146th Brigade, the 1/4th KOYLI, was to push across, advance south and clear the large Tessel Wood a mile south-west of Fontenay. Led by Major E.D. Wardleworth MC, the 1/4th KOYLI, supported by the 24th Lancers' Sherman tanks, in the words of Maj. Godfrey Harland of 'A' Company: 'poured out of Fontenay village [the western sector, the Germans still held the eastern part] and swept up on the hillside walking behind a wall of hideous noise and smoke and dust and flame which moved forward in jumps of a hundred yards at a time ahead of them.'

The plan was to clear the slopes and edges of the wood and to reorganize on the reverse slope. 'C' Company, under Capt. L.B. Keeble, and 'D' Company, under Maj. G.P. Roberts, led the attack, which was carried out with great dash in spite of heavy fire, which caused many casualties. Maj. Roberts, Lt. D.R. Evans and eleven other ranks were killed in action, 52 were wounded and 20 other men were listed as missing. Maj. A.B. Little and Capt. Lewis Keeble were each awarded the MC for gallantry.

Rex Flower of the mortar/carrier platoon wrote:

Our mortar officer, Capt. Dixon, gave out his orders. No. 3 detachment (us) to go with 'C' Coy on the left, No. 1 detachment to go with 'D' Coy. [On the way to the forming-up point (FOP)] We went down that slope like bloody bats out of hell! We just had to get to 'C' Coy on time, our very honour depended on it. Down we went into the smoke, dust, death and destruction, bodies and the noise of battle! We reached the cross-roads [in Fontenay]. There was a very dead German in the middle of the road. Flat as a pancake, a patch of blood and guts six feet across, everything gone over him. We went over him as well! Turned right and joined the Juvigny road at a fair clip. I shall never forget the military policeman. He was calmly directing traffic in that frigging lot. We got to 'C' Coy with about five minutes to spare.

L/Cpl. Geoff Steer of 'B' Company related:

The Bn Padre conducted a small service at 11 am and said 'God be with us' just before the barrage started. We gazed up the hill for about a mile and a quarter: it was all open fields, corn ready for cutting, peas ready for picking, no cover at all. Some of our shells dropped short – on the way up we saw dead Germans in the cornfields but we were also getting a pasting from the

German mortars especially the 'Moaning Minnies', their 6-Barrel Mortars. It was about 3 pm when we finally reached the wood along with the 24th Lancers. A good job – we were being counter-attacked by Tigers [Panthers] but the Lancers brewed two up, so the rest withdrew. All this time 'B' and 'C' Squadron machine-gunners kept up rapid fire on our flanks.

John Longfield of 'D' Company added:

Shells seemed to be exploding all over the place. A small splinter hit the man next to me. It went in through his foot and came out at his knee. He was screaming in agony. I called for the stretcher-bearers and carried on up the hill. Some of the 24 Lancer tanks were behind me. When they fired the sound was unbelievably loud. I felt as though I were being torn in two, like a piece of canvas ripped down the middle from top to bottom. In Tessel Wood, moving through thickish growth I came across an enormous crater. I was about to shoot a German sitting there on the edge of the crater, his arms resting on his knees. He raised his arms. He had no hands. I considered killing him to put him out of his misery . . .. We finished the day at the top of the hill pinned down by Spandau MG fire. I was told to take my Bren gun and sort him out . . .. [Later] We did not have any more trouble from that particular location. [John then watched two Lancer tanks being hit] The first tank by now was burning merrily. It was not long before it was red hot and remained that way for a fair amount of the night. The smaller tank also brewed up. The pair of them made an unpleasant firework display.

Capt. Lewis Keeble, second in command of 'B' Company, wrote:

It was the hell of a day – it was the most exciting day of my life. We were the left forward Coy, Gerald Roberts commanded 'D', the right forward, Derek Mayall with 'A' was behind us and Tony Little with 'B' behind 'D' Coy . . . our H-hour postponed. Two members of the company couldn't stand it and shot themselves in the foot in quick succession. The fire support was similar to or even greater than for Cristot. Off we go, the blast from a shell knocks me over, but only one little flesh wound. Up the hill through the first hedge, binoculars torn away, trousers ripped. Where are the boys? Not here. I go back 'come on'. Through the hedge again, still no boys. Back again 'COME ON!' They came. Through more hedges. Up to the edge of the wood. Bloody murder: people dropping dead. But we're there. Send success signal. Hitler *Jugend* prisoners. I said there would be no false glamour in this account. During the attack one of my platoons ran away and were brought back at pistol point by Tug Wilson, my 2 i/c. We dug in. I heard Gerald Roberts had been killed. 'D' Coy had ground to a halt and Tony Little had passed through them to the objective . . .. [Later] There was a great blast of artillery and MG fire. We were being counter-attacked by infantry and tanks. The same platoon ran away again. Tug got the spare Bren off the carrier. I got the spare 2 ft mortar, the CSM fed us with ammunition and this unconventional combat group put down some pretty rapid fire . . .. [Later] the enemy retired leaving two knocked out tanks and quite a lot of dead.

All day the 24th Lancers had suffered heavy and intense mortar fire and casualties. 'C' Squadron constantly engaged enemy tanks seen moving 2,000–3,000 yards to the west, and 'B' Squadron engaged targets south and south-east of Fontenay. On the right flank, Lt. Pip Williams got a Panther and Lt. Frank Fuller got hits on a Panther and two armoured cars. 'C' Squadron stayed on the western edge of Tessel Wood to protect the right flank of their Yorkshire friends. 'D' Troop of the 218th Battery of the 55th Anti-tank Regiment also added defensive fire power when the 12th SS Hitler *Jugend* counter-attack fell on 'C' Company of the 1/4th KOYLI.

The whole battalion mortar platoon was positioned in line along the base of a bank behind a line of bushes just short of the wood. Rex Flower recalled:

It was very, very hard labour to dig in under the hot sun. It was the hottest day up to now, in more ways than one as it was to prove. The bearing was straight over the wood. We got the ammo off and into the pit. We dug a shelf for it and put aiming posts up on the bearing and were all ready for action . . . then to our surprise the platoon Sgt. and driver appeared with the platoon truck packed with more ammunition. [At 17 hours] The vicious crash, crash of shells spoilt my reverie. They were dropping all over the field and they were enemy ones. The long awaited counter attack was on us . . .. We kept firing and firing.

The determined counter-attack was eventually beaten off. Flower continued: 'In the baleful flickering light of burning tanks, amid the smoke and smell of battle, we spent the night. Just in case the enemy came again. But he didn't come.'

The Battle for Fontenay by the Dukes

The original objective of the 11th Royal Scots Fusiliers was the taking of Fontenay, which in turn would allow the the 7th Battalion Duke of Wellingtons to come through and attack towards Rauray, 2,500 yards due south. The St Nicholas Farm on the Fontenay–Rauray road would be their first objective, as part of 'Walrus'. Because of the intense defence of the eastern sector of Fontenay by the Hitler *Jugend*, the 7th Dukes were now ordered to clear the village. At 1700 hours the battalion moved forward to an assembly position just west of Le Parc de Boislande, and zero hour for the attack was altered from 1845 hours to 2100 hours. Under command were two troops of the 55th Anti-tank Regiment and five platoons of 2nd Kensingtons (mortars and MMG), and in support 'C' Squadron of the Sherwood Rangers.

The plan was for the southern sector of Fontenay to be attacked successively by 'B' Company, then by 'D' Company under Major A.B.M. Kavanagh, each supported by 'C' Squadron of the Sherwood Rangers Shermans, and a detachment of AVREs. The Kensingtons protected the eastern slopes beyond Fontenay. 'A' Company, under Capt. J. Jameson, and 'C' Company, under Maj. Maurice Mountain, were in reserve. Fontenay had now been under intense attack for 16 hours. It was a village filled with destruction, smoke, dust and confusion. At zero hour, 'B' Company attacked and quickly made their way into the village.

It was slow, determined fighting. Within the hour, 'B' Company sent their success signal and 'D' Company went in to bite ever deeper into the SS Hitler *Jugend* defences. By 2300 hours both companies had secured their objectives. The tanks and AVREs withdrew in the gathering darkness, the reserves came and by midnight the Dukes had consolidated. However, they had not been able – because of the very late start (2100 hours) and the stiff defence – to clear their final objectives – the east edge of Fontenay, a triangular-shaped copse, and to capture St Nicholas Farm, south on the main road.

The defence had been strengthened during the day by two companies of the 21st Panzer Division, which had arrived from Caen, and by elements of the Panzer Lehr Division. These, together with the remaining fanatical elements of the SS Panzer Division, had held up the Lincolns, the Hallamshires and, above all, the 11th Royal Scots Fusiliers.

Captain Jim Howie, OC of 'F' Troop of the 55th Anti-tank Regiment, deployed his towed 17-pdrs on the north side of the valley running east-west and north of Fontenay. Brian Lott recalls:

> It was quiet for a time until the Germans started raining down mortar bombs and shells with devastating effect. One Bombardier was killed sheltering in a slit trench, head down exposing his neck and was hit by shrapnel. Several of the gun crews were hit too. Jim Howie was wounded on his backside and was stretchered away, with the words 'It's all yours, Brian' to his 20-year-old No. 2, Brian Lott.

The Polar Bears, aided by the Sherwood Rangers and the 24th Lancers had made a very good start to Operation Martlet, considering the dense early morning fog and mist which had reduced visibility to a few yards – and the ferocious and determined defences. So 25 June ended, and Monty now blew the whistle to start Operation Epsom rolling.

CHAPTER FOURTEEN

Operation Martlet

Stage II, 26 June – 'Feeling of Utter Desolation'

The GOC, Gen. Barker, now planned a triple attack in a general south-east direction from the Juvigny–Fontenay road towards the vital village of Rauray. This involved the taking and destruction of three fortified and well-defined farmsteads – St Nicholas Farm, La Grande Ferme and Le Manoir.

The Tyneside Scottish supported by Shermans of the 4/7th Royal Dragoon Guards (the third regiment in the 8th Armoured Brigade) were to advance from the north of Tessel Wood, 1,000 yards south-east to La Grande Ferme, with the 12th KRRC protecting their open right flank. This was the Tynesiders' first real baptism of fire. Led by a piper, the attack started at 0650 hours, 'A' Company up and leading.

They had to fight their way forward in the face of enemy tanks firing from cleverly concealed dug-in positions on the far side of the little river Seulles, which runs north–south into Fontenay. Snipers were active and the Tynesiders fell into a German battle trap. The hostile Spandau fire forced them to take cover along a bocage bank that was a registered DF target for the enemy *Nebelwerfers*. Under cover there, heavy mortar fire bursting in the trees caused many casualties. Several Shermans were knocked out. Within the first hour, Maj. McGregor, OC of 'A' Company, and Capt. Whitehead were wounded, and Lt. McDowell was killed. The tanks – try as they could – were unable to get through the high bocage hedgerows.

At midday, 'B' Company pushed through and got a platoon across the river, but they were isolated. Four Guards tanks were lost attempting to cross the stream, and Lt. J. Allan and Sgt. Smith, who had done so well, were ordered back. The attack faltered, and by 1120 hours had failed, with the loss of 48 Tynesider casualties. The battalion withdrew back to Audrieu and the Armoured Brigade disengaged.

Maj. J.D.P. Stirling, the historian of the 4/7th Royal Dragoon Guards, wrote: 'This was 'C' Squadron's battle, and they had a wretched day [supporting the 1st Tyneside Scottish on their way to Tessel Wood on 26 June]'. The scene at the start-line was described as 'a badly organised partridge shoot' because the infantry and tanks did not get lined up properly and some Shermans of the Royal Dragoon Guards were fired at by the infantry behind. Soon, Lt. G.J.G. Thompson's tank knocked out a Panther, but was in turn knocked out by another Panther.

Sterling continued:

> The squadron was overlooked from two sides. On the dominating high ground were from two to six Tigers and Panthers operating. On the left flank was a small wood in which four Tigers were sitting – cleverly placed so that it was impossible to get at them. They knocked out two RDG Shermans and their Spandau fire completely held up the Tynesiders. By late afternoon we had lost six tanks, 19 men casualties and had destroyed two Panthers.

Maj. T.M. Bell's 'C' Squadron was ordered under cover of smoke to withdraw back to Point 103, 'weary and disheartened'.

Austin Baker was a tank wireless-operator with the 4/7th Royal Dragoon Guards. He recounted:

> The whole squadron was now in the field with the tanks scattered around by the hedges. There appeared [on the morning of 26 June] to be Tigers and Panthers all around us. Between them they covered every gap. Six of the squadron were killed that day. The Tyneside Scottish came back across the field in a single file, led by a piper who was playing what sounded like a lament. I felt lucky to be alive.

Pte. Robert Nixon recalled:

> I saw the Sherman tanks go up in confident and steady formation and disappear into a hilltop wood near Tessel. I was very scared at the thought of my first action but the sight of the tanks charging into the wood eased my fears, because I thought there would be nothing left to fight. Imagine my dismay when an hour or so later the tanks or what was left of them came belting out back.

Nixon was mortared from a hedge alongside and was wounded, and with two of his mates, who were wounded by Spandau fire, he was driven back to the RAP in a carrier. He continued: 'I learned later the Tyneside Scottish was attacked ferociously by Tigers and infantry. Of about 12 Dundee blokes in my company only two of us came out alive.'

The second 'punch' of the day was on the left flank. At 0930 hours 'C' Company and 'D' Company of the 7th Dukes, supported by a barrage from the guns of the 143rd Field Regiment and backed by 'C' Squadron of the Sherwood Rangers, left their slit trenches at the edge of Fontenay. They advanced over the open ground astride the road leading south towards St Nicholas Farm, where concealed enemy tanks put three of their tanks out of action. The enemy was alert and the Dukes were met by heavy fire.

Both companies fought on with Brens and 2 inch mortars, but it was impossible to manoeuvre more tanks into the St Nicholas Farm and wood area. Suddenly a Panther tank came down the road towards No. 14 platoon of 'C' Company. L/Cpl. E.W. Dodd engaged it with a PIAT and knocked it out at close range. He was awarded the MM for this brave effort, but his platoon commander, Lt. W.J. Halse, was killed in action. The padre, Revd S.H. Chase, crawled forward to rescue a wounded man under fire and was awarded the MC. However, the attack petered out and Lt.-Col. Wilsey withdrew 'C' Company and 'D' Company back 300 yards to their original positions on the ouskirts of Fontenay. For the time being . . .

The third attack on the right flank was made by 'A' Squadron of the 24th Lancers and the 12th KRRC – both of the 8th Armoured Brigade – from the north-east corner of Tessel Wood, south towards Le Manoir Farm on the outskirts of Tessel-Bretteville. They actually reached La Manoir, but although 'A' Squadron knocked out two tanks as they advanced, they also lost several themselves. The 12th KRRC had managed to reach the outskirts of Le Manoir but received orders to abandon the attack. Under cover of smoke, the Lancers and the KRRC withdrew back to the start line. The Lancers' CO described it as a 'bloody day. The battlefield was full of burnt-out tanks, mutilated bodies everywhere, a feeling of utter desolation.' By the middle of 26 June, all three attacks had failed noticeably.

The general tried again. In the afternoon, the 7th Dukes were thrown into the attack once more. The whole regiment of the Sherwood Rangers, backed by all of the divisional artillery, would be launched south – with zero hour at 1530 hours – due south down the Fontenay–Rauray road. Martin Lindsay, the Sherwood Rangers' historian, told how:

> This time Colonel Stanley Christopherson took special trouble to hold a conference on the spot and 'tie-up' firmly with the infantry and the gunners. Ten minutes before the attack was due to start, Major John Semken, OC 'A' Sqn, came up the main street in Fontenay, squeezed his Sherman past the CO's in the very narrow street, got round the next corner and came face to face with a Tiger tank. [Perhaps one should ask how a 60 ton Tiger tank had managed to avoid the Polar Bear pickets guarding the road out of Fontenay towards Caen] His gunner had an AP round up the 'spout'. Six shots hit the Tiger and all at point blank range bounced off. But one shot hit the turret ring and the Tiger's crew baled out.

'A' Company and 'B' Company of the 7th Dukes, now assault companies, formed up further to the flanks of 'C' Company and 'D' Company as the barrage started at zero hour. This lasted for 20 minutes. Fortunately the enemy had chosen the grounds of Fontenay château as their prime DF target for mortar concentrations – where not one tank or Duke was assembled. At 1550 hours the tanks went forward, closely followed by 'A' Company on the left and 'B' Company on the right. St Nicholas Farm was soon captured and the advance continued a further 300 yards beyond.

When 'A' Company reached their objective, 'C' Company and 'D' Company with the reserve tanks were launched on to their objectives 1,000 yards short of Rauray, and by 1800 hours all of the Dukes' objectives had been captured. In two days' fighting they had suffered 120 casualties. At 2100 hours the 11th Durham Light Infantry arrived and passed through for the final attack on Rauray.

Martin Lindsay told how:

Fontenay Le Pesnel. Knocked-out enemy tanks and an anti-tank gun and gunner. (IWM, B5939)

A Sqn went on from strength to strength and knocked out 13 tanks (of which Sgt. Dring claimed four). Reaching the outskirts of Rauray, they bumped into German infantry dug so deeply into the ground that not even grenades would remove them. Lt. Ronnie Grellis dismounted from his tank and dealt with the Germans on foot. His private war was broadcast to the whole squadron . . . .. At night our infantry came up and dug in just short of Rauray.

At 2230 hours, Lt.-Col. Hamer of the 11th Durham Light Infantry was ordered by brigade to find out if Rauray was occupied and, if not, to move into it that night. At 0200 hours, news reached battalion HQ that the officer in command of the patrol had been wounded and captured, that the orchard round the village was occupied by Germans and that the rumble of tanks had been heard in the woods nearby.

The General's daily diary noted:

26 June. My attack went in yesterday – the first to break the strong crust the Boche have been able to build up during the lull. On the whole it was most satisfactory. Unfortunately the Boche took a lot of turning out of Fontenay and was in some strongly fortified houses at the East End which the Bn in that sector couldn't clear. In the evening the Boche had luckily withdrawn after the hammering we gave them. We knocked out 6 Tigers, 2 Panthers and 4 other tanks and took quite a few prisoners – all first class troops of 12 SS Pz. Div. I'm frightfully pleased with my chaps. They did excellently and are full of fight. These Tigers

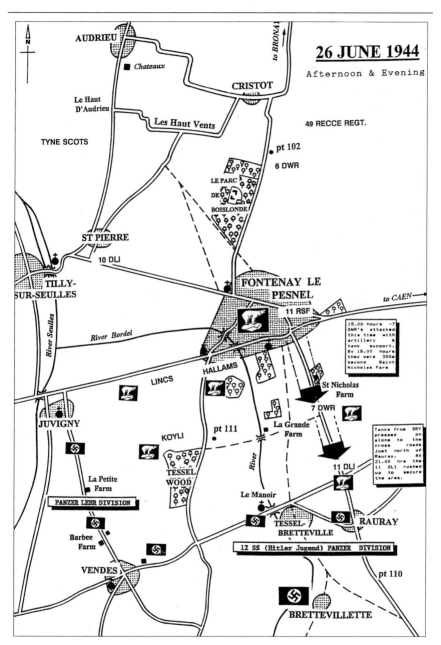

Fontenay Le Pesnel, 26 June 1944. (Bill Ashby)

Durham Light Infantry on the way to St Nicholas Farm, Fontenay Le Pesnel. Note the knocked-out Sherman and Panther. (IWM, B6042. Property of Lt-Col G. Barker Harland MC)

and Panthers are a nuisance, very heavy armour and we have to get a side shot at them. This battle is going to have considerable repercussions . . .. The 49 Div made the first break and we are all very pleased with ourselves.

27 June. [The attack] is going very slowly against the strengthening opposition and very difficult country. Yesterday we claimed 4 Tigers, 2 Panthers, 4 Mk IV and 2 SP guns so his casualties are mounting up, but one doesn't do this without losses on our side. His mortars are a perfect curse and one can't find the blighters. His rocket mortars are equally damnable.

CHAPTER FIFTEEN

Operation Martlet

Stage III, 27 June – 'Albacore'

A combined probe by the 11th Durham Light Infantry and the Sherwood Rangers now took place. 'B' Squadron sent two troops into Rauray to explore, and Lt. Ray Scott (a promising young actor), Sgt. Biddell and Sgt. George Green were killed. Their entire troop of tanks was knocked out by concealed Panthers. Rauray was eventually cleared by the 4/7th Royal Dragoon Guards. Martin Lindsay recalled:

> In Rauray we found nine enemy tanks including a Tiger and a Panther which had been abandoned intact and which we towed back to our lines. We sent it back to England covered with Sherwood Ranger signs! Major Hanson-Lanson went to have a look in Rauray for another abandoned Panther. A 'live' enemy tank hidden in trees shot him up from behind. He was wounded and Sgt. Crookes with him, died later of wounds.

Lt.-Col. Hamer, CO of the 11th Durham Light Infantry, sent Lt. Kenneth Hoggard's platoon into Rauray early in the morning under a heavy artillery barrage, which had little effect, and 88 mm guns took their toll of SRY tanks. Hoggard, despite being badly wounded, reached the centre of the village and sent back details of the German defences. They ran westward and sniped the 11th Durham Light Infantry Battalion position. It was only after the battle that, barely 200 yards away, was discovered a hidden officer's sniping and observation post, complete with sheets, mattress, chairs, flowers, wine and, of course, a telephone.

The brigadier now ordered a battalion attack at 1100 hours without tank support, since the German defenders had already accounted for seven tanks and two Anti-tank Regiment SP guns. H-hour was 1200. Platoons advanced in line abreast with fixed bayonets, 'B' Company on the right and 'D' Company on the left with a platoon of 'C' Company to mop up in the village. Spandaus and mortars caused 'B' Company heavy casualties in officers and NCO's, and they reached their objective with only 50 men left. Cpl. McArthur and Pte. Townsend took command of their platoons when their leaders had been killed. 'D' Company met stiff opposition and their OC, Maj. Low, was killed.

Around 20 teenage Hitler *Jugend* Snipers were killed. All were heavily camouflaged and bound to tree branches. One prisoner wept with rage at being captured alive, and even spat when questioned by Lt.-Col. Hamer. His reading matter was predictably a copy of *Mein Kampf*. The Red Cross flags of the stretcher-bearers were frequently fired on by Hitler's young men. Fortunately there was no immediate counter-attack.

Brig. James Hargest, a distinguished New Zealand observer of British combat tactics, wrote:

> The 49th Div of 30 Corps left division [49th Div of 30 Corps attacked and captured Fontenay and Tessel Wood on Sunday. It is 30 Corps' left division.] and worked along the Corps boundary. 8 Corps attacked Cheux [Operation Epsom] on Monday with 50 Div on its right flank. In any other army there would have been the closest liaison between the two corps and the two neighbouring divisions. But no! 8 Corps knew what transpired in 30 Corps only from liaison officers. The units side by side knew little or nothing of each other's progress!
>
> On Wednesday evening 60 hours after the 8 Corps attack I wished to pass along the road between the two Corps. I sought information as to whether it was safe. No one could tell me, infantry, artillery, and tanks – no one knew. I found the outskirts of Fontenay full of 49 Div troops. Neither neighbour knew anything about the other! The aftermath – on Thursday evening the enemy seized on the weakness and have driven a wedge between the two formations nearly 2 miles deep.' [CAB 106/1060]

The second part of Phase III – Albacore – was for the Hallams to pass through the 1/4th KOYLI holding the northern section of the large Tessel Wood. Lt.-Col. Hart Dyke wrote:

> The Brigadier Johnnie Walker said we were to advance along the road from Fontenay to Juvigny [due west] and then turn south along the Barbée Farm–Vendes road to seize the high ground south of Tessel Wood – and then get patrols into Vendes. The Lincolns and KOYLI were then to advance through us to the high ground south of Vendes.

Juvigny was believed to be held in considerable strength, so the Hallam's CO suggested a daring night march in dead ground using the track running down the east side of Tessel Wood – away from the main German defences to the Vendes–Juvigny area. Within an hour of dawn the whole battalion was safely digging in and deploying their anti-tanks guns, but a patrol sent into Vendes only 300 yards away suffered seven casualties – and within a few more hours, even worse. Around battalion HQ, Bill Ashby, commanding 'B' Company, was hit in the spine by a burst of MG fire. Hart Dyke wrote:

> This was a tragedy for me, as I felt very responsible for Bill. I had brought him to the Bn as Adjutant from the Queens. He died from his injuries several months later. The next morning a shell burst in the hedge in front of the wireless scout car and both operators and Peter Turrell were badly wounded. Johnnie Mott was lucky to get away with some splinters in his face and Philip Young, the sniper officer had an arm blown off and was killed. Our wireless aerial had obviously been spotted from the German OP in Vendes church.

Lt.-Col. Hart Dyke also received minor wounds.

For the last two weeks the 49th Recce Regiment had been mainly in reserve, based on Le Hamel guarding vital road junctions, often in an infantry role. John Russell of Y Troop, 6-pdr anti-tank guns of the 49th Recce Regiment, said:

> It was pouring with rain during the night of the 27th and we got our first rum ration. 'B' Sqn was ordered to protect the left flank of the Division advancing from Fontenay towards Rauray. We left harbour at 0500. [3rd Armed Car Troop – 6th Carrier Troop – 5th Carrier Troop – 4th Carrier Troop – Squadron HQ. Y Troop of the Anti-tank Battery – Mortar and Assault Troop moving towards a small wood on high ground ahead.] The Armoured cars

and carriers ahead were firing, high velocity shells were heard and they beat a hasty retreat as one carrier was hit. Over the radio 'Tanks-Tigers' were reported, three of 'em.

Panthers in fact attacked the rear of the column and the Red Cross ambulance. Y troop swung into a defensive box, No. 5 and No. 6 guns back to back, and 30 yards apart. The tank crews were badly at fault against the crack Panzer division. So unhooking, put down trails, dropped off extra ammo, I took the carrier and other vehicles under a nearby hedge. [6th Carrier Troop at 0800 hours were clearing the wood on foot, saw three Panthers emerge into the open from the north-west corner. Their long 75 mm guns were traversing slowly towards the vehicles in the hollow.] No. 5 gun opened fire, our first shot in anger. Our long training in UK paid off, the projectile was perfectly placed just below the turret ring. Gordon Bladon on No. 5 gun did it by the book. Instant result – flame, and again for the second Panther, a hit. The third tank tried to climb the bank to escape into the orchard out of view. Gordon put two shots into it. Also a PIAT bomb from the carrier Tp hit it and the Panther brewed up. [Later a Mk IV Special tank was seen in a hedgerow about 600 yds to the end of the wood. John Russell's 7 troop man-handled a 6 pdr into position and repeatedly hit it, knocked it out, but it did not 'brew up' and the crew escaped. Soon afterwards three Messerschmidt fighters appeared, chased an Air Op Lysander and attacked the recce troops. They were also attacked by friendly 'Churchill' tanks from the division next door!]

Troop Sgt. Monty Satchell of Recce Troop 'B' of Squadron the 49th Recce Regiment recalled:

Bloody hell what was that?' as a ricochet whipped over our turret. The medics half track was moving up. Our orders were to clear the corner of the cornfield, on the way to Rauray, of Spandaus and snipers. Driver Dave said, 'I could do with a Jimmy Riddle.' Everybody was tensed up and sweating. This was it – our first taste of action. I had to put my bloody head out of the turret to see properly. Two more Shermans had been hit up in front. 'Squadron advance, turn right, good hunting,' from Sunray over the radio. 'What do you see, Ron?' I said as MG bullets hit the turret.

Suddenly a German soldier stood up in the cornfield aiming a Panzerfaust at the carrier in front. 'Gunner, traverse left, 100, co-axial [37 mm gun], fire, give him a long burst. Nearly up to the woods. Dave our driver had done well weaving his way across the cornfield. 'Second target traverse right 200.' And so it went on. We all agreed after, we had been frightened in our first action. Monty was worried about the rations as Q [Bill Windsor] in his 3 tonner truck was only due up early in the evening. 'B' Squadron had started well.

The Kensington mortars and MMG were in the thick of it. 'A' Company was with the 146th Brigade and 'C' Company was with the 70th Brigade. Cpl. Pharaoh's 7th Platoon gun-carrier confronted a Tiger tank in the confused fighting in Rauray village. The carrier was hit but Pharaoh survived. The 9th Platoon of the 'C' Company supporting the Tyneside Scottish on 28 June suffered heavy losses. A Tiger tank burst through in the enemy counter-attack and destroyed both gun carriers, killing a complete crew: Cpl. Bushwell, L/Cpl. Wallace, Pte. Perry. Sgt. Bone was wounded and Lt. J. Griffiths won the MC. The 10th Platoon supported the 11th Durham Light Infantry, who lost heavily from the many hostile snipers. All three platoons fired on Bretteville and Quadeville, and engaged on 'map shoots' with great success.

On the night of 30 July and dawn of the 1st, German tanks retook Ringed Contour 110 in bitter fighting. The GOC, Maj.-Gen. Barker, sent the Kensingtons a special message on the 4th: 'Excellent co-operations given to the Brigadier and their individual Bns. Special mention of the gallant teams who remained fighting in the Bois de Boislande on 18 June and on the 110 feature on 1 July. These actions have given the infantry the greatest confidence.'

49th Division memorial at Fontenay. (Bill Hudson)

The gunners were in action – flat out – for the whole of Martlet supporting not only the Polar Bears but also their neighbours, the 15th Scottish Division. Maj. W.N. Richardson, Battery Commander of the 273rd Battery of the 69th Field Regiment RA, wrote an account of the battle of Fontenay. He recalled:

It is an axiom that gunners supporting infantry particularly B.Cs with Bn Commanders should preserve the closest liaison. My advice to people who haven't done the job before is, never to let the Bn CO out of their sight particularly if they are dealing with anyone so quick off the mark as Col Barclay. [of the 4th Lincolns. Richardson would have had his two troop commanders up in front supporting the leading two companies' advance. A FOO, Bill Ellison went with the forward right 'B' Coy under Maj. Barlow-Poole ('BP' of course), and another, Dick Hinchcliffe went with Jack Staniland's 'C' Coy as right flank protection. FOOs had the option of using Sherman or a carrier or of course on foot with 38 set.]

We then went forward in the thick fog. There was a good deal of small arms fire, some Boche, but mainly friendly, all unaimed but to some extent dangerous and certainly frightening. 'B' Coy went forward well and their C O was an inspiring leader. . ... As the fog lifted Dick started to shoot regimental and then battery targets at some tanks which he had seen poking their 88 mm guns out of a wood by Juvigny. As we shot at them our 24 Lancers Shermans were lying off in good position, popping off their 75s at them. The KOYLI went through about lunch time and with them were 'Boy' Carter and Ken Johnson [other FOOs of the 69th Field Regiment]. I went up to see 'D' Coy and found them well dug in and being shelled and mortared. There were a lot of dead Germans, captured German half tracks and motor cycles. Later on the Hallams went through the KOYLI and our Battalion [the Lincolns] HQ was in full view of Boche OP. It was in a little orchard and every time any vehicle came past on the dusty track up went the yellow dust and down came the Boche shells.

49th Division memorial at Fontenay. (Harry Cooke)

The tanks caused a lot of shelling. We were very lucky that day. Frank Blackstone, the Lincoln's 'S' Coy Comd. and I, had been up at KOYLI HQ at Tessel Wood with Col. Barclay at about 7 o'clock. There was a bit of a counter attack coming in on their left and they were being shelled hard . . .. [Later] We slept like logs. I never have been so tired before or since. The Fontenay full scale attack had been done, thank goodness and we had managed alright.

The 69th Field Regiment fired 700 rounds per gun in just over 24 hours during Operation Martlet and the 3rd Battalion Hitler *Jugend* Grenadiers took appalling casualties. In the cemetery at Fontenay-le-Pesnel there are the graves of 460 Polar Bears. Now along the road to Grainville stands proudly the memorial to the 49th Division's successful Operation Martlet.

CHAPTER SIXTEEN

Operation Epsom

'The Western Flank'

To the east, just a mile or so away, the 15th Scottish Division were struggling valiantly to take and keep the little Norman villages of Cheux, Le Mesnil-Patry, St Manvieu, Le Haut du Bosq, Mouen and Marcelet. The 11th Armoured Division Shermans and Cromwells joined in the attack on 28 June and forced their way across the River Odon onto the slopes – and, briefly, to the summit of the commanding Hill 112.

On the same day it was the 70th Brigade's turn to keep up the intense pressure. From Fontenay the Tyneside Scottish were to advance due south 2,000 yards between the left flank of the 7th Duke of Wellingtons, with the 11th Durham Light Infantry holding the Rauray road and the Lincolns on the right. Their objectives were the villages of Tessel-Bretteville and then Brettevillette, about 800 yards south-west of Rauray. Under another shattering barrage of an Army Group Royal Artillery and four field regiments, with 'C' Company and 'D' Company up, the Tyneside's attack was launched at H-Hour – 0700 hours. It was not good tank country, but the opposition was light, and behind the creeping barrage the first objective of Tessel-Bretteville was reached. So far so good, and at midday 'A' Company and 'B' Company leap-frogged through and were backed by a regiment of medium artillery. Capt. A.P. Whitehead wrote:

> The leading coys were met with heavy and accurate small arms fire soon after crossing the start line and enemy artillery and mortar fire began to fall on our back area. Opposition was particularly heavy on the right on 'A' Coy's front. The CO Lt.-Col. R.W.M. de Winton moved up 'C' Coy in support. Ground was being made and by 1430 hrs all companies were on their objectives but were engaged in stiff fighting in Brettevillette where they were being counter attacked in considerable strength by the 2nd SS Panzer Division infantry and tanks. Very confused fighting continued in the village. It was evident that it would not be possible to hold it and the CO ordered the companies back – 'D' Coy being only 300 yds from the built-up area. 'D' Coy 4 Lincoln was placed under command to protect the exposed right flank.

Casualties were heavy: the total of 117 included 9 officers. However, valuable ground had been won and many casualties had been inflicted on the enemy. The Tynesiders held their position until 30 June. Capt. J.D.P. Stirling wrote:

> Infantry and tanks went forward on the 28th towards the small wooded village of Bretteville. 'A' Sqn 4/7 RDG with 11 DLI and 'B' Sqn with 1st Tyneside Scottish. The place was stiff with dug-

in tanks and anti-tank guns and we lost several tanks reconnoitring the feature. For days and days nothing that anybody could do could shift them. We tried, the infantry tried and the gunners had a go with everything they had. It was still suicide to poke your nose out on to that forward slope. For two days we remained in this position, then withdrew into reserve at Les Hauts Vents.

One of the 9 casualties was Stirling himself.

By 1800 hours the Polar Bears held the line – the Hallams, the Lincolns, the Tyneside Scottish, and the 11th and 10th Durham Light Infantry. The Lincolns 'A' Company had already occupied La Grande Ferme, a stout old stone building between the villages of Bas de Fontenay and Tessel-Bretteville on the River Bordel. The 10th Durham Light Infantry moved through the 11th Durham Light Infantry in Rauray to secure another feature south of the little town. Two company commanders became casualties and, thanks to some gallant support by the Sherwood Rangers' tanks, a forceful enemy counter-attack was beaten off. Martin Lindsay, their historian, wrote:

> Our losses in trained veterans were grave indeed. In three weeks we had lost Sergeants Green, Biddell, Crookes, Bartle, Digby and Renney all killed. We would never be able to replace them. They were valiant soldiers and true comrades. 'B' Sqn now had only two officers left, Lt. Colin Thomson and Lt. Bill Wharton. And there were only seven tanks left in the Squadron.

Paul Crook, brigade major of the 147th Brigade, wrote after Operation Martlet:

> June was spent in tough but ineffectual fighting in 'Bocage' country against determined and brilliantly handled German troops. At one time we were up against the crack 12 PZ Division and later we fought against a 'stomach' battalion whose fighting qualities were derided by the Intelligence staffs at higher HQ. All I can say is that they should have come and fought against them themselves. They were well sited in positions from whence they could not leave, as they would have been shot by their tough regular NCOs behind them. They remained firing at us from their dugouts until we literally trod on them, causing unnecessary casualties particularly amongst [our] leaders.

The final two days of Operation Epsom, on 29 and 30 June, were the most savage of the offensive. The 11th Armoured Division had captured Hill 112, but Intelligence – perhaps Enigma/Ultra – had clearly indicated to Monty that really formidable counter-attacks by both the 1st and the SS Panzer Corps with the main thrust coming from the west, aimed at Cheux, might cut off the River Odon bridgehead. He ordered Lt.-Gen. O'Connor, GOC of the 8th Corps, to bring the 11th Armoured Division back in order to help defeat this new strong armoured counter-attack. In the five days of Operation Epsom, the 8th Corps suffered over 4,000 casualties. The Polar Bears had taken all of their objectives – at a heavy cost.

CHAPTER SEVENTEEN

The End of the 6th Bn Duke of Wellingtons

After their traumatic battle in Le Parc de Boislande – one day of victory, the second day of failure – the 6th Dukes were put into the 147th Brigade reserve for five days, from 19 to 24 June. Their morale was very low indeed. Their casualties had been a horrifying 16 officers and 220 men. Their well-respected CO, Lt.-Col. K.G. Exham had been sent back to England. They now had an interim CO, Lt.-Col. A. Warhurst, until their new CO arrived. Large intakes of raw reinforcements had to be swiftly integrated – not a happy business. The general wrote in his diary: '*Sunday 18th*. 6 DWR kicked out of Le Parc de Boislande by enemy counter-attack. Bad show after their excellent attack yesterday. 10 DLI failed to improve their position in St Pierre. Wed 21st: Spoke to officers of 6 DWR after their bad show. Looked in on Dick Oxley.'

Now under the command of Lt.-Col. A.J.D. Turner MC, who arrived on the evening of 26 June, the 6th Battalion Dukes took part, sadly, in their final battle action. Their task was to stop the gap between Juvigny and the western outskirts of Fontenay-le-Pesnel. The little river Bordel flowed east–west and ran through this piece of country, its valley thick with cover. The following account is derived from the Dukes' historian, Brig. C.N. Barclay:

> The ground made it difficult to approach unseen. The first half-mile was a forward slope, a great cornfield, criss-crossed by the tracks of armoured vehicles but with not a vestige of cover. After this came a stretch of fields, with their hedges running forward to drop sharply, in a wooded bluff, down to the river Bordel valley. Beyond it the orchards and fields rose gradually to the Juvigny–Fontenay road, along which the country was more open. 'C' and 'D' Coys went forward initially and being in full view were well mortared as they moved. There were casualties but they soon reached their objectives. 'A' and 'B' passed through and using all available cover managed to reach the top of the bluffs unseen and unmolested. There they were spotted and heavily mortared in a shallow ditch, the only cover. They continued to push on although 'B' Coy on the right came under fire from Juvigny – surprisingly – because the bridge there was meant to be in 'friendly' hands. Nevertheless the Dukes were now on their final objectives.

Then everything went wrong. The battalion mortar platoon suffered direct mortar hits and battalion HQ was shelled. Stretcher-bearers and carrying parties trying to get casualties to the RAP were heavily bombarded by mortars. The new battalion second in command, Maj. C.H. Forster, was killed when his carrier ran over a mine. Within 12 hours his successor, Maj. K.E.F. Miller ran over a mine in his jeep and was seriously wounded. 'C' Company, who had moved forward to a position on the right of 'A' Company, received direct mortar bomb hits on two slit trenches and their Company CO was one of many casualties. The reconnaissance battalion of the Hitler Youth SS Division under Gert Bremer was responsible for mortaring the Dukes with frightening ferocity.

The battered 6th Dukes, in some disarray, stayed where they were until the 30th. They were withdrawn again into brigade reserve, and then dug three separate and complete battalion positions in three days. Finally, they moved back by slow stages to the beachhead. By 12 August they were quartered in the United Kingdom at Colchester and provided reinforcements for the 7th Battalion.

A report from the Public Record Office (War Office 205/5G), made by their new CO, Lt.-Col. A.J.D. Turner MC, described the tragic situation Turner had encountered, the reasons for it and his recommendations:

REPORT ON STATE OF 6TH BN DWR (49 DIV) AS ON 30 JUN:

1. I arrived at 6 DWR on the evening of 26 June. From am 27 June until am 30 June we have been in contact with the enemy and under moderately heavy mortar and shell fire.

2. The following facts make it clear that this report makes no reflection on the state of 6 DWR when they left UK:
   a) In 14 days there have been some 23 officers and 350 OR casualties.
   b) Only 12 of the original officers remain and they are all junior. The CO and every rank above Cpl (except for 2 Lts) in battalion HQ have gone, all company commanders have gone. One company has lost every officer, another has only one left.
   c) Since I took over I have lost two second-in-commands in successive days and a company commander the third day.
   d) Majority of transport, all documents, records and a large amount of equipment was lost.

3. *State of Men*

   a) 75% of the men react adversely to enemy shelling and are 'jumpy'.
   b) 5 cases in 3 days of self-inflicted wounds – more possible cases.
   c) Each time men are killed or wounded a number of men become casualties through shell shock or hysteria.
   d) In addition to genuine hysteria a large number of men have left their positions after shelling on one pretext or another and gone to the rear until sent back by the MO or myself.
   e) The new drafts have been affected, and 3 young soldiers became casualties with hysteria after hearing our own guns.
   f) The situation has got worse each day as more key personnel have become casualties.

4. *Discipline and Leadership*

   a) State of discipline is bad, although the men are a cheerful pleasant type normally.
   b) NCOs do not wear stripes and some officers have no badges of rank. This makes the situation impossible when 50% of the battalion do not know each other.
   c) NCO leadership is weak in most cases and the newly drafted officers are in consequence having to expose themselves unduly to try to get anything done. It is difficult for the new officers (60%) to lead the men under fire as they do not know them.

7 DOW officers. Left to right: Walter Stone, John Lappin, Barry Kavanagh, Ken Evans. (John Lappin)

Conclusion

a) 6 DWR is not fit to take its place in the line.
b) Even excluding the question of nerves and morale 6 DWR will not be fit to go back into the line until it is remobilised, reorganised, and to an extent retrained. It is no longer a battalion but a collection of individuals. There is naturally no esprit de corps for those who are frightened (as we all are to one degree or another) to fall back on. I have twice had to stand at the end of a track and draw my revolver on retreating men.

Recommendation

If it is not possible to withdraw the battalion to the base or UK to re-equip, reorganise and train, then it should be disbanded and split among other units.

If essential that the battalion should return to the line, I request that I may be relieved of my command and I suggest that a CO with 2 or 3 years experience should relieve me and that he should bring his adjutant and a signals officer with him.

Being a regular officer I realise the seriousness of this request and its effect on my career. On the other hand I have the lives of the new officer personnel (which is excellent) to consider. Three days running a major has been killed or seriously wounded because I have ordered him to in effect stop them running during mortar concentrations. Unless withdrawn from the division I do not think I can get the battalion fit to fight normally and this waste of life would continue. My honest opinion is that if you continue to throw new officer and other rank replacements into 6 DWR as casualties occur, you are throwing good money after bad.

I know my opinion is shared by two other commanding officers who know the full circumstances.

In the field
30 June 1944

(Sgd) A.J.D. Turner
Lt.-Col. Commanding 6 DWR

This report, via brigade, division and corps, swiftly reached Gen. Montgomery, who was predictably very angry. He wrote to the Secretary of State for War, P.J. Grigg, saying that he had withdrawn the 6th Duke of Wellingtons Regiment from the 49th Division and on 6 July replaced them with the 1st Battalion Leicestershire Regiment. He described the Duke's CO as 'not a proper chap, displays a defeatist mentality'.

On 7 August Monty wrote to the unfortunate previous CO, Lt.-Col. K.G. Exham, in England about the disbandment. This was the end of the line for a brave, untried infantry battalion who had encountered the full ferocity of Hitler's *Jugend* and SS troops.

CHAPTER EIGHTEEN

Prelude to the Rauray Battle

'A Wee Bit of Bother'

There were a few days to go before the Polar Bears' next major battle, and reinforcements were pouring in to replace the dead and wounded young men lost at Fontenay and Tessel Wood. Maj. Harry Boyne, OC of 'D' Company of the Tyneside Scottish, had ordered Sgt. Gordon Cowie to report sick on 25 June, suffering from a severe form of enteritis. Cowie remembered:

> The RAP was filled with wounded Hallamshires, Yorks and Lancs (whose post it was). A Padre enlisted my help and a few non-wounded personnel to look after some of the Hallams. Handing out mugs of tea, cigarettes, etc. I noticed that the majority were not seriously wounded, but all appeared shocked and stunned and very pale underneath their camouflaged faces. It was their first time, actually the first few hours, of their first action. The noise from the 25 pdrs outside was deafening . . .. [A few days later] Major 'Bush' Nichol, our Bn 2 i/c arrived driving a jeep and very agitated. He ordered every available soldier [from the tented RHU near Bayeux] into the nearest 3-tonner saying 'every man is required now'. We were definitely scraping the bottom of the barrel for reinforcements, even the Bn tailor.

Pte. Ken West recalled that, on arriving from the 33rd RHU with his mate George,

> The RQMS, a tall, angular Scot, a typical regular soldier with a soft Scottish brogue welcomed our arrival. 'Welcome to the Royal Scots Fusiliers, laddies. We had a wee bit of bother yesterday and we're a wee bit shorthanded. . . . I would suggest you change ye're steel helmets for one o' these assault type on this pile – and camouflage netting on it too.
> Ken also handed in his khaki beret and received in return a larger khaki head-dress and an enormous brass cap badge, a tam-o-shanter.

John Longfield of 'D' Company of the 1/4th KOYLI said:

> Casualties meant reinforcements to whom we were, young as we were, old veterans. Like us they did not relish the idea of becoming a casualty and quite a few would say, 'I can't kill anybody', even when told it was often a case of kill or be killed, some could not face up to it. I feel sure that many a man died because when it came to the crunch, he hesitated for that vital fraction of a second before pressing the trigger. During training, guns were fired at targets, but there was not always enough emphasis that what it was all about was killing.

Another new reinforcement to arrive was Lt. John Lappin, who fortunately kept a diary:

> *Sat 1 July.* Reached Fontenay-le-Pesnil to join 7 DWR to find a real front line atmosphere. The Bn was standing too while its neighbours were being shelled and Jerry was jabbing away at the

forward positions. We were taken to the CO in his cute little dugout command post reminiscent of 'Journey's End', oil lamp and all. He seems a charming fellow, gave us a nice welcome.

Lappin met his new OC, Maj. Kavanagh of 'D' Company:

rather a breezy casual type and Bill Middleton the platoon Sgt, a droll Lancashire lad, very canny and capable. Also Lance Sgt. Walt Dawner, completely scatty, a good fighter. My predecessor Alexander got a 'blighty', 4 days back. The platoon did an attack on a Spandau overlooking the Tiger which was just behind. The Tiger gave them a dose of 88 mm HE and Alex came off worst with a piece of splinter in his neck. I became initiated into the practice of digging in. We specialise in it here.

Capt. Lewis Keeble of the 1/4th KOYLI recalled:

There's nothing like battle for promotion. During that three weeks at Tessel Wood, I had one lance corporal up to CQMS and another up to Sergeant. I'd have had my signals corporal Charlie Wainwright up to Field Marshal if it had been possible. Sergeants commanded most platoons, most of the time and were admirable.

Keeble also remembered:

The troglodyte doctor: being lost in the dark and fired on by own troops; the mutineering signaller saved by his Corporal; being shelled by Canadian mediums; the pacifist reinforcement; the drunken corporal; full body wash from a cup; a week in boots; tin hat lifted by a sniper; Tyneside Scottish rake our trenches; booby trap with football lace; shell reps; cider that corroded jerricans; Callard's rum; the Pioneer platoon massacred. And the battlefield is empty. One sees very few live, uncaptured enemy.

Lt. Brian Lott wrote:

Our CO Lt.-Col. E.C. Bacon [of the 55th Anti-tank Regiment] was unfortunately very tall and at Tessel Wood would stand on the side of the slit-trench talking to the men, sometimes with disastrous results. One [17-pdr anti-tank] gun was commanded by Bombardier Babington, my motor mechanic, the sergeant having been wounded. After a chat, the CO left, and the site was subjected to heavy mortar fire. I was requested 'For Gawd's sake keep the CO away, whenever he visits, we always get stonked.' Obviously the Germans on the other side of the valley had a wonderful view.

Maj. W.N. Richardson of the 69th Field Regiment described the battlefield around him:

On our left front was Tessel-Bretteville and further south was Bretteville. About June 28 the Tyneside Scots who had tried to get down to these [villages], got rather a bloody nose and 'D' Coy [the 4th Lincolns] was sent up to Tessel-Bretteville to give them a hand. On the following day 4 Lincolns took over their position. This is a rather fine village with beautifully built stone buildings and houses, reminiscent of the Cotswold's. Like all the villages in that area, it was badly wrecked by our shell fire and there were many dead cattle and horses about. The sweet sickly stench of dead animal was everywhere. There were also a lot of unburied Boche about. The worst place for this was the wood where 'D' Coy had been at the end of the Fontenay assault – there the tanks had run over the German dead in the road and it was really a horrible sight. Tessel-Bretteville is very close orchard country and from the best OP one could only see a thousand yards or so on a very narrow area. The company positions were well hidden and apart from Bn HQ and the reserve 'C' Coy, they got hardly any shelling or mortaring. The weather by now was pretty hot apart from one or two wet days. Quite a large number of Tiger and Panther tanks had been knocked out by the Shermans of 24

Lancers. Those chaps were a fine lot: the Squadron leader who worked with us at Fontenay was a most impressive soldier.

The gunners were nearly always in action. Maj. E.R.H. Bowring MC, the historian of the 143rd Field Regiment of the Kent Yeomanry, wrote:

On 17th June we fired a barrage in support of 6 DWR's attack on Le Parc de Boislande where both OP parties in support were blown up on mines within a few minutes of each other. The next day we supported 7 DWR in their famous attack on Point 102. From 25 June to 1st July we saw a period of intense activity. The guns were in action between Audrieu and Ducy Ste Marguerite and fired continuously in support of the three brigades in their battles around Fontenay, Rauray and Tessel-Bretteville – also in support of 50 Div on our right, 15th Scottish on our left. We will long remember the attack of 11 RSF on Fontenay, where despite the thick fog it was necessary to bring down 'Uncle' targets very close to our own troops in order to dislodge the Germans from their positions.

The sappers, too, were kept busy. Spr. Bill Hudson of the 757th Field Company RE reported that:

clearance of minefields and booby traps went on most of the time around Cristot and St Pierre. Almost as important was the horrible task of bulldozing graves for the hundreds of dead cattle and horses killed by shellfire striking every Norman field and a serious health hazard. Roads were repaired and in some back areas improvised shower baths were rigged up.

Pte. Jack Snook drove a 15 cwt truck for the divisional RASC. He recalled:

In that cramped bridgehead, ammunition, always a top priority, was required in almost unheard of quantities. The roads were crammed night and day with endless convoys of ammo lorries. They were bombed, ran the risk of road mines, occasionally sniped but no guns were ever kept waiting. We all took too much for granted, our food, water, petrol, oil, our letters, NAAFI rations, medical aid, RE supplies and the conveyance of troops over many miles were all by kind permission of the RASC. No one missed his daily bar of chocolate and rations of cigarettes, much less a meal . . .

According to the 69th Field Regiment's FOO, Maj. Richardson: 'Lt.-Col. Peter Barclay kept the 4th Lincolns active with hard patrolling and the Boche opposite us got little rest. He was enthusiastic about codenames. I can remember HAMMER, AXE, SAW, GIN wood, the LATTICE and the YELLOW HOUSE. We had to know them all and found it not too easy at times.'

Between the Lincolns and the Hallams at Tessel Wood was the No Man's Land of the valley around La Grande Ferme. Boche patrols located the Lincoln's Bn HQ which was shelled hard on most days. Maj. Richardson told how 'one stonk hit my 'Monster' [Richardson's Sherman] driver, Longhorn, jeep driver, Schofield, and batman, Winder, with shell splinters.'

A mile or so back at the 25-pdr gun pits incoming fire was often very accurate. Gnr. John Mercer wrote:

A second group of shells rained upon the gun position. Earth was scattered everywhere. 'No. 2 gun has been hit,' was the cry. Dougie Marshall and Johnny Feaver had been killed. Penhaligon the taciturn Cornish driver of the quad had been seriously wounded as several shellcases in the gun pit had exploded.

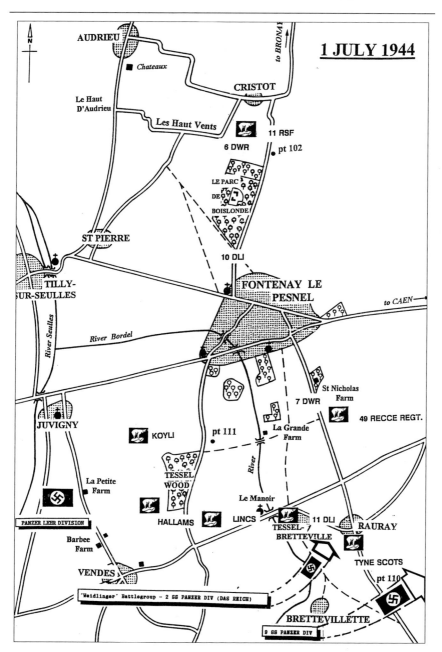

Fontenay Le Pesnel, 1 July 1944. (Bill Ashby)

The KOYLI had one disaster which could have been avoided, as described by L/Cpl. Geoff Steer:

> It had been a very trying day [the 29th] for No. 10 Platoon 'B' Coy [of the 1/4th KOYLI]. We were dug in at Tessel Wood. The heat was in the 90s and Jerry watched especially when the grub came up at about 5 pm. They also gave us a burst or two from their 6 Barrel Mortars. Our officer, Lt. Trumper and Sgt. Ball shared a dugout just to the left of mine. We were told that during the night the Pioneer Platoon would pass through our lines to go to the west of Tessel Wood to lay an anti-tank minefield. The mines, 6 to a box, already primed, and then return through our lines, having given the password. Nearly midnight we were awakened by this terrific explosion. Our blankets were blown some 50 yards away. The hedgerow bushes were on fire. We thought Jerry was shelling but there was no 88 mm whistle. The medics arrived and led Lt. Trumper and Sgt. Ball go down the hill to the RAP. We never saw them again. We stood too as dawn broke. What a sight! Parts of bodies everywhere, paybooks, dogtags and personal items. The 2 inch mortar team were killed by blast, Privates C.J. Smith and F. King. Corporal Thompson gave me a hand, we collected all the bits and pieces, placed 18 in one grave. Later HQ sent up all the crosses with their names on. Major Little our Coy CO thanked us for a job well done. We had lost all the Pioneer platoon and 4 of our No. 10 platoon. The explosions were a chain re-action, each blown up by blast.

Of course, it was exceedingly dangerous to cart several hundred *primed* anti-tank mines, by night, through a wood.

Rex Flower of the mortar platoon said: 'It was a very dangerous thing for 'S' Coy Pioneers to do, carrying mines, ready armed with detonators in place. Twenty six were killed. I knew most of the dead as it was my company.'

Under their new CO, Lt.-Col. Disney Barlow OBE from the KSLI, the 1/4th KOYLI now stayed dug in, absorbing punishment for another 25 days and nights. On the 'other side of the hill' the opposition was now two fresh divisions. The battle group *Weidinger* of the 2nd SS Panzer Division, known as *Das Reich*, had arrived via St Lô. Later they became notorious when it was discovered that on their way from Toulouse they had been harassed by the Maquis. In sadistic revenge they massacred the wrong village – 642 inhabitants of Oradour-sur-Glane – as a reprisal. Also now in the line were the 9th SS Panzer Division, known as *Hohen Staufen*, just arrived from the eastern front. The *Weidinger* battle group now held Brettevillette, and the 9th SS Panzer Division were behind them advancing towards Cheux, with the 10th SS Panzer Division behind them beyond the River Odon, heading north-east towards Caen and Carpiquet.

CHAPTER NINETEEN

The Rauray Battle

'Locked in Mortal and Bloody Combat with the Polar Bear Butchers'

At dawn on 1 July the Polar Bear Division had seven of its nine infantry battalions in the front line. The 11th Royal Scots Fusiliers were on the right near Juvigny and in touch with the 50th Tyne Tees Division, who were next to them, the 1/4th KOYLI held the western edge of Tessel Wood, the Hallams defended the south-west corner, just north of Vendes, linking up eastward with the Lincolns at Tessel-Bretteville. The line continued: the 11th Durham Light Infantry were near Rauray and finished on the left, with the Tyneside Scottish holding the high ground to the south, known as Point 110. They were in contact with the 6th King' Own Scottish Borderers of the 44th Brigade of the 15th Division, who held the ground east of them. Only those units near Point 110 had a good field of view. The visibility of the others was restricted by high hedges and trees.

At 0450 hours a Tyneside Scottish patrol returned from Bretteville and reported hearing sounds of considerable enemy tank movement south of the village, and that some wounded Tynesiders were still lying in the village unheeded by the enemy. A little later, Maj. Angus, OC of 'C' Company, who were in the forward right position, reported that they were being mortared and shelled by the enemy in considerable volume and that machine-guns were firing into their locality immediately to their front. By 0640 hours both 'C' Company and 'B' Company reported that they were being strongly attacked by German infantry supported by tanks. This counter-attack was by an infantry battalion of the 2nd SS Division and a tank battalion of the 9th SS Division. At 0650 hours the enemy laid a smokescreen and infantry began to attack the Tessel-Bretteville to Point 110 sector of the allied front. The main thrusts were between the junction between the Lincolns and the 11th Durham Light Infantry battalions and 'B' Company and 'C' Company of the Tyneside Scottish. Five Tiger tanks approached 'B' Company of the Tyneside Scottish, while others near Brettevillette shot HE shells at 'B' Company of the 11th Durham Light Infantry and 'C' Company of the Tyneside Scottish.

Sgt. Gordon Cowie, who had just joined 'D' Company in reserve, recalled:

1 July was actually my first day in action. It was not nice but I was very proud to have taken part in this battle. Later we learned that we had won a Battle Honour for this action. The CO, Lt.-Col. R.W.M. de Winter, 'alerted' the whole battalion, moving up the tank support of the 24th Lancers and calling for artillery DF targets. Capt. Buchanan brought his 3 inch mortars into action, also firing on prearranged DF targets. In the dawn light, enemy troops had managed to get in close, coming from Brettevillette and Queudeville, and the Tynesiders' anti-tank 6-pdrs were soon in action. Sgt. O'Brien's anti-tank gun, operated with the greatest coolness and courage by its crew, knocked out five tanks in their first six shots, two of them at point-blank range. The attack was now clearly in considerable strength, and the whole corps artillery, backed by naval warship fire, was ranging along the battalion front. 'A' Company, under Maj. Mirrielees MC, on the left flank was forced back from their five-sided, field which was occupied by the enemy. On the right, 'C' Company was also compelled to pull back its forward platoons, now down to 8 or 9 men, to retain some link with the neighbouring 'B' Company of the 11th Durham Light Infantry. Although hard pressed, Maj. K.P. Calderwood's 'B' Company still held firm in the centre. However, soon the SS troops had worked their way round the flank of 'B' Company and had surrounded it. However, the carrier platoon fought their way forward to bring up supplies of ammunition.

During the rest of the morning, fresh attempts to infiltrate into the British lines were made. Spandau parties and snipers continued to cause problems around the village of Rauray, where there was a lot of close fighting. Similar parties worked their way between 'C' Company and 'B'

2nd Kensingtons Bren Carrier passes a knocked-out German tank in Rauray. (IWM, B6137)

Durham Light Infantry anti-tank gunners inspect a knocked-out Tiger tank at the Bretteville crossroads. (IWM, 6045)

Company of the Tyneside Scottish. During the morning's fighting, another gap had developed between 'B' Company and 'A' Company on their left. Tanks and Panzer Grenadiers had attacked along the line of the road to Cheux [the 49th and 15th Division boundary]. 'A' Company had been forced to give ground and moved over temporarily to join with the 6th King's Own Scottish Borderers of the 44th Brigade, holding the right flank of the Scottish division. The tanks then swung round, and 'B' Company spotted them 300 yards behind their position heading northwards, and they reported the situation. Tanks from the 24th Lancers engaged them and knocked out six, which stopped the advance. More tanks could be heard in the direction of Brettevillette, and the area was heavily stonked by artillery and mortars.

Capt. A.P. Whitehead's battalion history related:

> As each successive attack broke down on the Bn line, the enemy subjected the whole area, especially the 110 m ring contour to murderous artillery and mortar fire, softening up for the next attempt. One of these attacks was headed by British soldiers in British uniform driven on in front of the SS troops. The CO ordered up a platoon of 'D' Coy in reserve under Lt. Murray to the relief of 'B' Coy and succeeded in reaching them on the ring contour.

Between 1300 hours and 1430 hours the enemy put in fresh attacks. 'B' Company were attacked twice and 'C' Company reported troops concentrating in front of them. These were dealt with by heavy fire from the artillery regiments, which broke up the attacks. During the afternoon, Crocodile flame-throwing tanks assisted the Tyneside Scottish and the 11th

Durham Light Infantry in clearing away the Spandau teams and snipers that had infiltrated. They sprayed the hedgerows to force them out of hiding. Many Boche were shot trying to escape rather than surrender.

Capt. Whitehead continued:

> By about 1500 hrs the full fury of the German counter-attack had been worn down. No enemy formation could hope to reach its objective through the screen of artillery. It now remained to clear the Boches from within our own lines and restore the defensive position. A company of DLI were placed under command. The Tyneside counter-attack was for 'D' in reserve, with the surviving carrier crews, to clear the ground between them and 'B' Coy and for the DLI to retake the five-sided field once held by 'A' Coy.
>
> At 1600 hrs a large number of enemy infantry and tanks were spotted by observers from 'B' Coy and the 6 KOSB forming up near Quedeville for yet another determined attack. The combined artillery, MMG, and mortar fire of both divisions, together with naval gunfire, was directed with devastating effect. It was enough to end the German plans to break through on this sector of the front.
>
> At 1700 hrs with gallant tank support from the 24th Lancers, the 40 remaining survivors of 'B' Coy covered by 12 Bren guns and 4 Sherman tank Besas moved forward clearing the hedges of Germans as they went. By 1800 hrs all enemy had been cleared from within our lines, the five-sided field had been regained. 'D' Coy relieved 'B' Coy on the ring contour.

Sgt. Gordon Cowie remembered having just returned from hospital:

> Ernie Parker, my troop Sgt., told me that we were to counter attack up the left hand side of the field on our right and that I, because I was 'fresh' would lead 'D' Coy with my section. I thought that was very kind of Ernie to give me such a star role! The object of course to relieve 'B' Coy which was still more or less surrounded and take over 'A' Coy positions which had been overrun and were now occupied by the enemy.

Cowie slung his Sten across his chest, then acquired a rifle and a bandolier of fifty rounds. He continued:

> I had my tea 'laced' with rum, but Colour Sgt. 'PIPEY' McKay had rum laced with tea. So together with Taffy Jones, the Bren Gunner, the No. 2, Vinyard from Ipswich and followed by the Adjutant, Captain Alexander, now OC 'C' Coy, and about 30 or 40 men behind me in single file set off at H-Hour, 1700 hrs. I felt somewhat exposed. Everyone including the CO looked white and tense. I felt OK although do not know how I looked. Like the others I was to be frightened many times like this. Being an NCO in any case one had to set an example. I think I did this day.

There were many gallant deeds performed that day. Pte. Hugh Allan was badly wounded in the legs by a mortar bomb. Sgt. Sam Swaddle ignored heavy machine-gun fire to drag the wounded man to relative safety, and then carried him 1½ miles back to the RAP. Allan remembered: 'Sam and another man, Bill Barclay from Edinburgh, carried me all the way taking turns each, over their shoulders.' One of the Durham Light Infantry was wounded and was caught on barbed wire. Pte. Jim Barnes ran out and rescued him under fire and brought him back to Sgt. Gordon Cowie's slit trenches.

Rex Flower of mortar platoon of the 1/4th KOYLI recalled:

> We heard the skirl of bagpipes and to our surprise a Scots regiment [the 1st Tyneside Scottish] came right through our positions, attacking to the left of Tessel Wood. I think their objective was Brettevillette and Rauray. They came back later, minus a lot of men and sadly the pipes too! Some tanks went with them but I didn't see them again either.

The Tynesider losses were horrendous. Around 100 men including two young officers, Lt. Bolton and Lt. Wallace, were killed that day. Another 300 were wounded, missing or captured. At Andrieu, where the battalion were placed in reserve, 200 South Wales Borderers, 100 Herefords and 50 Glosters arrived to join them. All surviving rifle company personnel were grouped into two companies, 'B' and 'C', with a new 'A' Company formed from the South Wales Borderers and a new 'D' Company from the Herefords. The RQMS Manson obtained replacements for all lost or destroyed equipment.

On the evening of the 1st, Maj.-Gen. 'Bubbles' Barker sent the poor battered Tynesiders a message: 'My congratulations on the magnificent stand made by you today. You have today made a great name for yourselves, not only in the Division, but in the army as a whole. I deplore the casualties you have sustained but am gratified to know that the gallant band who remained on point 110 were successfully relieved.'

The Durhams' Story

David Rissik, the Durham Light Infantry historian, briefly recollected the part that the 11th Battalion played in the Rauray counter-attack, in which it suffered some 200 casualties, including two company commanders killed and another wounded:

> It was a day of bitter fighting. The Germans launched their most determined and well planned counter-attack since the initial landing. A whole division seemed determined to punch a hole three to four miles wide in the British positions. Among many outstanding incidents of a memorable day was an immediate counter attack under Capt. Robert Ellison with a platoon of 'A' Coy, a troop of tanks and two sections of carriers under Captain J.B. Nicholson. This effectively broke up a German attempt to infiltrate between the DLI and [the Lincolns of] 146 Brigade [just west of Tessel-Bretteville].
>
> When some positions of the Tyneside Scottish had been overrun, early in the evening 'C' Coy were called up to counter attack. It was personally led by the Coy CO Capt. Bill McMichael, exactly according to the Barnard Castle battle school 'book'. While a platoon under Lt. Keith Pallister moved down the 5-sided field and engaged some Spandaus and a heavy MG, McMichael took the rest down the right flank. Down the alley between them, tanks brought down covering fire. When Pallister got held up, McMichael and Corporal Rowe threw 77 grenades and 'C' Coy made short work of the Germans who made off in all directions.

Ronald Dinnin, the MTO of the 10th Durham Light Infantry, recalled: 'There was at some times infiltration of the Brigade's position but each time they were made, they were successfully restored by the DLI. In one instance a 'flame-thrower' tank was used for the first time. Unfortunately there were heavy casualties on both sides.' After the battle was over, the 11th Battalion needed 200 and the 10th Battalion 150 reinforcements.

The German counter-attack also came in onto the 4th Lincolns' front, and 'B' Company under Maj. W.E. Pattin resisted stoutly on the left forward sector. However, the enemy SS penetrated a short distance into the battalion area, when they were promptly counter-attacked by 'C' Company at 0800 hours – with complete success. To keep the situation under control, 'A'

Company of the 7th Dukes came under command to strengthen the left flank. However, in two days of fighting, 22 Lincolns were killed, including Maj. J.M. Staniland and CSM B.H. Ringham.

The Sherwood Rangers also helped to stem the tide. 'C' Squadron supported the 10th Durham Light Infantry and lost two tanks, and Sgt. Nelson did magnificent work fetching back their wounded crews under heavy fire.

The Suffolk Yeomanry, the 55th Anti-tank Regiment, played an important part in the defence of Rauray on 1 July. 'A' Troop of the 217th Battalion were with the 11th Durham Light Infantry and 'C' Troop were with the 10th Durham Light Infantry.

Lt. W.S. Vaughan, 'C' troop commander, Sgt. W. Hall and Bdr. L.W. Sparrow were the heroes of the day, winning the MC, DCM and Croix de Guerre, respectively. Sgt. Hall and his detachment knocked out five Panthers. Hall manhandled his gun 400 yards under fire to get into action, with excellent laying and aiming by Bdr. Sparrow. Sgt. Sturgeon of 'B' troop and his detachment knocked out another Panther, making the Suffolk Yeomanry bag for the day six tanks in all. 'B' Troop was with the Tyneside Scottish, and their OC reported that:

A third gun in the troop was confronted with a Panther head on and partially hull-down at 600–700 yards. Remembering all that had been said during four weary years of training on the 'engagement of hull down targets at long range' this detachment showed commendable restraint for some time. Eventually human nature got the upper hand and they opened up. The first round went straight through the turret probably killing the tank commander. The Panther immediately proceeded to reverse, still head on, back behind the crest and three more rounds merely glanced off the frontal glacé plate. The Germans miscalculated their position in relation to the gun and turned broadside on a fraction too soon. One further round achieved a satisfactory 'brew up'. The APTC taught us the value of manhandling the guns and the use of dummy guns to draw enemy fire. The effect of the new Sabot ammo was found to be devastating. But only four of the ten 6 pdrs which started the day were fit for action at the end of it.

The gunners were superb that day. Maj. W.N. Richardson of the 69th Field Regiment RA recalled:

A Boche counter attack came in early in the morning. Billy was with the Bn [the 4th Lincolns] – 'C' Coy had a sharp encounter clearing the 'Pheasantry' on the left and our OP shot well. Unfortunately some guns didn't and they had several short rounds in 'B' Coy. Dick was rightly furious. I acted as CPO and later went up to take over from Billy. By then the position was quite quiet as far as the Lincolns were concerned but on our left where 70 Bde were, there was a terrific battle going on. The infantry 6 pdrs and gunner 17 and 6 pdrs had a very good day, so did the 75's in the Tanks. Something over 40 enemy tanks were knocked out. The centre of the battle was Rauray and an excellent cartoon was later given to General Barker as a memento – but unpopular as a Christmas card later on.

Gnr. John Mercer, in his book, *Mike Target*, wrote:

It was now July 1st 1944 and my twenty-first birthday. Instead of being in the centre of a warm family party in England, I was in the centre of a pitched battle. I was being showered with earth from exploding mortar bombs. Under the enemy bombardment lasting ten minutes, orders directed from the halftrack [of the 185th Field Regiment's observation post] ten feet to my right sent our shells whining overhead to fall with a crash on targets invisible to me. Mike target after Mike target was called. I was aware of many shells falling short and exploding behind me. On the left some Sherman tanks were moving up to reinforce our troops. One was struck by an AP shell fired from an 88 mm gun. It 'brewed up', its crew jumped out in haste and it caught fire and exploded. One man was in flames.

After the counter-attack battle of Rauray, Troop Sgt. R.D. Sheldrake with 'A' Battery of the 55th Anti-tank Regiment wrote:

> It fell to my lot to help get the wounded back on my jeep. Time after time, Dave and I took wounded men back to the RAP. But it wasn't half enough. We were supporting the DLI's who were wickedly mauled, being reinforced sometimes twice in one day when they lost 75% casualties . . .. I had seemed to have become immune to the suffering. I was almost ashamed to find that the dead meant nothing to me, that even the stink of flyblown flesh was something I could live with.

He recalled how a relieving troop commander from the 53rd Division straight from England was badly wounded, and died of his wounds because 'the next second we were all flat on our bellies (at THQ talking to me, Guv and our BC, pointing out the landmarks). An 88 mm airburst arrived. Thanks to that sixth sense we had learned at great cost, almost everyone was safe, everyone except the new Troop Commander, wearing a beret [not a steel helmet].'

The Lancers' Story

The main onslaught in the Rauray battle was delivered against the 70th Brigade by skilful German infiltration, pre-dawn and then later under cover of smoke. Much of the credit for beating off the four determined attacks, apart from the intense artillery fire, must go to the 24th Lancers. Leonard Willis, their historian wrote:

> There were reports of 70 enemy tanks massing south of Fontenay. Opposed to them were the Sherwood Rangers Yeomanry and 10th DLI south of Rauray and 24th Lancers with Tyneside Scottish in Rauray village itself. 'C' Sqn had two troops east of the village, two to the west and Squadron HQ covering the road running north and south through the village. 'A' and 'B' Squadrons dominated the right and left flanks respectively, but Major Bill Luddington's 'C' Sqd bore the brunt of the battle. At 0645 a force of fifteen Panthers and a Tiger tank attacked the Tyneside Scottish right flank positions, passed through them and fought their way into the west side of Rauray. The attack was eventually stopped by 1st and 3rd Troop 'C' Sqn and a rapid counter attack by our infantry, supported by two troops of 'A' Sqn on the right flank, drove the enemy out of the village into the woods behind. By virtue of the dense orchard, thick country, the Lancers were unable to engage them but the Tyneside infantry and the anti-tank gunners [of the 55th Anti-tank Regiment] got eleven of them before their positions were over-run and most of the gun crews killed.
> The second attack was against the Tyneside Scottish left forward Company, to the east of the village. The Lancer tanks were unable to go south of the key orchard, which was dominated by two Tiger tanks. A further attack overran the left forward Tyneside company, but the enemy's advance towards Rauray was halted by allied tanks, which destroyed all of the six visible Panthers supporting the attack.

Capt. Douglas Aitken, MO of the 24th Lancers', took up the story:

> Throughout the rest of the day repeated smaller attacks were made, usually three to five Panthers supporting a company of infantry, they were all beaten off. Sgt. Wilcox Troop Sgt. 2nd Tp 'C' Sqn camouflaged his tank, waited completely in the open, disguised as part of the

49th Division Christmas card, 1944. The cartoon was inspired by Lord Haw-Haw's reference to the division as 'The Polar Bear Butchers'.

The 'Butcher Bear' is seen standing at his chopping block at the sign-post to BAUBAU. He is dressed in his blue & white apron and has his 'steel' slung round his waist. He is snarling and a few drops of blood drip from his great jaws. His right paw is toppling over a Panther. His left paw is poised over a butchers knife stuck in the belly of an SS bastard. More SS bastards each with a gory belly wound, lie beside him. Left around him 'brewed up Panthers & Mk IV specials and one Tiger; each show their swastikas. A few bodies lie around the brewed up Bosch tanks. There is a background of 'bocage' through which can be seen the muzzles of British 75's & 17 pdrs, also a Bren or two all firing. Above the bocage two conventional flagstaffs fly the burgees of the —

24 Lancers & Tyneside Scots!

hedgerow. When the enemy tanks were seen and clear of the orchard, he called up 2nd and 1st troop tanks who speedily came up level with him, fired furiously for about 30 seconds and then retired to their concealed positions. Sgt. Wilcox was awarded the MM. At about 6.00 pm the Tyneside Scottish counter attacked to recapture their forward position supported by 'C' Sqn and by 6.30 pm had recaptured all the lost ground. It was a graveyard of smouldering Panther tanks. Lt.-Col. W.A.C. Anderson, the Lancers' CO was awarded the DSO and Major Bill Luddington the MC. The action demonstrated how the defences had the advantage over the attack. We had an ample supply of tanks in reserve to replace those lost in battle. The Germans did not, and the loss of so many tanks and SP guns was very serious for them. Altogether the 'bag' on the 70 Brigade front was 34 Panthers of which 31 were destroyed in the Rauray area. 'C' Sqd took out nine plus two SPs and 'B' Sqn a SP gun and 'A' Sqn killed about 200 of the enemy. All for the loss of three Shermans and three brave 'C' Sqn troopers.

Our tank boys now have greater experience and the infantry have at least appreciated that the PIAT could knock out a Tiger, never mind a Panther.

The voices [on the radio] of the tank commanders were calm and blasé. 'Hello, Charlie Able, there are five Panthers creeping towards the corner of the orchard on your right. Can you see them? Good. Blast them to blazes. Hello Charlie Able, well done – I saw one hit. How many did you get?' and so on. By lunchtime 'C' Sqn had got five Panthers and a SP gun. Poor 'A' our most notorious Sqn were in reserve that day and very angry about being out of it. The Tyneside Scottish we were supporting claimed 42 tanks which was considered fantastic. In typical British fashion the BBC announced that night a total bag of 30, not to mention hundreds of Jerry infantry. A poor day for the Germans.

It was indeed. In three days of battle the *Hohen Staufen* Division had suffered 1145 casualties, the battle group *Weidinger* 636 and the Hitler *Jugend* 1240. Jack Snook, divisional RASC, said:

We turned our small radio on to the Forces Network to hear the news. Imagine our surprise when the German Forces broadcaster nicknamed by us as 'Lord Haw Haw' came out with the phrase, 'You Polar Bear Butchers!' I said to Freddie, my mate, 'Hey that's us.' Haw Haw went on to say that if any man with a Polar Bear flash on his shoulder was captured he would be shot right away without any trial whatsoever. He said that British soldiers with a Polar Bear flash on their shoulders had massacred SS German tank crews who had come out of their tanks with their hands up, to surrender, only to be mown down without mercy.

The General wrote in his diary:

2 July. Yesterday the old 49 Div made a great name for itself and we are all feeling very pleased with ourselves. After being attacked on my left half, all day by infantry and tanks, we were in our original positions after a small scale counter attack by the evening. We gave him a real bloody nose and we calculate having knocked out some 35 tanks mostly Panthers. One of my Scots Battns [the Tyneside Scottish] distinguished themselves particularly. We gave him a proper knockout with our artillery with very strong concentration on any point where movement was expected. 'Bimbo' Dempsey is coming to see me at 2.30. My tanks gave me great support yesterday and accounted for quite a number of Panthers. Bobby Erskine came over this am to give his congratulations.

The division was now widely known as the 'Barker Bears'. The Rauray battle of 1 July was a major honour, not only for the division but specifically for the Tyneside Scottish, the Durham Light Infantry, the 55th Anti-tank Regiment and, of course, the 24th Lancers. A 49th Division memorial now stands proudly near the military cemetery between Rauray and Fontenay-le-Pesnel.

CHAPTER TWENTY

Holding the Line

'Listening All the Time'

For the next three weeks the Polar Bears continued to hold the 3,000 yard line from the Rauray area west towards, but not including, Vendes. Most of the time, vigorous patrolling was carried out, and reinforcements received and integrated. Brig.-Maj. Paul Crook of the 147th Brigade wrote in *Came the Dawn*:

Early in July we changed commanders in addition to the replacement of 6 DWR by 1 Leicesters. Our Irish Brigadier [Mahoney] although physically brave as a lion could not mentally cope with the complexities of handling a brigade group and armour in action, and started to do some very strange things. Fearing for the safety of the soldiers, I had to report these to the GSO1 at Division, Dick Jelf. The Brigadier did in fact suffer a nervous breakdown and was abruptly invalided home.

His replacement, Brig. Henry Wood, who had been commanding a battalion of the Queens in the bridgehead, Crook regarded as 'a very high grade officer in all respects, as well as a friend'. On the same day, 3 July, he continued:

Lt.-Col. Montgomery-Cunningham, the massive unflappable, splendid CO of 11 RSF was killed. His Jocks adored him and he was a tremendous loss. He was replaced by Duncan Eykyn a friend of mine from Staff College days. Three Bn Cos in 147 Bde had been written off in less than a month and the only CO to survive was Felix Wilsey with the 7th Dukes. He was an outstanding CO, always courteous and kindly as well as brave and efficient. John Drive, our splendid Staff Captain left to go to Staff College, and Jack Crosland, a new General Staff Officer joined us.

Capt. John Lappin of the 7th Duke of Wellingtons Regiment had his views on the 'management': 'Saturday 8th July. Our GOC Division, General Barker came to see us – waited all afternoon – Rather ancient but quite a nice old stick. They say he knows his modern war alright – fair enough!' However, within the first three weeks of campaigning, two out of three Polar Bear Brigadiers had been replaced – not a good start at all.

Lt.-Col. Hart Dyke wrote:

The grand strategy of the campaign caused us [the Hallams] to remain in our exposed positions south and east of Tessel Wood for three weeks. Sporadic enemy shell and mortar fire from three directions caused daily casualties. The enemy augmented these by regular 'stonks' between 9 and 10 am and 4 and 6 pm. Even in one's slit trench one was not safe. The RSM was buried and although dug out quickly was never the same and had to be replaced a month later. But 'D' Coy at the SW corner of Tessel Wood had the worst of it. They suffered severely. I eventually had to move them.

The MO, Gregory Dean, CQMS Jackson and CSM Langdale were wounded, and the new adjutant, Capt. Kesby, was killed by a shell within 24 hours of his arrival. Hart Dyke wrote:

One is responsible for so many men's lives and it is difficult to avoid seeing the casualties, to give the men every possible fire support. All ranks learnt two things very quickly. A high standard of discipline to ensure that plans did not go astray and unnecessary casualties suffered, and secondly, the truth of the adage – DIG or DIE. Before leaving England we had succeeded in obtaining a pick or a shovel for every man in a rifle company. They were so valued in Normandy that the men carved their initials on them.

On 10 July a strong fighting patrol was sent out to snatch a prisoner for unit identification. In close-quarter fighting, 'A' Company, under Maj. Nicholson and Lt. Poyner, killed 14 enemy and wounded another 8, but the Hallams lost 25 casualties from the enemy artillery strafe which followed. Lt. Poyner was killed and no prisoners were taken, but epaulettes and papers identified the enemy unit. Lt.-Col. Hart Dyke was convinced now 'that any attack needed tank support OR one must attack by night, as artillery support in bocage country was of little value and only advertised an attack'.

Hart Dyke also evolved new platoon tactics for the bocage:

The Bren guns allocated for air attack defence were now made available to the rifle companies since the *Luftwaffe* was a spent force. Platoons were organised into two Bren gun sections of two NCOs, four men and two Brens each, plus one large rifle section and platoon HQ with the 2 inch mortar. In the advance the Bren sections advanced up parallel hedgerows, one Bren covering the other while the rifle section remained in reserve available to carry out a turning movement under the platoon commander covered by the mortar. These tactics reduced the number of men advancing at any one time and the death roll of platoon commanders. In defence this organisation was highly successful, giving each forward section two Bren guns for cross-fire. The rifle section specialised in patrolling.

The description of patrols varied according to the rank of the participant. John Longfield, then a private with the 1/4th KOYLI, wrote:

We carried out nightly patrols either fighting or reconnaissance. Of course each man did not go out every night but we all went out several times. As the nights passed, no matter how dark it was, we got to know where we were when out in No Man's Land. Often this was by smell. Dead men and dead cows smell very differently and as we crept along we knew where we were by the various hedges and the smells! We went out as quietly as possible, tried to get right up to the German positions, hurled 36 grenades into them and then opened fire. Bullets and bombs would usually come in the opposite direction and after the exchange we would retreat to our own lines. One night we were pinned down in a cabbage field. Hugging the ground as closely as possible, I could hear the Spandau bullets smashing the cabbages. I let fly in return of course and fortunately managed to keep lower than the German bullets. When we ran out of ammunition, as was inevitable, we made a break for it towards our own lines.

The next day Longfield's company CO gave him a rocket for leaving so many empty Bren gun magazines behind.

The story by the young platoon commander, Lt. John Lappin of the 7th Duke of Wellingtons Regiment, is a little different:

Monday 10th, with KEV [Kavanagh, his Company CO] to recce the front line positions at Tessel-Bretteville – a snug little position. The big snag is patrolling. Personally I think the Lincolns are asking for trouble. They have had two platoon commanders killed in two nights on patrol. No Man's Land is in front of us, about one mile in which Jerry puts out the odd Spandaus at night.

On the 13th, Lappin led out a small fighting patrol:

By this time it was light: off we went by the same route and walked straight out of the corn into the trees in front of the house. There we found several weapon pits with signs of occupation but the whole bloody lot were asleep! I dropped off a Bren gun there to cope with the occupants when they awoke, and went round into the house. That was easy – it was empty but in the back garden were three more Jerries in their dugouts. Simpson got one with his Sten and I got the two others with a grenade followed by Sten. Strangely enough I had no compunction about it. It just seemed the obvious thing to do. By this time the hullabaloo had roused the other Boche and the Spandau teams woke up on our right and started something. My right hand Bren was outnumbered so decided to withdraw but not before getting at least 3 Boche in the process. Simpson got another with his Sten and Wright bagged another with his rifle. Getting too hot so we withdrew into the cornfield, made for base, Jerry firing wildly at us from the trees. None of my blokes were hurt.

L/Cpl. Simpson was recommended for the MM. Fusilier Ken West of the 11th Royal Scots Fusiliers recounted his experience on patrol, which was under the brand-new Canloan platoon officer, Lt. Wilson, who was nicknamed the 'Bank manager'. Wilson said: 'We're off at 1400 hrs on a standing patrol [to the east of Juvigny]. Just beyond that clump of trees there's a farm, we'll go through the farm and take up a position on the far side of the wood. We are borrowing a section from 15 platoon – that makes us about twenty-five in all.' Wilson and his batman led, followed by signaller Cpl. Jackie Thompson and his rifleman escort, then the experienced Sgt. Louis Hill, and the leading section. West led the next section on the opposite side of the road. They made their way along the hedgerows towards the farmyard, which was surrounded on three sides by a high stone wall. 'Through the yard, out of the southern gate, straight across the field to the wood – pretty straightforward,' said Sgt. Hill. 'Recce patrols have reported no enemy in the wood.' Soon after, Spandaus opened up on the leading section and killed Lt. Wilson and two fusiliers. Fusilier Ken West continued:

Our own Bren guns fired back to try to stop this hail of lead. Our rear section reported that a further Spandau was firing now from the left flank of the wood preventing anyone from getting back to the hedge. We had been ambushed, caught in a simple trap! Tracer bullets were now being fired over the top of the wall into the left of the barn filled with new-mown hay. Within minutes the whole of the barn was ablaze.

By using drains and ditches, the patrol, 'some covered in cow muck and stinking like a sewage-works,' managed to make their escape, leaving the three dead behind.

Many of those who fought in Normandy were aware of the lethal power of the dreaded *Minnenwerfer*, the multibarrelled mortars nicknamed 'Moaning Minnies' because of the disgusting and frightening noise they made. They probably accounted for two-thirds of all allied casualties. Because they were so mobile, it was essential to try to eliminate them by every possible means. Initially the gunner regiments would plaster the landscape with 25-pdr shells on a reported mortar site. The Kensingtons had a vested interest in the matter: their 4.2 inch mortars were invaluable to the Polar Bears in the front line, in both attack and defence. Under Lt. G.A. Hunt, their adjutant, a counter-mortar office was set up at divisional HQ to call on fire from corps and divisional artillery, plus all 4.2 inch and 3 inch mortars. The codename for counter-mortar activity was 'Poppycock', followed by the compass bearing of the suspected mortar position. A number of reports enabled cross-bearings to be made, then targets were engaged and heavily plastered.

Lt.-Col. Hart Dyke recalled:

> At Tessel Wood all the mortar platoons got into their stride and the constant practice given them in neutralising enemy mortars gave them great confidence for the future. The gunners also came into their own. The 49th Division produced a wonderful counter-mortar and counter-battery organisation. Compass bearings called 'shell-reps' and 'mortar-reps' were sent in by each Coy as soon as an enemy gun or mortar fired on us. Harold Sykes or Mickie Carter our FOO's [of the 69th Field Regiment] did the necessary when we got a tri-section.

Rex Flower from the mortar platoon of the 1/4th KOYLI described life in the front line:

> We had to stand to the next night, an attack was expected. Nothing happened, only the usual quota of enemy shit. Sgt. Kohlman was wounded, an old friend from icelandic days; Pte. Kennett, was killed; my old friend Bill Avery left us through shellshock. In Blighty we had shared everything. A reservist who did his turn in India and Burma with the 2nd Bn. The shell fire was really a bit much! Constant shellfire plays on the nerves. We were always listening all the time.

However, on 3 July, he wrote: 'Our turn to visit the Army Baths unit, in a large field with a lot of water heaters, rows of shower heads under awnings. There was no luxuriating. 'Just get the dirt off, Jack.' As we left the shower we were given a clean towel and pants. It was very efficient!'

Unfortunately the fog and chaos of war often meant that the fallen were not always accounted for, although most regimental padres made determined efforts to track down and retrieve 'their' dead. Lt. John Lappin of the 7th Dukes noted in his diary:

> *Monday 3 July.* A filthy day. I read the burial service while we buried two lads of the DLI lying in our platoon area, caught in the open by a burst of Spandau. I hope I got some real feeling into those prayers. Poor lads. We were relieved by the RSF back to our old positions in the orchard next to the Lincolns.

On the evening of 6 July, most of the British Army, including the Polar Bears, watched 400 Lancaster and Halifax bombers unleash their dreadful load on Caen, just 10 miles away. The damage caused by the 3,300 tons of bombs to human life, fabric and buildings was immense. Little loss and few casualties were suffered by the Germans, who had shrewdly drawn back their forces into the eastern suburbs.

For 10 days, 4 Lincolns were dug in near Tessel Wood until relieved by the 7th Dukes on 9 July. They had sent many patrols out and vigorously mortared the opposition, but in so doing suffered casualties. Maj. J.M. Staniland, Lt. Fowler, Lt. Merrill and Lt. Wallace were all killed in action. After a well-earned rest at Ducy Ste Marguerite (where visits to Bayeux produced unlimited supplies of cheese, butter and cream), they relieved the Hallams on 16 July. Two Polish deserters told them that the village of Vendes, to the south-west, and until now heavily defended, was now empty. It was now a period of heavy rain, so all of the roads turned from thick dust to axle-deep mud.

Both of the Durham Light Infantry battalions, terribly battered after the Rauray action, spent 4 days near Bayeux, absorbing reinforcements, resting and recovering. ENSA shows and cinemas were now put on. Clean battledress and shoes [instead of boots] made the war seem some way away. On 7 July they were up in the line again in the Tilly area, and by coincidence they were next door to their sister battalion of the 50th Northumbrian Division. So no less than five battalions of Durhams were clustered together protecting the bridgehead. On 11 July the 10th Durham Light Infantry supported the 50th Division in an attack on the Juvigny–Hottot road. 'C' Company and 'B' Company led, but the latter suffered heavily as it moved across open ground, and took 50 casualties, mainly from mortar fire. They received magnificent support from 'C' Company of the Kensingtons, who fired nearly half a million rounds of MMG ammo during the day. Two days later, the 11th Durham Light Infantry relieved the 10th Durham Light Infantry. It sounds rather absurd, but the 11th were pleased to move up. They had been in reserve and were almost overcome by an overpowering smell. Patrols located an abandoned Camembert cheese factory a mile away – upwind.

The Tyneside Scottish, after their traumatic battle defending Rauray, were back in the line a week later, when they took over a defensive position from the 11th Royal Scots Fusiliers, just north of the Pont de Juvigny. They spent another 10 days in the line patrolling vigorously. However, on the night of the 11th they heard much activity in and around the battalion lines, including the sound of tanks in motion. At first light a whole armoured division was parked in the region, with tanks, carriers and lorries scattered over the place. It was not the 11th, 7th or Guards Armoured Division who were in action further to the east. Closer inspection revealed a division composed of rather cleverly made rubber dummies. Just before midnight, the whole area was heavily bombed by the *Luftwaffe*. One bomb landed on the battalion signal office, and the CO, Lt.-Col. de Winton, was wounded and evacuated. The second in command, Maj. D.N. Nicol, assumed command. The dummy division attracted the *Luftwaffe* like wasps to jam. Bob Sheldrake recounted:

> The first stick of flares fell right across us hanging there like candelabra showing our vehicles in sharp outline. The din of the diving [*Luftwaffe*] as they screamed in towards us, followed by the bombs that cracked and split the earth. Griffiths crying out that he was hit. Rocketing, whistling bombs slammed into the ground. We ducked and a giant spade was shoved in behind the pit wall and caved the whole wall down on top of us.

Sgt. Bob Sheldrake's 'A' Battery of the 55th Anti-tank Regiment said: 'The infantry around us had numerous casualties. A huge bomb destroyed a signal section and an AA gun crew.' Lt. John Lappin of the 7th Dukes recorded in his diary:

> *Tuesday 18th July.* A 'black' day for 'D' Coy. Having been relieved, we had hardly settled down – having dinner – when the Hun shelled us [Condé-sur-Seulles] with 88 mm. The first shot whizzed past my HQ and exploded in front of Coy HQ. When the turmoil had subsided, I found Sgt. Downs with a nasty smack on the left shoulder. Webber the sniper was badly hit and 'Kev' [Lappin's company CO] had a flesh wound in the arm. The CO ordered him back to the RAP. I took over until Charles returned. A stretcher-bearer told me Sgt. Murphy was also killed. Charles poor chap is very 'jittery'. We must all be getting rather bad-tempered. I had a row with Middleton. All very silly. *Wed. 19th.* A morning of shocks. Two lads from 18 platoon killed by booby traps. The old story, nosing around for souvenirs. The second shock was first class news – back for 3 days' rest camp at Bayeux.

There Lappin enjoyed seeing Cary Grant in *Mr Lucky*. Back in the line, the Dukes were holding the line at Cagny – one of the savage Goodwood battlegrounds. Lappin continued: 'Caught with my pants down by our Div General and two Brigadiers, sitting behind my HQ in shirt sleeves, no hat on, writing home. However, the old gent was his usual pleasant self. All was OK.'

The New Boys – the 1st Royal Leicesters

Brig. W.E. Underhill, the regimental historian for 'The Tigers', wrote:

> At 2100 hrs on Saturday 1st July the Brigade Major arrived with orders for the Bn to move to France on the next day to replace the 6th DWR who had received such heavy casualties. Some officers and men were out of station until midnight. There was a deficiency of 21 vehicles destroyed by the 'Buzz-bomb' four days ago. Vehicles were not waterproofed for a beach landing, etc.

Even Barclays Bank opened on the Sunday morning to close the regimental accounts. Underhill continued: 'So at 1400 hrs to the second 1st Battalion the Leicestershire Regt left Purley on the first lap of a journey which was to take it through France, Belgium, Holland and, finally, end in Germany almost a year later. The troops shouted to their well-wishers. 'Monty has decided he cannot do without us!' ' From Southampton they sailed on the *Princess Maud* across the English Channel, landed dry-shod on the beaches of Courcelles and concentrated at Cancagny on 4 July. Under Lt.-Col. Novis they moved by march route to St Cristot and joined the 11th Royal Scots Fusiliers and the 7th Duke of Wellingtons Regiment of the 147th Brigade on 6 July. They had five days when most officers and NCOs had a short attachment to the units in the line. On 13 July they went into the line near Fontenay, having relieved the 4th Royal Welsh Fusiliers of the 53rd Welsh Division.

CHAPTER TWENTY-ONE

The Capture of Vendes and Barbée Farm

'It was a Charnel House'

By 14 July the Polar Bears again had seven battalions in the line in preparation for Operation Cormorant. The 15th Scottish's objective was Evrecy, 5 miles south-east of Rauray, passing through the 53rd Welsh Division to the east of the Polar Bears. The newly arrived 59th Lancashire Division was to advance through the Polar Bears with their objective of Noyers and Missy, 3 miles south of Tessel Wood. As their part in Operation Cormorant, the 49th Division's objectives were to capture Vendes and to clear the Juvigny woods astride the River Seulles.

Brig. Johnny Walker's brigade was entrusted with the task of capturing Vendes and La Barbée Farm, just north-west of Vendes on the Juvigny road. Ironically, Lt.-Col. Hart Dyke of the Hallams had discussed such an attack with a neighbouring brigadier from the 59th Division. His advice was: 'do not attack Vendes frontally, but pinch it out by an attack from the east'. Predictably, the Hallams were chosen for the attack on Vendes. Hart Dyke said:

> I told Johnnie Walker this attack was NOT on, but I could take Vendes with tank support OR without it, by a night attack. I would lose very heavily in a frontal attack by day, as artillery was of little use in this country where trees prevented close support and the Boche were dug deep into the thick [bocage] banks dividing the fields.

All available tanks were allocated to the 59th Division and a night assault was ruled out. Hart Dyke continued: 'I went away with a heavy heart, but the Brigadier put a company of KOYLI under my command to help in the attack on Barbée farm.'

Maj. Tony Nicholson's 'A' Company were given the task of the frontal assault on Vendes, with 'C' Company and 'D' Company remaining behind near Tessel Wood in their firm base. Maj. Derek Dunhill's 'B' Company of the 1/4th KOYLI were given the objective of La Barbée Farm.

The Hallams' Story

Lt.-Col. Hart Dyke recorded:

The enemy had good OPs in Vendes church and Petite farm. There was just room in the command post for Peter Newton [OC of the support company], Jerry Bedward [IO], the two signallers and myself. Covered slit trenches were provided close by for the gunners, orderlies, reserve signallers and Arthur Cowell and his A/Tk HQ. The attack on Vendes [at 0645 hours] met the fate which I had feared. Defiladed from their front the enemy machine-gunners were almost invulnerable as the rubble from falling buildings only added to the protection of their slit trenches. The Hallams tried a frontal attack and then from a flank to advance across No Man's Land and were subjected to cross-fire. Smoke was used to cover the last 50 yards to Vendes church but forward movement beyond La Bijude farm was suicidal. 'A' Coy now screened a second attack by Major Mike Lonsdale-Cooper's 'C' Coy towards Barbée farm [taken by the 1/4th KOYLI] and then assault Vendes from the west [right flank]. Despite artillery, mortar and MMG fire the enemy were infiltrating back into the orchards and close back to back fighting was going on around Barbée farm. 'C' Coy had two platoons almost wiped out.

Maj. Tony Nicholson of 'A' Company now reported a slackening of fire from Vendes:

So the CO ordered up 'D' Coy in reserve to push straight down to Vendes. But, alas, they never arrived. I now heard from the Brigade that the 59 Division attack had failed completely. My left flank was in the air and threatened by enemy tanks. Tony [Nicholson] said he could hold on where he was but Derek [Dunhill of the 1/4th KOYLI] was doubtful if he could. The Padre [Thomas] with superb courage took the armoured medical half-track across the open to Barbée Farm and evacuated the wounded.

Under cover of a twenty minute protective box DF fire plan at 1700 hrs the Hallams and KOYLI Companies were withdrawn. An 88mm shell landed close to the trench occupied by Cpl. Graham Roe and Pte. Topliss, burying the former. But Topliss ran as fast as he could down the field adjacent to Tessel Wood clearly suffering from shellshock. Graham Roe recalls:

My Coy CO reported to the Colonel that the enemy was filtering back behind us and that we were now engaged in close hand to hand fighting. The CO told the Major that the South Lancashires (59 Division on the left flank) had suffered many casualties and had been over-run in places. We were given permission to withdraw under a huge covering fire plan. We had to traverse a very long open slope. Many of my comrades were hit on the way back and we helped each other as best we could, first at a trickle and the CO met us, shouting for us to double in before we were knocked out by shellfire which was pouring in on us from every angle. The walking wounded were gathered into the jeeps, but above them were two stretchers supported by metal tubing. I tried a rough count of the survivors with me from 'C' Coy. Those I could see totalled 17. We had started with about 100.

The next day it was learnt that the enemy had withdrawn from Vendes, La Barbée and La Petite Farme. Padre Thomas and Maj. Lonsdale-Cooper were awarded immediate MCs, but in a month of action the Hallams had suffered appalling casualties – 33 officers and 460 other ranks.

Corporal Graham Roe, 'C'
Company, Hallamshires.

The 1/4th KOYLI's Story

At 0655 hours, Maj. Derek Dunhill's 'D' Company crossed the start line and, in spite of heavy enfilade fire from Vendes, about fifty men soon reached La Barbée Farm. Cpl. G. Lee won the DCM for pushing his section forward to take a farmhouse. Pte. John Longfield wrote:

> The Hallams were attacking from the north and we, 'D' Coy, from the east. It was a very hot day. We carried all our usual equipment including water bottles full of water. As Bren gunner, both I and my No. 2 carried full magazines. Our attack went forward with the usual mortar, artillery and small arms fire landing on us. I was firing the Bren from the hip and eventually we got to, and took, Barbée farm. [John shot a Gerry with a stick bomb in his hand.] We fired at the Germans and our Corporal threw a 36 grenade at them. Unfortunately it blew all the flesh off his face. Within 2 or 3 minutes I was the only one of us left alive. Then to my astonishment a Hallamshire Bren gunner dashed across the orchard and jumped in the ditch with me. Battles got very confusing at times.

The Hallamshire was shot in the head by Longfield's side. A German soldier then appeared and threatened him with his rifle. Longfield's Sten gun jammed – they often did when they were badly needed. Longfield said: 'The German smiled. This really enraged me. But he did not have a bullet up the spout. I hurled the Sten gun at him, pushed the dead Hallamshire off his Bren, pulled the trigger and really blasted the Boche with what was left in the magazine.'

In the mid-afternoon the three officers and 60 other ranks of Hallam's 'C' Company had reached their objectives, but at 1700 hours the enemy launched a counter-attack on La Barbée Farm. Now surrounded on three sides, the two companies (the KOYLI and the Hallams) withdrew under the box barrage, walked slowly back, covered by Maj. Dunhill and CSM D. Wilkinson and six other men. The former earned the MC and the latter the DCM. The 1/4th KOYLI suffered 48 casualties that day, including 6 dead.

Three days later, Maj. D.J. Mayall's 'A' Company and Maj. A.B. Little's 'B' Company, together with the Tyneside Scottish, set off again to take both farms, now defended by a reinforced German company and two Tiger tanks. After a very heavy pounding by guns and mortars, the enemy withdrew. Rex Flower was one of a burial party to visit the battlefield around La Barbée and Vendes. He said: 'The bodies had been in the hot sun for six days. The stench was awful, indescribable. It was a terrible thing to see that these had been young men in the prime of their life. It was a charnel house.'

Maj. Richardson of the 69th Field Regiment AA with the Lincolns recalled:

Vendes was indescribable. It had been bombarded very hard for nearly four weeks and the damage was frightful. Dead cows, horses and a few dead Boche were lying about. Telephone wires, tiles, glass, stores, bricks and abandoned equipment lay in the streets. We found time to look at the Boche positions at Vendes and Petite and Barbée Farms. The reason for our high casualties at Tessel Wood was plain. The whole position was very badly overlooked.

CHAPTER TWENTY-TWO

Caen

Mosquitoes, Night Bombing and Joining the Canadians

Between 21 and 24 July the division was withdrawn from the front line and then moved – after the ill-fated armoured divisions' battle in Operation Goodwood – to new positions south-east of Caen, relieving brigades of the 51st Highland and the 3rd British divisions. They also now joined the 1st Corps, itself part of 1st Canadian Army, and this partnership was to continue until the end of the war.

In the last 10 days of July and early August, most units managed to get back to the rest areas at Ducy St Marguerite and Chouain. Some units encountered the Prime Minister, Winston Churchill, on the 21st as they marched back out of the line.

The Tyneside Scottish went back to Foliot for 4 days of rest and recuperation, before moving to near Demouville to relieve a unit of the 3rd British Division. The 1/4th KOYLI celebrated Minden Day in the line near Grentheville with dust, shelling and mosquitoes. Here, Lt.-Col. Disney Barlow, and six men he was talking to, were all killed by a Boche concentration. The Royal Scots Fusiliers were in a defensive position at Frenouville, where they remained until 9 August. Their patrols encountered poorly trained troops hastily brought up to stop gaps in the enemy line. In his book, *An' it's Called a Tam-o'-Shanter*, Fusilier Ken West of 'D' Company vividly described day-to-day life in and out of the line:

> Huge amplifiers blared out recorded music by the hour. Glen Miller and his orchestra entertained us with their entire repertoire from 'Moonlight Serenade' to 'Amor, Amor'. 'Little Monty' Montague from the Welsh Fusiliers said their music was a decided improvement on the bagpipes. He was promptly subdued by a horde of gentlemen from the other side of Hadrian's Wall.

West described his company commander, Maj. Rowell, as a 'tall, young looking man, his manner was sharp and his questions incisive. He knew what he was doing and he would brook no laggards in his company, of that there was no doubt. 'D' Company will be the smartest on the parade.'

Turning to CSM Cookson, he ended with 'Dismiss the Company, Sergeant Major.'

> The next day we saw our new Lt. Colonel D.A.D. Eykin, slimly built with a full moustache neatly twirled at the ends. The face was kindly and the eyes alert as they checked the men for

whom he was now responsible. The questions were mainly concerned with the wellbeing of the Fusiliers, both mentally and physically. From that day onwards, he was known affectionately as 'Dad' Eykin the father of the 11th Bn Royal Scots Fusiliers.

An open-air service was taken by the Padre Capt. Wylie, which was described by Ken West:

for all the members of the Church of England, Church of Scotland, Odds and Sods as other denominations are called. 'There is a small corner of a foreign land,' we sang together. 'Praise my soul the King of Heaven' and the 23rd Psalm. The Colonel read the lesson followed by a lusty response of 'Onward Christian Soldiers'. We prayed for our dead comrades, for the wounded and for those posted as missing. The service ended with a lone piper playing the lament, 'Flowers of the Forest' and the blessing. The singing had silenced the noise and battle.

Paul Crook, the Brigade-Major, described the new battlefields south-east of Caen:

Behind us were the ruins of the shattered city, though happily the towers of the Abbeys were mostly intact. Nearer were the skeletons of large factories in the outskirts of Colombelles. The terrain consisted mainly of open cornfields which had been cut and we set about digging in our positions in the stubble. Apart from increased shelling and bombing we were divebombed throughout the night, not by German aircraft, but by French mosquitoes. Trying to sleep in a slit trench was literally a nightmare. The only solution was to cover up every part of one's skin and sweat it out. We were literally covered with bites; a few men were so badly bitten around the eyes, they were evacuated as casualties.

Pte. George Marsden, now with 7th Dukes, had a macabre story:

We dug in at Cagny and were bombarded by some flying creatures as big as bumble bees which flew into our faces. So we wore a mosquito net suspended from our helmets. One night we had a meal of Spam, jam and some smelly [Camembert] cheese sandwich with a mess tin of lukewarm tea. I reached up in the dark for a sandwich, found something soft, lifted it down close to my face. It was three fingers attached to half of a human hand.

Sgt. Bob Sheldrake of 'A' troop of the 217th Battery of the 55th Anti-tank Regiment recounted:

After three days' rest we moved across the bridgehead, through the airborne area. Night found us in the badly battered village of Demouville; enemy bombers found us too and we got the first raid of a number which were to try the nerves and stamina of the hardiest types. The flares of the attacking aircraft showed up the gutted buildings often just one wall and a chimney stack. The stumps of once proud trees jutted up like fangs of decayed teeth, gaunt and white in the swinging, sinking lights. It was a macabre, silent place. Nerves drove one of the gunners who had been withdrawn once, and put in again, to put a burst of Sten bullets through his foot. The troop was better for his going; nerves are catching and panic can mean death to men who are living, day and night, seemingly only by the grace of God.

The Hallamshires and the 146th Brigade were in reserve around Cuverville, and then relieved the 1/4th KOYLI. Lt.-Col. Hart Dyke made a recce of the new area: 'It entailed walking about large areas of country under enemy observation, in daytime, visiting companies. Everyone else was underground. It was like 'Musical Chairs', praying that any shelling would occur when one was in a position, so that one could jump into cover.' Their next move on 1 August was to relieve the 1st KOSB of the 3rd British Division at Troarn.

Signaller Harry Teale of the 147th Brigade HQ had a lucky escape:

Today was the 26th July. As we went down the road past Colombelles a battery of 88mm dual purpose guns went into action from two miles away. The first shell was a direct hit on the front truck and Bill Sinclair, Ken Thomas, Harry Hartley and two defence platoon soldiers were blasted off the road. I stopped [the second truck] in the shelter of a ruined building and walked back – all had been killed instantly. There was nothing I could do. Our rear HQ came to pick up their bodies later on. It was our worst week, being a small unit of 65 men our friendships were very close. L/Corporal Eric Dale-Chapman and I celebrated the same birthday. He was killed on the 28th from a mortar shell burst, now buried in Ranville Cemetery.

Fusilier Ken West of the 11th Royal Scots Fusiliers, on the outskirts of Frenouville, met an irate French farmer protesting at the damage done to his cornfield when an RAF Typhoon had just crash-landed. Beside himself with rage, the farmer was told in French, by West's mate George: 'C'est la guerre, Monsieur.' West continued:

The blue overalled farmer bemoaned his losses. In five years of war the Germans had never burned his fields. The British had dug holes, defiled his ground, driven tanks and lorries through his crops. In three weeks we had ruined him and killed his cows. George suddenly lost his cool: 'You ungrateful little bugger, we've come to liberate you lot. If you're not satisfied we'll all go home and let the soddin' Jerries reoccupy your land . . .. I'll never come here again for my bleedin' holidays.'

Both of the Durham Light Infantry battalions were in Emieville, about 5 miles due east of Caen. The 10th Durham Light Infantry had their HQ in a luxurious old château complete with racing stables. However, there was a steady drain of casualties as they lost anything up to 15 men a day. A mild form of dysentery affected many. Every kind of defence was mounted against the savage and ubiquitous mosquitoes. Some tried nets, others smoked and some wrapped themselves in old curtains. Medical services tried their best with lotions, creams and ointments, but nothing worked. L/Cpl. Singleton of the 11th Durham Light Infantry anointed his trench with petrol, rested from his labours, lit a quiet cigarette and ended up in the RAP.

The newly arrived Royal Leicesters spent from 24 July to 10 August in the line at Le Poirier with a 2,000 yard front. Their historian, Brig. W.E. Underhill, wrote: Patrolling very active, as was enemy shelling and mortaring. This was a very difficult time for the Bn. It was six weeks before they got a proper fight with the enemy, when they suffered many casualties, including Lt.-Col. Novis, the CO, almost all from shelling and mortaring. Maj. I.D.M. Liddell then took command.

Lt. Brian Lott of the 55th Anti-tank Regiment saw:

One evening an American Flying Fortress flying over and started bombing the large steel works factory in Colombelles where a Canadian AGRA was stationed. More Forts were behind but a quick thinking Mustang pilot shot the leading Fort down, thereby avoiding a disaster. Even so some of the Canadians were killed.

As Lt. John Lappin of the 7th Dukes recounted, 1 August was a bank holiday: 'The day started with the heaviest stonk I've been in. I had a feeling the Hun had heard of our reputation and was determined to extinguish our platoon. Afterwards I counted 6 Moaning Minnie craters and about 20 mortars [landed] in the platoon area.'

Two days later the Dukes were bombarded by Jerry leaflets. Lappin said: 'They just provide a laugh. If he were to compare the Spandau to the Bren, his mortar fire to ours, the Tiger with our Shermans, he might make more impression on our chaps.' Then on 5 August Lappin continued: 'Small influx of Canadians into my area. Most picturesque shoulder titles "Governor General's Footguards." A pleasant crowd.'

Food, particularly at the very front line, assumes enormous importance, as Bob Sheldrake recalled:

As the position became more static the compo rations disappeared. We sometimes got fresh meat instead of tinned, dried prunes and rice instead of tinned fruit and pudding. The fresh tea was an improvement. On arrival back from visiting 'B' Echelon [battery supply lines], I had to sort out the rations to give each gun crew and THQ their fair share. Try cutting up a piece of raw meat, fat, lean and bone included, into five parts, so that one part should be rations for six men, the next seven and the other three, for eight men. Try sharing the tins of condensed milk in the same proportions. The Guv's new batman, Andy Anderson was worth his weight in gold, for he could really cook. Each gun crew self-supporting. From now on we began to have roast beef, etc.

Capt. Lewis Keeble of the 1/4th KOYLI remembered:

Came Minden Day and my château cellar was selected as the RV for a little convivial booze-up for all officers of the Regiment who could get there. Quite a lot did. Staff officers from various Divisions, one or two from 6th Airborne, including Richard Todd the film star. They gathered in the cellar, baying their fatuous upper class greetings. . .. The enemy can't have been more than 400 yards away.

A few days later Lewis was wounded by *Nebelwerfer* fragments: 'I got back to the RAP still shaking badly. Tom Dean our magnificent MO, did a rapid diagnosis and immediate treatment: a quadruple neat gin. He kindly dug the fragment out. No sweat, as they say.' On 5 August, Lt.-Col. T.W.A. [Mouse] Harrison-Topham arrived to take command of the KOYLI, who had had various encounters at Grentheville, Bourguebus, La Hogue, Chichebeville and Benouville, with Moult Station, Ingouville, Lion d'Or and Bonnebosque still to come.

The General's Diary

General 'Bubbles' Barker wrote:

12 July. Jim Hall (ADC) wants to go back to do some Regt soldiering. As his Battn has had rather high officer casualties, he will be welcome. Jim Hare is sending me a Rhodesian named Parsons in his Rgt.

15 July. I had a house the Boche had left empty, in front of our lines, booby trapped. It went up this morning with considerable shouting from the Boche and is still burning! A steady stream of Poles 'PW' continue to come in. I am going to try some propaganda – loudspeaker and leaflets. The Americans are making pretty slow headway. Considering we have attacked practically every Panzer Div to our front, it is disappointing. I fear they have a lot to learn.

21 July. I am going to be with John [Crocker of the GOC 1st Corps]. It is very sad to leave Gerry [Bucknall]. I am very fond of him, he is good and his staff excellent – better than JC's [the 49th Division moved from the 30th to the 1st Corps].

23 July. I passed through Caen these last two days, like a town after three years fighting in the last war. Most depressing. The Cathedral seems more or less intact. . ... This torrential rain has played hell there, already churned up by bombs. [The *Luftwaffe* were active also and bombed corps and division HQs on 24–27 July].

26 July. The mosquitoes are perfectly damnable. I can't sleep with my head covered. I am asking for anti-mosquito stuff for the troops.

1 Aug. I must have had a thousand mosquitoes in my caravan last night. I killed about 500. [To his wife he wrote] – Will you send me a Flit gun and some Flit? I now go around in an Armoured Car as there is so much shelling: stupid to use a jeep.

2 Aug. I am just off with 'Buggins' [Brennan the CRA] around some of his gun positions. *3 Aug*. I like to see all the chaps and what they are doing. I think they appreciate my coming around. I gave the Boche a very uncomfortable night as I chose 20 targets and had harassing fire kept on them all night. The Canadians are usually referred to as 'Canooks'.

4 Aug. I hear that Gerry Bucknall this a.m. was going home and being replaced by 'Jorrocks'. I am frightfully sorry as he was a first class show.

5th Aug. Heard today 'Bobby' [Erskine] has gone home too. I believe his chaps did make a pretty good mess of the party on the British right flank. I always felt that B's desert training would not be any good in this form of warfare. However I am very sorry indeed.

8 Aug. Heard this evening the thrilling news that Himmler has been shot and Goering wounded – will probably be on BBC tomorrow. . ... I am pleased with my new ADC – Frank Parsons. He's a proper chap.

CHAPTER TWENTY-THREE

Break-out from the Caen Sector

'Eventually the Dam Burst'

Brig.-Maj. Paul Crook wrote:

So while we fought on against a determined and skilfully handled enemy without dramatic progress or publicity, [General] Patton's troops enjoyed a startling and very lightly opposed advance with the consequent excited press attention. Subject as we were to shelling from three sides – we were on the extreme eastern corner of the Allied Line based at Caen, and as such received much enemy attention. Life was uncomfortable in addition to the mosquitoes and casualties inevitable. On 7 August an offensive [Operation Totalize] was launched by 1st Canadian Corps of which we were a part. It was preceded by a massive night air-attack by bomber Command which succeeded in destroying all the villages and consequently blocked all the roads.

Most of the young commanders involved thought that the bombing killed very few Germans, many wretched French men and women, and simply held up the advance. Paul Crook again: 'A further air bombardment took place the next day in daylight and was a disaster as we witnessed the Polish Armoured Division being decimated alongside us.'

On 9 August the 7th Dukes, with a squadron of tanks, attacked towards Vimont. An anti-personnel minefield and mortaring took a heavy toll. Maj. L. Hill of 'D' Company and CSM J. Robinson of 'C' Company were killed, and Maj. C.H. Mountain, Capt. H. Gardner and the IO, Capt. J.P. Symonds, were wounded. So on the next day the 11th Royal Scots Fusiliers resumed the attack. Vimont, a village 5 miles south-east of Caen, on a crossroads in bocage country, with the River Laizon flowing through it, was their objective.

At 0640 hours on 10 August under a barrage, 'C' Company on the right and 'B' Company on the left set off. Six supporting tanks were blown up on mines beside the main Caen railway line, and heavy artillery and machine-gun fire was coming in. By 0900 hours both leading companies were holding ground on the far side of the river Muance, but neither tanks nor Crocodiles could dislodge the large number of enemy machine-guns. So the brigadier ordered the fusiliers back to a defensive line at Bellengreville. The fusiliers returned to Vimont, now cleared, 3 days later and moved forward to Moult. By the 10th it was clear, unfortunately, that Operation Totalize had come to a grinding halt.

Brig.-Maj. Paul Crook recalled:

The morale of the Canadians became low, but under our splendid GOC 'Bubbles' Barker, we were not aware of this. Eventually the dam burst and the hinge of which we formed part creaked open. We visited the edge of the Falaise Gap and saw for ourselves the gruesome evidence of an army in defeat, bodies of men and horses everywhere, equipment, vehicles, guns abandoned, buildings destroyed and hedgerows scarred.

The famous killing grounds west of the Argentan-Falaise 'Gap' had trapped Von Kluger's armies. Operation Tractable started on 14 August for General Crerar's 1st Canadian Army for another big set-piece attack towards Falaise.

The Hallamshires had found Chichebouville empty on 9 August and kept probing south-east towards Billy, but for the Polar Bears the real hot pursuit – finally – got going on 16 August. Scores of sharp little battles were fought against shrewdly placed enemy rearguards.

The Recce Regiment historian recounted:

We began to move forward and to do our real job of reconnoitring in front of the Division. The enemy had withdrawn on one front to the high ground around Argences Ref 1761 and 49 Recce Regt, advanced on the right flank making rapid progress in spite of blown bridges and mines. Enemy resistance was weak except on the line of the river Dives east of Mezidon Ref 2456. In the next two weeks we advanced 50 miles and took 600 POW. Each day resolved into a rapid advance from bridgehead secured by the infantry, to the next obstacle where we examined the bridges before the infrantry came up.

On 8 August the 4th Lincolns moved by MT to Sollers, and from there on foot to Bourguebus in the wake of the fierce battle of Goodwood, and then south to 'Star Wood'. They bypassed the village of La Hogue, which had been totally destroyed by a thousand bomber raid. On their left flank a counter-attack was repulsed by the Royal Scots Fusiliers. By the 13th the Lincolns had reached Conteville, but in a few days they had lost their adjutant, Capt. C. Corben, their acting CO, Maj. R.D. Stokes – a pre-war officer who had served in Norway and Iceland – Capt. I.F. Cooke and battalion IO and Capt. Knight of 'B' Company. On the 15th the advance continued to Billy, and Airan was captured the following day. Capt. Russell, OC of carrier/mortar group, pushed ahead 7 or 8 miles [a huge distance in that long, hot summer] to seize two important bridges. Under fire, Pte. Simmons of the pioneer section lifted 150 mines under fire at a range of 300 yards. For this great effort he received the MM.

On the 17th the division's objective was to get a bridgehead over the river La Vie, towards St Laurent, but the town of Mezidon needed a real battle to clear it. The Tyneside Scottish started from Le Torp, and by late afternoon 'A' Company was in the western outskirts. Next, 'D' Company, embussed in scout cars and half tracks of the Recce Regiment, followed, but with both bridges over the river Dives blown, by nightfall the Tynesiders were only halfway through the town. House to house fighting ensued through most of the night. Cpl. Williams of 'D' Company knocked out two enemy LMG posts. Capt. A.P. Whitehead recalled:

'Somewhere in the Falaise Gap.' (Michael Bayley)

Even stiffer opposition was coming from the high ground rising steeply from the east of the town . . . enemy artillery, mortar and small arms fire was landing in streets. It was impossible to bring forward any rations. Considerable casualties were sustained and inflicted. Bn HQ were losing a lot of men and the IO Lt. Craig Mitchell was killed. But by 1500 hrs the following day French civilians appeared, as the enemy withdrew, harassed by the divisional gunner regiments. 'A' and 'D' Coy gained possession of the eastern ridge. The French population of the town displayed incredible enthusiasm at their liberation. Many did not know whether to laugh or cry as they attended the funerals of our men.

David Rissik, historian of the 10th Durham Light Infantry wrote: 'But at Mezidon the wheel of fortune turned for the 10 DLI. The advance through Mezidon was led by the Tyneside Scottish and the 10th Bn with 11th Bn in reserve. The Mont de la Vigne some four miles beyond there was where bitter resistance was encountered and a fierce encounter battle ensued.'

The Durhams had to cross two streams (the river Dives), each about 20 feet wide. Although they were fordable they had sheer banks of up to 20 feet high. At the top of the hill was a château in a thick wood. Against this natural defensive position the leading company suffered heavily and Maj. Keith Sanderson, their OC, was killed. So Lt.-Col. Sandars ordered a two-company attack with artillery support for 2030 hours. The streams were crossed but, according to a member of 'D' Company, 'hell was let loose from Spandaus firing from the hedgerows. I saw a lot of chaps fall wounded and the rest blazing away at the hedgerows. Cliff Thomas got to within 30 yards of one post, threw a grenade but was killed by a Schmeisser higher up.'

Capt. Riley, their OC, got a bullet through the shoulder, Sgt. Brown cleared a cottage and Pte. Jenn took three German prisoners. David Rissik wrote:

> We stormed the chateau and Sgt. Brown and Pte. Ward did great work clearing it. We captured 14 PW and Corp Fisher and L/Corp Edwards knocked out several posts singlehanded . . .. Only forty members of 'D' Coy were left and 'C' Coy had five casualties including Major Oliver Mason their OC, who were wounded and captured. It was now dark and it took a long time to bring up food and ammunition and to evacuate the numerous casualties. Just after 0300 in the early morning a vigorous counter-attack came in under a heavy mortar barrage, many Germans shouting in English. Both Durham companies were forced back fighting anyone they could identify. A second German company appeared at dawn and the luckless Durhams fought their way out in small groups and consolidated at the foot of the hill. The battle was over. Casualties and prisoners were over two hundred. It was a black day for the Durhams.

Sgt. Bob Sheldrake of the 55th Anti-tank Regiment remembered:

> Following in the wake of the Tyneside Scottish we came to the village of Canon (a suburb of Mezidon) of happy memory. There were people at home and ready to welcome us: on the trees hung peaches for the picking and there was cider in the cellars. We came upon a piano and drums – someone – the unknown someone who turns up at such times – played for hours. I remember sitting there, banging away at the drums, feeling just a bit cidery, while the men milled around and sang and the war seemed very far away, its din muted by the clinking of glasses. As we made our way back along the street an enemy bomber roared low overhead, guns chattering as shells smacked into the ground at my feet. For a brief moment the air was full of death as he gunned the length of the street.

Brig. Underhill, historian of the 4th Lincolns, wrote:

> On 18/19th, after a brief rest in Quetieville [4 miles north-east of Mezidon] as dusk was falling we moved off once more, 'C', 'B', 'D' and 'A' Companies through tortuous tree-lined lanes to the village of Le Mesnil-Mauger, clear of the enemy, who was ensconced in high wooded ground on the far side of the river Vie. With high, slippery banks and swollen with recent rain, it was running swiftly – a serious obstacle. Behind us crimson mushrooms of flame from villages indicated unusual enemy air activity. Now the leading Coy was met with a cascade of mortar bombs and shells and heavy bursts of MG fire. Major Caldwell eventually found a small footbridge, across this 'C' and 'B' filed – a difficult operation in the dark and progress was slow. Simultaneous with the mortar barrage green flares were sent up and *Luftwaffe* bombers flying low, bombarded the strip between road and river.

Alas the footbridge led only to an island in mid-stream. A bomb landed in the midst of 'B' Company, causing 37 casualties, including Maj. Caldwell and Capt. Ainger, both of whom were wounded. Two more bridges were now discovered. 'D' Company crossed the first and 'A' Company crossed the second, but they both ran into trouble.

Brig. Underhill recalled: 'They were caught in a triangle of an unfordable river, the other side, a deep ditch and the base, the line of fire of a 20 mm cannon which killed Capt. Metcalf of 'D' Coy. Daylight showed the need for a drastic reorganization and the Lincolns were withdrawn to a more defensible area near the village of Le Mesnil.'

Lt. John Lappin of the 7th Dukes wrote in his diary:

Tues 15th. I was a lucky dodger! Bob Smith, a patrol commander of 'A' Coy was killed today. He took out a big fighting patrol towards Argences, bumped Spandaus and lost four men probably POW.

16th August. L/Corp Dearden came back today looking bronzed and fit, a likeable, intelligent fellow with several old members of 16 Pl wounded early on, just returned from a 'blighty' cure.

17 Aug. Travelling in transport – that made one think. The Jocks and Leicesters have moved forward with little opposition, taken prisoners. The road to Lisieux stretched away before us bordered by orchard and pleasant little farms, woodlands and cornfields, little damage to buildings or crops.

CHAPTER TWENTY-FOUR

The Sad End to the 70th Brigade

'Intense Gloom and Despair'

After the savage battles around Mezidon, in the afternoon of 19 August, the three battalions of the 70th Brigade were given the depressing news that the brigade was being disbanded and replaced by the regular 56th Brigade consisting of the 2nd Battalion, South Wales Borderers, the 2nd Gloucesters and the 2nd Essex.

Capt. A.P. Whitehead, the Tyneside Scottish historian, related the sad story:

> In an atmosphere of intense gloom amounting almost to despair the CO Lt.-Col. Nicol, announced that the whole Brigade was to be broken up or rather transferred to 59 Division the whole of which was to be broken down. This sudden and unexpected bombshell was a terrible shock to all the disappointment was so bitter that after the fine record the Bn had achieved during the hard days, now that the first round of the campaign had been won, it was not allowed to share in the fruits of victory.

The GOC, 'Bubbles' Barker, addressed all officers and warrant officers on the 20th at Moult, expressing his sorrow at losing the brigade and his sympathy with all those concerned.

Capt. A.P. Whitehead wrote:

> On the 21st the Tyneside moved to Fresnay, and their officers were addressed by Monty on the next day. He expressed his deep sorrow that he had had to order the breaking down of the formation in this way . . . on the whole casualties had been lighter than had been expected . . . it was vital that units should be brought up to strength. It was a bitter pill to swallow but all would have the opportunity of finishing the job, even if with other formations.

The CO, 8 other officers and 164 other ranks were posted to the 7th Argyll and Sutherland Highlanders in the 51st Highland Division. Maj. Mirrielees, 4 other officers and 101 other ranks went to the 5th Battalionn Black Watch, and 3 officers and 57 other ranks moved to the 7th Battalion Black Watch. However, Maj.-Gen. Barker arranged for some Tynesiders to stay with the Polar Bears. Maj. Alexander, Capt. Mackenzie and 12 other ranks were posted to the 11th Battalion Royal Scots Fusiliers, and some from the Hereford area and South Wales moved to the 2nd Battalion South Wales Borderers.

Eventually the battalion was placed on 18 October 1944 in suspended animation, as Whitehead continued: 'and if the call should come again the Tyneside Scottish will be there – "Harder than Hammers", as always'. In the Second World War they lost 9 officers and 267 other ranks, all killed in action.

The blow was particularly unwelcome to the 11th Battalion Durham Light Infantry who, unlike the 10th Battalion and the Tyneside Scottish, were still at full strength and maximum fighting efficiency. During the final disbandment in September, each rifle company, complete with its own officers, was divided among the Green Howards, the Dorsets, the East Yorks and the Devons of the 50th Tyne Tees Division. Many of the 10th Battalion Durham Light Infantry joined their 'cousins' of the 6th, 8th and 9th brigades in the 151st Brigade of the 50th Division. Ronald Dinnin, the MT officer of the 10th Durham Light Infantry was posted initially to the 2nd Battalion Essex Regiment, later to the 1st Leicesters and finally to the Hallamshires, whose MTO had been killed.

The 185th Field Regiment RA had supported the 70th Brigade. Their CO, Lt.-Col. Mackay Lewis, wrote: 'We moved and fired from two of three positions each day on the breakout. We halted at Mezidon to say farewell to 70th Brigade with whom we had firm and cherished associations, engendered in training and cultivated in action. It was altogether a very sad affair.'

CHAPTER TWENTY-FIVE

The New Arrivals

The 56th (Sphinx) Independent Brigade

When they landed on the Normandy beaches, the 56th Brigade, with their Sphinx insignia, were under the command of the 50th (Northumbrian) Division and very quickly occupied Bayeux, to a delicious welcome. Each man found himself in the unaccustomed role of a conquering hero! After two days they came under command of 7th Armoured Division for a drive south towards Tilly. Although their first battle was a failure Lt.-Col. D.W. Biddle CO of the 2nd Gloucesters was awarded the DSO. Back with 50 Div for six weeks and on

The Sphinx emblem.

Aug 8th 56 Brigade came under command of 59 Division for an attack on Thury-Harcourt. Here 2nd Gloucesters lost 48 casualties and when they joined the Polar Bears they were commanded by Lt.-Col. Butterworth as his predecessor had been wounded a week before.

The 2nd Battalion South Wales Borderers had served with the Polar Bears in the ill-fated Norwegian Campaign in the spring of 1940. On D-Day, four years later, they were the only Welsh Battalion to land with the assault troops on the beaches at Asnelles. Their first serious battle was at the Chateau de Sully, and the next was on 8 July at Granville and the Boix de St German, where they suffered 130 casualties. Early in August they again suffered heavily at Courts Genets and Fourneaux-le-Val. When they joined the Polar Bears they were commanded by Lt.-Col. Barlow.

'The Pompadours', the 2nd Battalion Essex Regiment, were raised in 1755 and took their name from the deep purple facings of their eighteenth-century uniform. From 12 June the wood near the village of Verrières was known as 'Essex Wood', where Tiger tanks took an appalling toll. A week later the Pompadours took part in the three-day battle for Tilly-sur-Seulles against the Panzer Lehr Division. Again casualties were heavy, and after 16 days in action they were a very, very tired battalion. Lt.-Col. G.G. Elliott had taken over from Lt.-Col. Higson after the 12 June battle. For most of July the 2nd Essex were at Parfouru l'Eclin, under most vicious stonking from Launay Ridge. Then, from 8 to 17 August under command of the 59th Division, after several daring night marches they captured Forge-à-Cambro east of Thury-Harcourt.

Brig. Ekins commanded the well-respected Sphinx Brigade when it joined the Polar Bears at Pedouze on Saturday 19 August.

CHAPTER TWENTY-SIX

The Swan to the Seine

Hot Pursuit

Lt.-Col. Hart Dyke described the Hallamshires' advance:

18th August I sent a carrier-mortar group to reconnoitre as far as Mery Corbon [3 miles east of Les Pedouzes on the main Caen–Lisieux road]. They found the bridge over the river Laison destroyed. By working on the fallen masonry the carriers forced a passage so I sent them up to the bridge on the river Dives three miles north to cut off any enemy retreat. I established my command post at Lion d'Or. That night our HQ slept in a lovely country house in the village and made use of the tomatoes from the garden and how lovely they tasted. The countryside was at its best just now and it was hard to believe we were not on manoeuvres in England during a lovely sunny spell.

The sappers put a Bailey bridge over the river Dives while the Hallams' rifle companies crossed by boat at Lion d'Or.

During the night of the 19/20th the Polar Bears pushed on towards the river Touque, led now, as usual, by the armoured cars of the Recce Regiment, but often bumping resistance. Their line of advance from Mezidon on the river Dives via Rumesnil (11 miles due north) to Bonnebosq (3 miles north-east), up to the river Touques (8 miles east), across to St Philibert-des Champs (3 miles east and north of Lisieux), 5 miles north-east to Cormeilles and another 10 miles north-east to Pont-Audemer on the vital river Seine.

The Recce Regt. historian:

On the evening of the 20th we moved into a harbour at 294595 and were immediately greeted by a 'stonk' from infantry guns which put 5 men, 3 m/cycles and a carrier out of action. Added to this was a night of heavy rain and we felt far from being 'liberators'.'
[The next morning No. 1 troop had a very brisk action at Bonnebosq.] We plastered them with Brens, Besa and 37 mm guns firing HE . . .. We were undoubtedly masters of the situation, withdrew slightly to let the infantry supported by two Churchill tanks firing 95 mm and 7.92 mm enter the town from a flank. One final objective was La Chapelle Hainray three miles north, met with wild enthusiasm – a smiling throng swarming over us. Jerry had left behind Teller mines strewn all over the road.

The 11th Royal Scots Fusiliers rode on trucks, tanks and captured vehicles through St Plait, Dumont, Baignard, Ouilly-le-Vicompte, across the river Tourques, Lieurey, St Martin, Appeville and across the river Risle.

For the attack on 22 August to take Ouilly-le-Vicompte, the whole 147th Brigade was deployed. 'B' Company and 'C' Company of the Fusiliers led, and took 20 prisoners against 5 casualties. The GOC, 'Bubbles' Barker,

BRIAN JONES – "THE FIRST THING I'LL DO WHEN I GO HOME ON LEAVE TO DUBLIN IS TO GO UP TO THE GERMAN EMBASY & I'LL SPIT ON THE DOORSTEP!"

IVAN STRAWSON "I'VE HAD THE BAR COUNTER AT HUNSPLET TAILOR MADE – EXACTLY THE RIGHT HEIGHT TO PROP YOUR ELBOW UP ON"

BERTIE HOOGVLIET

GEORGE BUTTLE

CHARLIE PEACHEY.

BOB ARCHER (TOJO)

Members of 2nd Kensingtons. (Michael Bayley)

visited battalion HQ to congratulate the Fusiliers. The Royal Leicesters also played a significant part. Their pioneer platoon stretched ropes across the 20 foot wide river Touques and their first battle was a complete success, despite a fierce counter-attack in the afternoon. The rifle companies nearly ran out of PIAT and small arms ammunition, and half of the 20 stretcher-bearers were hit. One of them, Pte. W.A. Ratcliffe, received the MM. Despite heavy shelling which, cost the lives of Lt. Jeyes and eleven other men, plus another 35 wounded, the Leicesters defended their bridgehead and by evening the supporting tanks were across. By the morning of the 23rd the 11th Royal Scots Fusiliers and the 1st Leicesters had broken out of the bridgehead, and the enemy, who had been pounding the Lincolns on the left flank west of the river, were now sent scuttling back towards the river Seine.

The 7th Dukes were west of Mesnil Mauger on the 19th. By the 21st they were in heavy rain at Les Trois Pois, and by the 23rd they had reached St Gratien, just west of the river Touques. They crossed the river between the Leicesters and the 11th Royal Scots Fusiliers, and advanced towards the river La Vallette, where the bridges had, of course, been blown and mined. Lt. John Lappin's route took in St Laurent Dumont and Cambremer:

> our first real civic welcome, whole village, men, women and children out to welcome us. Two local gendarmes giving away cider which flowed freely. From Ouilly-le-Vicomte to St George-du-Champs [on the 24th]. We looked like the Battle of the Flowers as we had flowers in our

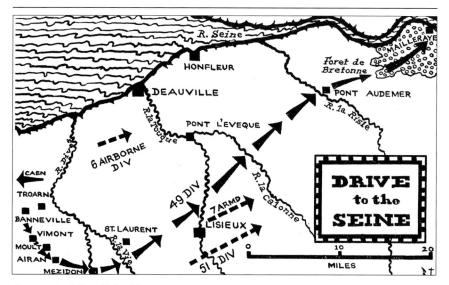

Swan to the Seine. (Brian Thexton)

tin hats and the trucks were festooned on the way to Cormeilles. A little battle was in progress
at the bridgehead of La Villette. 'B' Coy waded across further down from the main bridge. 7
Dukes had a good day's work advanced 12 miles, forced a bridgehead, and took 12 PW.

The first action the 'Pompadours', the 2nd Battalion Essex, had on
joining the Polar Bear Division was on the 24th, as Lt. A.A. Vince wrote:
'Cormeilles is a pretty little town set in some beautiful wooded country with
numbers of small streams and rivers winding through the valleys. A dusk
attack was planned and men from the FFI [Resistance] were allotted to each
of the leading companies as local guides.' 'B' Company led and took the
western part, straddling a river with a blown bridge. 'A' Company then
entered the main square, civilians appeared in a flash with white flags and
Cognac. Finally, 'C' Company consolidated on the high ground to the east.

Lt. A.A. Vince:

Champagne and wines were unearthed, hidden from the Boche. It was the old story of
'cigarette pour Papa' and 'chocolate pour bébé'. We met several RAF types dressed in blue
overalls, clogs and little French berets. They said 'Christ, I thought you blokes were never
coming!' Shot down in raids over France, they had escaped and gone into hiding, coming out
at night to work with the Maquis [FFI].

On the same day, the 25th, the 2nd Gloucesters had a fierce engagement
at the village of Epaignes, where 12 were killed and 41 were wounded.
Tommy Short with 'C' Squadron of the 49th Recce Regiment said:

Alas – for some the magic soon came to an end (the reception of the French crowds, people
trying to board your armoured vehicles, girls were clinging to you and crying). The heavy

armoured car with its crew of Sgt. Roy Ogleby, A. Roberts, the gunner operator and me, the driver, had reached Epaignes on the road to Pont Audemer when it was hit by 20 mm shells. The vehicle caught fire almost immediately – the ammunition inside exploding into an inferno. My chum Roy Ogleby and Roberts were burnt to death but I managed to get the low side door open and fell to the ground wounded. Sgt. Ogleby had been recommended for a commission and A. Roberts was a tall quiet lad who spent most of his free time at the end of a day's fighting writing long letters to his wife.

Tommy spent two years in hospital recovering from his wounds. At Epaigne, the Recce Regiment deployed three squadrons against the enemy defences, inflicting more than 100 casualties – the last stand was made south and west of the River Seine. The last 8 miles to the river was covered in 4 hours. 'A' Squadron arrived first at Quilleboeuf, 'B' Squadron went to Vieuxport, where 300 prisoners were taken. However, on the night of the 27/28th at Ste Opportune a determined counter-attack by Germans fleeing eastwards was beaten off.

On the division's left flank were the 6th Airborne Division, astonishingly mobile, and on the right flank were the 7th Armoured Division (the Desert Rats), back once again in their African form, sweeping ahead while the 51st Highland occupied Lisieux. Gen. Barker was pushing the Polar Bears east and north-east to the river Calonne, the 147th Brigade on the southern centre line and the newcomers, the 56th Brigade, taking over on the northern flank from the 146th Brigade. The Recce Regiment, now pushing and probing, led the advance towards the river Seine at Quillebouef from St Philibert, Cormeilles and Pont Aldemer on the river Risle. They reached the river Calonne on the 24th, and by the evening the 7th Duke of Wellingtons Regiment had got two companies over the river.

Lt.-Col. Dick Jelf, the divisional GSO1, often visited the divisional battalion COs. Lt.-Col. Hart Dyke of the Hallamshires recalled:

Both Dick and John Freeman the [146th] Brigade Major were always very welcome. They had the art of saying the right thing, of making you feel the Bn had done well, and, as the CO I always felt a great pride in showing anyone around the Bn. It gave them a picture of our difficulties and it gave us a feeling that we of the 49th Division were all one party and a damn good party too.

Brig.-Maj. Paul Crook of the 147th Brigade wrote:

We carried out three night river-crossings in five days. Although enemy resistance was very slight we could never take this for granted. There, at each river, patrols had to be sent out to locate the enemy and then a full-scale night attack with its supporting fire plan arranged, assault boats allocated, the crossing made and then the bridging equipment brought up. All this required a great deal of active staff work at Brigade Headquarters all through the night and one hardly slept for a week. Dawn was spent anxiously awaiting reports from the troops across the river. We were lucky enough to liberate a Benedictine monastery and the delighted monks were gracious enough to give us a liberal stock of their lovely liqueur.

John Longfield of 'D' Company of the 14th KOYLI described a typical day during the advance to the Seine:

We stood to one hour before sunrise, breakfast, a skirmish with any Germans in front of us, a whole day's advance (we once covered 23 miles on foot in one day!), probably another

Fusiliers of 11 RSF, Melle, 1945. Front row, left to right: Ernie Naylor, Kenneth West, David Spittlehouse, Jim Moore. (Ken West)

Part of the mortar platoon at Bonnebosque, Normandy. (Rex Flower)

skirmish in the evening. Then dig slit trenches, eat. Stand to until an hour after sunset, then sleep – except when on guard. So we did not get a lot of sleep. Men fell asleep while digging trenches, some even fell asleep while walking.

Maj. Eric Bowring wrote:

> Once the advance was under way [the 143rd Field Regiment RA] we changed gun positions daily and sometimes two or three times in a single day. We occupied 14 positions in 10 days. These were an exciting and breathless ten days full of the welcome of the civilians with their Calvados and cider. Alternatively FOOs supported the Recce Regt, tank squadron and advance guard battalions and some good shooting was enjoyed during brief but fierce encounters with enemy rear-guards on the rivers Vire, Touques and Risle.

The Polar Bears were given the task of destroying all of the enemy between the river Risle and the river Seine, if possible preventing them from crossing by the ferry sites. (The bridges were all of course blown, except for one at Rouen.) Finally, they were to clear the Forêt de Bretonne. Lying in a huge loop of the river Seine, this huge forest some 7 miles east–west, 6 miles north–south, could shelter a brigade or two of fleeing *Wehrmacht*. On the morning of the 27th, the 146th Brigade advanced north-west towards Quillebouef, and the 1/4th KOYLI had a brisk action taking the Ferme d'Elbeuf, supported by guns, 3 inch mortars and the Kensingtons MMG. 'D' Company suffered 10 casualties, and L/Cpl. T. Fleming was awarded the MM.

John Longfield recounted:

> From haystacks in barns in the farmyard, Germans dropped down all over the place. Bullets were flying round in such quantities that I am surprised that anyone survived. As the yard cleared I fired at Germans crossing the gate to get out at the other end of the farmyard. I was in an absolute fury because they weren't all dropping down. The other fellows had come over the wall and we swept through the farm and out at the other side. Officers were calling us to come back but all the men wanted to do was kill Germans and they only came back when all in sight had been disposed of. We took 8 prisoners. Heaven knows how many we killed . . ..
> [A few days later] We suffered a bit of shelling. I woke up in a dimly lit dressing station.

Longfield was later downgraded from A1 to A2 and joined the 5th Kings Liverpool Irish. Rex Flower with the mortar platoon had recently lost his 'old friend Pte. Maunton killed, along with Sgt. Grey from icelandic days when their flame-thrower Wasp carrier went over a mine'. On the Swan, as the brigades leapfrogged forward, Rex continued:

> nasty weather meant that mortar pits and 'slits' were brimming with water . . .. [Later] Douggy Longstaffe was seen running around in circles, shouting and waving his arms about whilst mortar bombs were crashing down. He was slapping himself. We thought he had gone bomb happy. He had dived into a wasps nest.

By the time the 1/4th KOYLI had occupied l'Angle, a village north of the forest on the evening of the 28th, they had captured 130 prisoners for the loss of 28 casualties. They found a tremendous amount of German equipment abandoned, including thirty-one lorries and cars in running order, and they had to round up hundreds of horses running loose that had been used to haul *Wehrmacht* guns and wagons. Capt. Lewis Keeble of 'C' Company carried out several model battle school attacks on pockets of resistance in the Forét de Brotonne, coordinating mortars and MMG. He remembered: 'The whole forest was stuffed with stores and equipment of all kinds – some dumps even had fuses and explosive charges laid to them which had not been set off.'

The Lincolns received a welcome draft of reinforcements on the 24th – 'A' Company, for instance, by then totalled only 44 in all ranks. From Le Plessis they continued their zig-zag course, and by the 28th they had reached Quilleboeuf on the River Seine. A 'pheasant drive' through the forest produced a bag of 1 captain, 5 subalterns and 90 other ranks. Around the blazing village of St Nicholas they gathered in another 88 prisoners. Many were Russians, others were members of the TODT labour organization. On 30 August the FFI came over from Yvetot and were supplied with much booty, that is arms and ammunition. The FFI 'Chef' was M. Rousseau, a good contact and interpreter. He was lent a battledress and Lincoln flashes, and rapidly promoted himself to the rank of Captain.

Another 85 reinforcements arrived, since every defensive action by the Germans had taken their toll. Lt.-Col. Hart Dyke recalled: 'We reached the river just west of Vieuxport but were unable to dislodge the enemy holding Aizier. I ordered 'D' Coy to carry out a turning movement to surround the enemy, but they lost their way in the thick wooded hills.' By darkness the enemy had gone, but the Hallams captured 64 prisoners during the day.

Lt. John Lappin of the 7th Duke of Wellingtons wrote in his diary:

Sunday 27th. Corneville sur Risle. This was the first pukka scrap I'd been in and I thoroughly enjoyed it throughout. We had accounted for 10 dead, 15 PW – all pukka Germans. Our casualties were 7 wounded, unfortunately I lost 2 NCOs. A bitter blow. I got a Schmeisser machine pistol in place of my 'lost' Sten. A word about the partisans [FFI]. Their info was very valuable but they would get mixed up in the fighting. It was really incredible to see them going round our boys during the scrap offering '*un peu de cidre*'. Three of the local lads insisted on joining us. We armed them with a captured rifle, a Schmeisser and a Spandau. Thank goodness they had no chance to fire them! *28th.* Outside Pont Audemer. 50 or 60 Jerry prisoners were marched back to the cage. We got a whiff of that unmistakable smell as they passed. Lack of soap I suppose. Rest area – billets, a bath of hot water in the school-master's kitchen – a good lady did my laundry; a folding bed, sleeping in sheets. Heaven!

29th. Back to visit the bath unit with Kev and to the Field Cashier in Corneville. Normandy has been very cheap for me. I drew 1000 Francs, the first pay since leaving England. I arrived for drinks at Bn HQ mess – Eric Mattock, Jeff Lord, King, etc. The Brigadier dropped in for half an hour. What a pleasant chap he is. Thank goodness we'er well led from the General down to 'Kev'.

30 Aug. Reinforcements came from South Staffs and a Capt. Ellis.

As a result, Lappin, who had been a captain for a week reverted back to lieutenant, 'being surplus to war Establishment'.

Bob Faxon was with the 6-pdr Anti-tank Battery of 'A' Squadron of the Recce Regiment. In an infantry role his troop were searching lanes and farms on 27 August. 'Friendly' artillery fire unfortunately killed two men of the carrier troop just outside Ste Opportune. Sgt. Dave Robson set up an observation post on high ground opposite a church when a large force of Germans were spotted advancing. Their two 6-pdrs were deployed in the nearby village but two heavy armoured cars from the Recce Regiment returning from Quilleboeuf with a large party of German prisoners arrived at the same time.

Caught in cross-fire from enemy MG the guns were temporarily abandoned but rendered safe by taking the firing mechanism. They were retrieved at dawn on the 28th. The MO Capt. Sutcliffe and his orderly 'Doc' Connolly with a stretcher rescued a wounded German. Faxon recalled: 'The local priest asked if he could bury three of our men in his churchyard. They were given a moving funeral service. Most of the small children of the village took part and covered the graves in flowers.'

Lt. Brian Lott's Anti-tank troop was sent to the Forêt de Brotonne. The GOC gave the Loyal Suffolk Hussars the task of collecting the thousands of horses abandoned by the fleeing *Wehrmacht.* Lott described events:

> The forest was absolutely littered with German equipment, particularly horse transport – I recall seeing a few tanks, some of them Shermans with German insignia. We pushed the dead horses into the river, but round the other side of the horse-shoe river bend, our troops were busy pulling them out due to river pollution. Bad co-ordination. Just after the battle for Le Havre, Lt.-Col. E.C. Bacon was succeeded by the 2 i/c Major Brian Gooch [who subsequently wrote the unit's history].

The unsung heroes of the Swan to the Seine, apart from the Recce Regiment, were the sappers. The 294th Field Company historian wrote: 'After the break out from Caen, we started the long trek up to the Seine, lifting mines, checking verges, filling craters and bridging. In one period of seven days we built five bridges for the Division to cross the rivers Vie, Touques, Celonne, Risle and a tributary of the Risle.' On 29 August one of the Recce officers carried out a survey for likely ferry sites across the River Seine. The Sapper historian recorded:

> On the last day of August we built and started operating two Class 8 ferries at Mailleraye-sur-Seine. With these and storm boats we ferried quite a large number of vehicles and men including the Belgian Brigade until they were dismantled five days later. Memories of rafting across the inconvenient 'Bore' will live with the company for a long time. Altogether, the Sappers bridged seven rivers between the 15th/31st August, although some enterprising Bns [including the Hallams] made their own bridges of telegraph poles and planks.

Spr. Bill Hudson was with the 757th Field Company. He described a tragic event on the River Seine:

> The bore of the Seine – a fourteen foot wave which came down at low tide – meant we were unable to bridge, but we constructed three rafts to ferry infantry and recce across. They were anchored mid-stream at low tide but were still swept down towards Rouen and had to be towed back with storm boats. On the third day a lorry load with 15 South Wales Borderers came aboard. The driver didn't stop when ordered and got to the far side of the raft which tipped and the lorry slid into the Seine. There were no survivors, as all were in full marching order.

The 55th Anti-tank Regiment guns arrived in Rouen late at night and waited in the streets for the Royal Engineers to complete a pontoon bridge at Elbeuf. Sgt. Bob Sheldrake wrote:

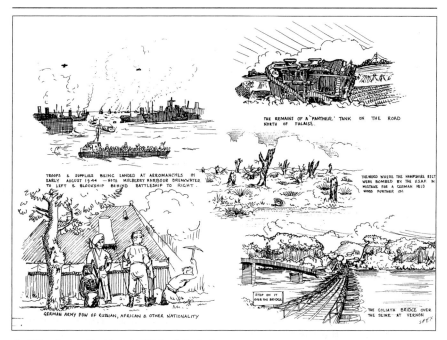

2nd Kensington 'incidents'. (Michael Bayley)

Here in Rouen we came face to face with the terrible shortage of food. They [the French civilians] gathered in their hundreds and stood, silently watching us eat. We were at first indifferent, then mystified and then it was borne into our thick skulls that it was the food they were interested in. We gave away every sweet, every biscuit, every spare bit of food we had, many gave away every precious cigarette as well. For every person helped there was a hundred angry at not having been included.

Bob Faxon of 'A' Squadron of the Recce Regiment said:

A local man – on 30th August – rowed across the Seine and offered to take six of us in his small wooden boat. I still remember unbuckling my equipment in case we had to swim! Once across, our small section marched into Lillebonne to be met by a strong force of Resistance men who helped us patrol the area. After we left 'A' Sqn repaired and launched two German rafts and brought the Bren gun carriers over to the north bank. Sadly one sank with the loss of two of the French FFI Resistance men. A few of our men 'borrowed' bicycles and took up a defensive position at a cross-roads on the Le Havre road . . .. [Later] The Anti-tank battery was disbanded and I joined the Assault Troop.

The general's diary and letters home gave an account of that exciting two weeks when the Polar Bears had their heads down pushing and shoving their way towards the River Seine:

12th Aug. Intercepted an air report of large columns of Boche vehicles and tanks moving from Flers to Argentan, pulling out of the salient at the junction of the British and American armies. No doubt the RAF has been dealing with them satisfactorily. My Sappers had lifted 1,000 anti-tank mines from my sector, probably double that still to be lifted. Went back to

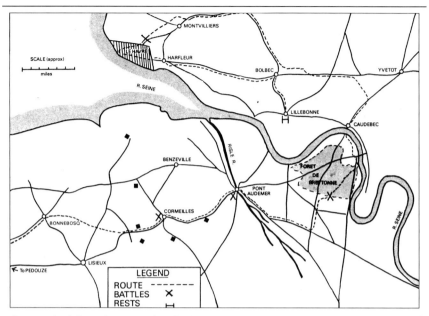

Swan to the Seine – the approach to Le Havre.

the small flat we are running for officers and sergeants on the beach, 24 sleeping and 10 per day for the day. It is much appreciated. 14 Aug. We picked up another 500 mines yesterday. I must say the Boche does fight with great courage and determination. We've given him a hell of a time and he has not let up at all.

19 Aug. Two days ago we captured the first flying bomb site [near Mezidon] and exactly directed on London. Very well hidden with very thick concrete shelters around. The Americans are on the Seine at Louviers some 60 miles due east of me.

21 Aug. This pleasant country has been completely ravaged, most villages ransacked by the Boche SS troops as part of their plan. Sheer bloodiness. Have now a new Brigade [the 56th] in my Div in place of the old one [the 70th] I have had up to now. Very sorry indeed to lose them as they have done magnificently. Said goodbye to 70 Bde officers and visited 56 Bde.

26 Aug. My HQ in the Aga Khan's training stables . . . .. I expect the Boche to fight gallantly [penned in front of Port Audemer] till he's overcome. It gave us the opportunity to kill more of them. I am thoroughly enjoying myself as you may imagine. Operation becoming more and more like our Exercises at home – swanning forward with Advanced Guard and the Recce Regt ahead and civilians and villages with shops.

27 Aug. What annoys me is these ruddy Poles and Russians are fighting as well as the Boche. The civilians say the Russians have behaved worse than the Boche. It's great times. I am thankful to be able to be in it. I'm one of the few of the more antique Div Commanders remaining!!

28 Aug. The Maquis [FFI] are appearing in large number. They seem to have dealt very quickly with any traitors who have given their chaps away to the Gestapo.

30 Aug. These are great days and the sight of so much booty is very morale raising.

1 Sep. I meet every ruddy river at its broadest and I am still here with no proper means of getting my chaps across the Seine. Our equipment is not designed for tidal rivers apparently and my rafting has made little headway against the fast current . . . . Buggins [the CRA] has got for me a lovely Nazi flag – one of those enormous ones you see hanging on the walls behind Hitler when he makes his speeches in the Reichstag.

CHAPTER TWENTY-SEVEN

The Taking of Le Havre

'Din of Battle, Organised Chaos and Danger'

Meanwhile, almost unbelievable events were unfolding. The 43rd Wessex Wyvern Division had forced a vital bridgehead over the River Seine at Vernon, and the might and pride of the British Army had surged across. Led by the 11th (Black Bull) Armoured Division charging north to Antwerp, the Guards Armoured Division to Brussels and the Desert Rats to Ghent, northern France and most of Belgium was liberated in the space of a few days. Paris had fallen and many intelligent key officers were taking bets that the war would be over by Christmas. Opening the English Channel ports to shorten the supply line from the invasion beach Mulberries was now vital.

The task of capturing Le Havre – a great ocean port surrounded by water on three sides – was given to the 1st Canadian Army. In effect, this task was allocated to the 1st British Corps, consisting of the Polar Bears, who would invest the port from the left (south-east and north-east) and the 51st Highland Division from the right (north-west). The latter had just returned from settling

Polar Bear attack on Le Havre, supported by the 'Funnies', flails and scissor-bridge. (IWM, BU859)

old scores by the recapture of St Valery-en-Caux, where they had been in terrible trouble some four years back. It was known that Le Havre was heavily defended by coastal artillery batteries, which – like Singapore – could only fire out to sea. The land defences were incomplete, but the garrison of more than 11,000 troops, under Col. Eberhard Wildermuth, had a whole series of inland concrete bunkers harbouring 76 field, medium and anti-aircraft guns.

However, first the Polar Bears had to cross the river Seine. 'A' Squadron of the Recce Regiment had ferried 80 men and 12 vehicles over on Class 5 rafts, although two carriers were lost when rafts capsized. Once across, the plan was for the 56th Brigade to lead, taking a northern route with the 146th Brigade following on a southern route. Operation Astonia was the codeword for the Le Havre investiture.

After the Recce Regiment, the 4th Lincolns were the advance guard of the division. DUKWS had been promised but they never arrived, and one company crossing on 1 September at Caudebec-en-Caux found themselves paddling with shovels when the storm boat's outboard motor packed up – and a complete absence of paddles. As the marching troops swung briskly on their way westwards, civilians cheered, and excited adults, children and dogs from lonely farmsteads raced through meadow and orchard to greet them. By 0730 hours on 2 September they linked up with their transport, who had crossed rather gingerly across the badly damaged railbridge in Rouen, many miles to the east. By early evening they were in St Aubin Routot, preparing to attack Gaineville, thereby covering the main approach to Le Havre from the east. The 1/4th KOYLI moved from l'Aigle on the evening of the 1st to cross the River Seine behind the Lincolns.

Capt. Lewis Keeble, OC of 'C' Company, recalled: 'It was a shambles for which fortunately we were not to blame at all. The engines of the horrible little boats kept breaking down. The flow of the river caused us to drift all over the place. Then we had a perfectly revolting march [of 7 miles] in pouring rain to reach La Fresnaye.' Lt.-Col. Hart Dyke accompanied 'C' Company of the Hallams by boat across the river, while Maj. Johnnie Mott, second in command, led the rest of the battalion on the south bank eastwards to cross at Rouen. Hart Dyke recalls:

It was a hard pull as we [Jerry Bedward and myself and two signallers] with only one pair of oars were being steadily swept downstream towards Le Havre and the enemy! . . .. [but later] we steamed into Lillebonne after ten at night to be met by a wildly cheering multitude. The local cinema had just finished its evening show attended by some German soldiers. Little did I know that the wretched Bn was sitting with the rest of the division in one vast traffic jam on the west side of the river sixty miles away.

The Lincolns put their set-piece attack in on Gaineville on the evening of the 2nd. 'B' Company, under Maj. Flint, advanced with great dash, and by sheer fire power cleared a way, but 'A' Company were held up on the right by thick, strong barbed wire cattle fences. Sgt. Bland took out two machine-gun posts for which he was awarded the MM, and by nightfall Gaineville – an important outpost for the defence of Le Havre – was taken.

The 1/4th KOYLI now had to clear the approaches to Harfleur 2 miles west and only 4 miles from the great dock area. The KOYLI must have been expecting to clear their objectives before breakfast – they were dubbed, Eggs, Ham, Sausage, Bacon, Marmalade and Kidney. Supported by tanks of the East Riding Yeomanry, the KOYLI battled their way against determined resistance and by nightfall were in the outskirts of Harfleur, but they suffered 45 casualties. Capt. Lewis Keeble recalled:

> In broad strategic terms we bumped the outer defences of Le Havre at Harfleur and were stopped . . .. Having liaised with Derrick Dunhill at 'Eggs' I brought 'C' Coy forward while he moved off with 'D' Coy to 'Bacon'. We advanced perhaps 150–250 yards under desultory artillery fire and then they hit us. Very intensive artillery fire. Very intense MG fire and everyone went to ground.

Capt. Lewis Keeble was hit in his left arm, but eventually crawled back to safety. Rex Flower of the mortar platoon said:

> My eagle eye noticed white blobs in the field – yes, they were 'mushys' and we got a nice bagful each. Later on saw some tomatoes ripening in a garden. Well, I couldn't help seeing them, could I? The enemy had plenty of artillery here, with infantry in concrete emplacements. My old Coy 'A' lost some KIA inc. my old friends Ptes Carter, Hodgson, Mellor and 'Slash' Woolhouse from Rotherham. We stayed in the farm for 8 days.

The 1/4th KOYLI were involved in two battles for Le Havre. The first was not a success. Maj. Godfrey Harland of the 1/4th KOYLI recounted:

> Douglas Wardleworth (Bn 2 i/c) and I were told to go and meet the German envoys, bring them in a staff car to Brigade HQ. This we did. They handed their 'Commanders' (*Wildermuth*) letter to Brigadier Johnnie Walker. He then phoned 'Bubbles' Barker with the vital reply. The envoys told us that Hitler had personally ordered defence of Le Havre to the last man and last round. The General's answer: 'I wish you good luck and a Merry Christmas'. The German envoys were totally mystified by his reply!

Brig.-Maj. Paul Crook of the 147th Brigade described Operation Astonia:

> The port of Le Havre was a formidable place to attack being one of the strongest fortresses of the Atlantic Wall. Three sides were protected by water, the Seine Estuary, the sea and a flooded area. The approach from the east was made difficult by a flooded valley dominated by high ground, whilst a minefield and anti-tank ditch barred the approach from the north. There were many concrete strong-points manned by infantry guarding the A/Tk ditch as well as gun positions in concrete casements. In the town itself were two forts and many roadblocks, pillboxes and fortified houses, together with AA and A/Tk guns. The strength of the garrison was estimated to be at least 8,000 including 4,000 artillery and AA personnel and some 1,300 Naval personnel of doubtful fighting value. It was clear to both sides that the attack had to be made from the north. To carry out the assault we were greatly strengthened by detachments of Flails (mine destroying tanks), Crocodiles (tank flame-throwers), Kangaroos (armoured personnel carriers) and assault engineers. It was the biggest collection of 'armoured funnies' [from Hobart's 79th Armoured Division] ever assembled in one place.

For the final assault the 146th Brigade was positioned on the eastern flank while the 147th and 56th brigades were to the north. The 51st Highland Division was in position to the north of the 56th Brigade to assist in Operation Astonia. Most battalions carried out street fighting exercises in the next few days. Ammunition loads were revised to include a greater proportion of grenade

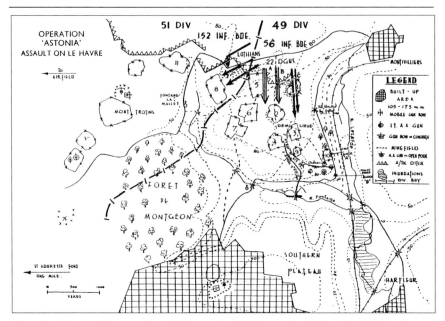

Operation Astonia. The assault on Le Havre, 10 to 12 September 1944.

and Sten gun ammunition. During the 4th and 5th the FFI and patrols brought information of the enemy's strengthened disposition. Indeed, 'A' Squadron of the Recce Regiment captured an entire company on the morning of the 3rd. During the next 9 days the Recce Regiment provided a Phantom wireless net of 15 stations covering every unit to help the GOCs' information network.

In the next few days it rained depressingly as the Polar Bears and the 51st Highland tightened the encircling net. Brig.-Maj. Paul Crook recalled:

> The defences were softened up for two days before the assault by shelling from Royal Naval ships at sea and bombing by the RAF. From the Field of the Cloth of Gold we were able to watch with awe and pleasure the massive raids by the air forces on the defences. They were accurately carried out and had a heartening effect on the morale of our troops and consequent disheartening effect on the enemy. Captured prisoners subsequently stated that the bombing was very frightening but there were comparatively few casualties both to the German troops and civilians owing to the excellence of the dugout shelters. The breakdown of communication prevented the German commanders from knowing what was going on and stretching their resources and fire power.

Meanwhile the GOC, 'Bubbles' Barker, wrote:

> *4th Sep.* I'm fed up learning the Canadians are mopping up the Le Havre peninsula and have asked J.C. [John Crocker, the corps commander] to have it stopped and merely have credit given where due. The 49 Div have done everything and got across the Seine under very difficult circumstances.
> *5 Sep.* I have written to the Public Relations chap at Army Camp HQ and said I'm fed up with learning about the Canadians on the Havre Peninsula.

6 Sep. The monks at Fécamp gave us a case of Benedictine, made in the monastery there. They buried all they had and the Boche gave them a large supply of sugar to make more, just matured for us! I have just come back from watching the RAF do some very accurate bombing of the Boche positions in front of me. Ammunition dump went up in the Foret de Mongeon with a lovely mushroom of smoke. It is very galling to hear of the other Armies forging ahead with no opposition and be left here with the sticky end.

8 Sep. I only wish we could leave this Canadian Army. They have such an inferiority complex that they concentrate almost entirely on themselves. It's maddening not to be able to deal with [the investment of Le Havre] any quicker, but it is a tricky undertaking and we cannot chance a reverse at this stage. I want no more casualties than I can help.

The plan of attack was comprehensive and thorough. Models of the town and its pillbox defences were made, and studies by all ranks, plus the corps, divisional, brigade and battalion plans were explained by the COs to their men. In addition to the splendid 'funnies', 12 field regiments, 4 medium regiments and 2 heavy regiments of artillery were in support. RAF Bomber Command raids were called Alvis (1645–1745), Bentley (1845–1900), Buick (1900–1930) and Cadillac D+1 completed by 0800 hours). The Royal Navy provided two heavily gunned monitors to bombard from offshore. HMS *Erebus* with 15 inch shells was hit on 5 September and retired hurt to Portsmouth, but was back again on the 8th, only to be hit and retired again.

The methodical surrounding and investment of Le Havre was a miracle of competent administration and supply. Blending naval and aerial bombardments with the huge supporting artillery and mortar barrages required complex planning. The GOCs of the 49th Division and 51st Division were given sufficient time to get their own, and supporting arms, into place.

In the first aerial bombardment by the Lancasters and the Halifaxes, on the night of the 6th, a thousand bombers dropped 1,500 tons of bombs, much of it on the Grand Clos Battery, but bad weather delayed D-Day for the attack from 9 to 10 September. The RAF dropped 4,900 tons of high explosives on the city and HMS *Erebus* and battleship *Warspite* engaged the perimeter defences. Spare a thought and a prayer for the 5,000 French civilians who were killed during Operation Astonia.

Zero hour was now to be 1745 hours on the 10th. The 56th Brigade would seize the two dominating hills to the north, standing above Montivilliers, 3 miles north-east of the town centre, supported by the 'funny' tanks of the 30th Tank Brigade. Simultaneously the Highlanders would press southwards on the coastal flank from Octeville-sur-Mer, while the 147th Brigade would push inland towards the Forêt-de-Montgeon. Finally the 146th Brigade had the task of advancing, south of the main escarpment and west into the vital dock areas.

The 56th Brigade Attack

Their objectives were the strong points in and around Fontaine-la-Mallet, and then to seize the bridges spanning the river Lezarde, which ran at right angles from the Forêt-de-Montgeon. It was a textbook attack with two squadrons of flail tanks of the 22nd Dragoons leading (a full account is given in Ian Hammerton's *Achtung Minen*), followed by two squadrons of the 7th Royal Tank Regiment's Shermans and assault squadrons RE with their Bombards. Through the huge minefields, nine lanes had to be cleared, which intense rain had turned into bogs. The South Wales Borderers were on the right and the Gloucesters on the left, supported by 'gun' and Crocodile flame tanks. Then the 2nd Essex mounted in Kangaroos with tank and AVRE support would pass through, capture two key strongpoints and the two bridges over the river Fontaine, finally establishing a footing on the southern plateau/escarpment.

The Gloucesters followed their flail tanks, 'D' Company in the lead, followed by 'B' and 'A' companies, and finally 'C' came through to take their objective – a pillbox strongpoint. With them went the observation post party of the 185th Field Regiment. Under Capt. Thompson, the FOO, was Gnr. John Mercer and Jim Pearce. They were captured in an orchard by Hauptmann Kurt Langner of the 86th Alpine Division and his men. They were taken to a large, deep bunker near Fontaine-la-Mallet, but by dawn Capt. Thompson had persuaded his captors to surrender.

The Gloucesters swept through the enemy fire in fine fettle, but the 2nd South Wales Borderers had a much harder time and suffered heavy casualties. Their objectives were three woods on a ridge. In each wood was a huge concrete dug-out some 30 ft deep, surrounded by trenches and protected by mines and wire. 'D', 'A' and 'B' companies, aided by flails, flame-throwers and tanks, were ordered to capture each wood. 'D' Company led, crossed a minefield under heavy fire, went over the wire and forced the enemy in trenches and dug-outs to surrender. 'A' Company followed through, but were disorganized by heavy fire from the second wood. The support vehicles suffered badly, so Maj. Collins brought up 'B' Company to take the second wood from the flank with flame-throwers, and then captured the third wood. Pte. Gallagher won the MM by stalking and capturing six Germans.

Lt.-Col. G.G. Elliott, CO of the 2nd Essex, wrote in his campaign memoirs:

> We were to drive [in Kangaroos] through whichever of the gaps [in the minefields] which were open, straight to our objective, 'A' Coy strong points 9 and 9A and the two bridges; 'B' Coy strong point 10, and 'C' Coy to follow just north of SP3, ready for the last phase. The bombing and artillery bombardment had so disturbed and cut up the ground that movement by foot or vehicle became a major problem. The woods became an absolute tangle, even with the help of artificial moonlight, it was most difficult to advance.

Of the nine lanes, three were completed on the right (Laura), none in the centre (Hazel) and one on the extreme left (Mary). By 0815 hours on the 11th, only two lanes remained open: one for wheels, one for tanks. Around 29 flail tanks and 6 Avres were knocked out, mainly due to mines, but some because of anti-tank fire. Lt.-Col. Elliott recalled:

I saw four tanks of 7RTR 'go up' on mines almost simultaneously. The crocodiles and infantry followed hard after. The SWB had considerable trouble suffering 60 casualties in their second company directed on SP6. Unfortunately the SWB FOO was taken prisoner and after the initial bombardment, no arty. fire was directed on SP8 [which caused most of the defensive fire].

The brigadier unleashed the 2nd Essex at 2200 hours. Col. Elliott sent the Essex on foot through 'Mary', 'the most reliable gap'. Half an hour later all objectives were taken, but at 0200 hours, said Col. Elliott:

I found Major Brown and his HQ of 'B' Coy comfortably established in the cellar of the ruined château sampling the captured victuals. Having cleared the Northern Plateau and seized 3 bridges intact, I considered we had done enough for the night. We only had 8 casualties in the battle of Le Havre. Nevertheless it was an exciting experience.

Now the Gloucesters came back into the history. Lt.-Col. Butterworth, their CO, heard on the wireless link that the 147th Brigade on his left were held up by a mined road. He asked for permission from brigade and from the GOC for the Gloucesters to continue into Le Havre. So, mounted on tanks and carriers, they pushed forward and soon reached the Place de la Liberté, which seemed an appropriate objective, almost in the centre of the town. Well-armed FFI appeared from nowhere and helped to round up prisoners. By late evening the Gloucesters had reached the Forte de Tourneville (the old fort of Sanvic) and dug in for the night in the adjacent cemetery.

The 147th Brigade Battle

Brig.-Maj. Paul Crook recalled that night:

And what a night! There were flail tanks flashing away detonating some mines and missing others. Armoured assault. Engineer vehicles were chuntering around and tanks following up. There were the noises and effects of our own supporting fire from a variety of weapons – finally, of course there was the din of battle, organised chaos and danger.

Crook had prepared the plan of attack with Brig. Henry Wood:

We had to pass through 56 Brigade and capture a feature on the southern flank overlooking Harfleur. We started at 2300 hrs with an attack by 1 Leicesters. The tracks were still found to be heavily mined and progress was slow. There were some anxious moments but by noon [on the 11th] the Bn finally captured its objective east of the Forêt de Montgeon and a vital bridge leading into the port.

The Leicesters, after a week's rest and reorganization near Pont Audemer, were now commanded by Lt.-Col. F.W. Sandars DSO. The key road, though carefully tested by sappers, was still heavily mined and vehicles blew up and blocked it. Communications with supporting gunners and Kensingtons were not very good, but a 'stray' troop of tanks helped 'shoot' 'C' Company under Maj. Denaro and 'B' Company under Maj. Liebert on to their objectives. The enemy did not put up much opposition after the fearful bombardment, and by 1000 hours about 450 prisoners had been taken. However, Maj. John Gorman was killed by a sniper.

By late afternoon the main action was over. The two main problems were the evacuation of thousands of prisoners and the honest handing-in of a captured German cash office. The 11th Royal Scots Fusiliers also had a relatively easy time, despite the enemy using glass mines in the roads. Some 600 prisoners were taken – about half by 'B' Company. Maj. Charnock and Lt. Dunlop were wounded, but the fusiliers suffered few casualties. Brig.-Maj. Paul Crook wrote:

> 11 RSF were then given the task of clearing the whole of the southern flank which proved harder than expected, owing to the number of strong points and fortified houses which had to be tackled. 7 DWR next advanced through Montivilliers in Kangaroos and dismounted at the bridge captured by the Leicesters and 'A' and 'B' Coys marched straight through into the centre of Le Havre.

Lt. John Lappin's diary for the 11th read:

> Things were going well – the General eager to get into Le Havre decided to push the Dukes forward into the town on armoured troop carriers, 'D' Coy leading, my platoon in front. We tore down the road towards the town. The Canadian Kangaroo crew kept us amused. Two Kangaroos struck mines and were disabled, but only 2 casualties. The General and Brigadier took a look at our catastrophe and decided to pull us out of the battle. We sat down in the suburbs and had the unpleasant job of watching the Glosters going in to do our job for us. They seemed to have a whole regiment of tanks in support. Just before dark we moved up to occupy the high ground overlooking the river. What a mess! It was another Caen, not a house worth having, everything blasted and cratered.

The 146th Brigade Battle

On the southern flank they had two tasks: to simulate an attack to draw enemy resistance off the 56th Brigade on the northern flank; and later on to clear all enemy east of the river Lezarde, then bridge the river and pass through into Le Havre. G.F. Ellenberger's history of the KOYLI noted that a copy of Shakespeare's *Henry V* was available. For the first time since 1415, the British Army stood before Harfleur: 'If I begin the battery once again, I will not leave the half-achieved Harfleur till in her ashes she lie buried.' (Shakespeare) Will got it right as usual.

At 2130 hours on the 10th, two German officers arrived at 'Eggs' and were conducted by Maj. Wardleworth and Maj. G.C.W. Harland to brigade HQ, where they said that they could not accept Brig. Walker's terms, as their higher command (AH) had ordered them to resist to the last. Lt.-Col. Godfrey Barker Harland's book, *Battlefield Tour*, gave a detailed account of the 1/4th KOYLI's second battle to capture their objectives, codenamed 'Kidney' and 'Marmalade'. Between 4 and 10 September, seven separate KOYLI patrols went out to probe and investigate enemy defences, minefields and obstacles. They reported that there were no minefields in front. In the event, 'D' Company lost 14; the RE section and covering party lost 9; 'B' Company lost 9 and 'C' Company suffered 10 casualties – all from the minefields in front.

During the day the 1/4th KOYLI suffered 56 casualties, including 11 killed, but they were helped by the flails of the 22nd Dragoons, which arrived at 0830 hours (3 hours after zero hour), and the tanks of the 9th Royal Tank Regiment, 'Kidney' and 'Marmalade', which were superb, well-camouflaged, deep concrete dug-outs and bunkers, were eventually taken. At 0935 hours, 'Marmalade' was taken with 57 prisoners, 10 more than 'C' Company's remaining strength. By 1230, 'Kidney' had been taken as well, with another 63 prisoners.

Maj. Godfrey Harland recorded: 'The fire power produced from guns, tanks, mortars, MMGs and flame-throwers was spectacular and the trees and buildings in "Kidney" were set on fire.'

Rex Flower recalled: 'In this attack, the whole of the mortar platoon was firing together, all six mortars! That meant a lot of 'shit' going over the top of Jerry. We were firing on and off for hours both HE and smoke. We got through a huge amount of ammunition.'

The Lincolnshires moved forward at about noon and entered Harfleur against slight opposition, greatly helped by the AVRE petards carried on a Churchill tank, which at short ranges of 80–120 yards delivered a heavy and very sensitive 'bomb' at the target. By nightfall the Lincolns, with HQ in Harfleur, were finally established in the outskirts of Le Havre, having suffered 14 casualties, including Maj. M.C. Russell MC.

By the afternoon of the 12th, Le Havre was captured. The garrison commander, Col. Eberhard Wildermuth, in his pyjamas but wearing his medals, gave himself up in the Fort de Tourneville. At 1530 hours Fort Ste Addresse surrendered and the total number of prisoners came to 11,300, of which the Polar Bears were responsible for 200 officers and 6700 other ranks.

The Gloucesters had the privilege of storming the main fortress, and there they found the garrison well-prepared for surrender, all equipped with full suitcases. They also liberated 4 RAF prisoners, 30 Algerians expecting to be taken away as slaves, 30 Italians and a few French 'comfort' girls. CQMS Burnett of 'D' Company was the first to arrive with a lorry – not for the girls, but to make the most of a very well-stocked wine cellar. In hot pursuit came all of the other Gloucester CQMSs.

The battalion formed up again quickly (perhaps reluctantly?) and hurried on to the sea, nonchalantly collecting prisoners en route. The bag was 1500 by the Gloucesters, whose casualties during the day were only 40. They captured the naval admiral and his staff, together with his cellar, which provided two bottles of best beer per man in the battalion. The only sad note was the loss of Maj. J.K. Lance, who was killed leading his company into Le Havre. Four years earlier the Gloucesters had been in the British Expeditionary Force retreat from Waterloo to Cassel, so revenge was sweet for those who fought in both campaigns.

After various adventures clearing the docks and the main Mole – a strip of land 1 mile long and 100 yards wide, and studded with large concrete pillboxes – Lt.-Col. Hart Dyke and his Hallams had every reason to be

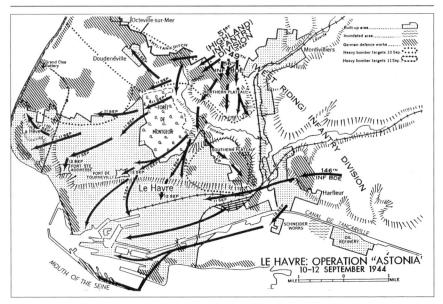

Operation Astonia. The assault on Le Havre, 10 to 12 September 1944.

The Hallamshires. The surviving officers from those who landed with the battalion at Le Havre. This photograph was taken before the assault.

pleased. He said: Our total bag was 1005 PW, three Dornier Flying Boats and a submarine. We retired to sleep very tired but satisfied with the day's work. We had cleared a built up area six miles by two miles in extent for only 15 casualties.

The Kensingtons took part in the huge barrages and fireplans on Le Havre. 'C' Company had some excellent MMG shooting from carriers in hulldown positions from a long ridge in front of the infantry. A section would sneak up, fire a couple of belts at the mass of barbed wire, earthworks and concrete emplacements, withdraw behind the ridge and bob up elsewhere. 'D' Company fired their mortars with an air observation post ranging the 12th Platoon and the 14th Platoons on to their targets. On 10 September all platoons fired non-stop for at least 3½ hours – the longest spell yet. The mortar barrels overheated and had to be cooled off.

Sgt. Bob Sheldrake of the 55th Anti-tank Regiment watched the bombardment:

> flack coming up into the sky, as if in mad anger, filling the path of the approaching aircraft with angry, deadly puffs of smoke, the spread out bombers, worked by robots, spilling out their bombs, shovelling them into the target area – the resulting eruptions, roar and rumble, great columns of black smoke flinging up into the air, covering the whole with layer after layer of muck.

On the 12th, Sheldrake and the rest of his regiment helped to marshal, and then lead back, some of the hundreds of prisoners to cages. He continued:

> With two gunners we went to a square in the dock area where 300 Germans were put into our batch. One officer led at the head of the column, through the rubble strewn streets of Le Havre, shepherded by two gunners, one on either side and my lonely self bringing up the rear. They straggled along carting their worldly possessions with them in a long snake avoiding the craters . . . . I began to realise that they were just ordinary men, dragged into this thing as we all had been.

With the lack of *Luftwaffe* activity, the 89th LAA Regiment RA were now using their 40 mm Bofors guns as light field artillery. H.J. Nicholls, battalion HQ subaltern with the 308th Battery, related:

> Our self-propelled guns were sent into REME, a troop at a time, to have the breech casing drilled and a bracket fitted to take a sight clinometer. 'C' Troop fired 2000 rounds on the perimeter defence of Le Havre. A German 150 mm heavy gun fired thirteen shells on 'C' Troop position and an officer, a sergeant and a gunner were killed and others were wounded . . . . [Later] 308 Bty received 5 cases of brandy, 192 tins of cream (Danish with labels in English!), one case of Libby's asparagus tips, 200 pounds of Danish butter and 150 tins of peaches.

Many Polar Bears made 'detours' to the Benedictine Abbey at Fécamp to purchase the famous liqueur: 'A large bottle for 116 francs (11 shillings and sixpence) and miniatures at 11 francs each. Happy Days!'

A heavy smoke barrage was part of the Operation Astonia plan. The 118th Company RASC had to rush back to the beachhead to pick up these 'emergency rations', and arrived back at the outskirts of Le Havre with an hour to spare. Many Polar Bear units had 'acquired' *Wehrmacht* vehicles in the Forêt de Bretonne, abandoned for lack of fuel. Their new owners turned, of course, to the ubiquitous RASC for supplies. The only way this extra demand could be met was by the RASC themselves, who 'acquired' working Boche lorries. The 146th Infantry Brigade REME workshops at Bourneville and La Brière recovered and repaired hundreds of enemy crocks that littered the countryside. Around 60 additional load carriers per brigade were provided by the resourceful REME. When Wasp flame-throwing equipment on carriers proved to be in demand by the infantry battalions, the carrier crews mounted extra armoured plate on the front, sides and back. The REME cut the plate from abandoned German armoured vehicles and welded it into place. On one occasion a battery of captured *Nebelwerfers* was repaired and put back into action against their previous owners.

The General's Diaries

The General wrote:

12 Sep. We have taken some 6–7000 prisoners and the Jocks [the 51st Highland Division] a good many also but old 49 has really done the job. I am delighted. I feel I put the chaps into battle with a good plan and they had therefore been able to do justice to their efforts and their high morale and courage. The show went through like clockwork in spite of the v. strong defences. Casualties are remarkably light. My tanks of all sorts co-operated superbly and the gunners were quite excellent. My HQ is now in the Place de la Liberté which is very appropriate. I'm afraid the civilian pop. did have many casualties in our bombing. The RAF was v. accurate at the time of the attack but seem to have been wide of the mark previously. We have taken vast stocks of German food and also beer and wine. I am giving the beer to the troops and the wine to the civil pop. The Boche started to crack about mid-day yesterday, we having put in the attack at 5.45 pm on Sunday. We always seem to attack on Sundays. We had considerable trouble with deep-seated mines which often blew up tanks after others had passed. Luckily the weather had remained perfect. This will be a memorable day for the Div and myself.

13 Sep. The real cause of our success was that the Boche went down into their deep shelters for the bombing and our artillery and did not get to their positions till too late – we got into them too quick. We had to outflank every strong point before they gave in. The co-operation of the infantry and tanks was quite excellent . . .. stocks of Boche Beer, Champagne (Moet & Chandon), Brandy, Danish butter and cheese, chocolate, cigars, tinned fruits – everything.

14 Sep. Last night I gave my Brigadiers, including two of my Armoured Brigades and my chief staff officers dinner in Balbec – champagne, trout, v.g. beef and duck. It was a great party. In the middle came the BBC broadcast about 49th Div – rather too much about us, I thought. My div has just received 60 immediate awards covering the period from D-Day to the end of July. Five of my COs have got DSOs.

The Polar Bears' casualties in the taking of Le Havre were 19 killed and 282 wounded. Brig.-Maj. Paul Crooke's assessment of Operation Astonia was: 'Although he received plenty of support, in the end it was the British infantry soldier who had to go forward and attack fortified positions in the face of enemy fire. It was due to the dogged courage, determination and skill that such a successful outcome was so rapidly achieved.'

Of course, the RAF bomber raids, the Royal Navy monitor gun-ships and the immense artillery fireplans terrorized the defending *Wehrmacht*, but it was the poor bloody infantry who had to take and occupy the ground. The

GOC, 'Bubbles' Barker, issued an order for the day: 'Today has been a memorable one for 49th Division. After an attack against very strong defences, in a matter of hours the Division supported by the Armour has broken through and relieved the port of Le Havre which is essential for the maintenance of the American Army.'

However, a day or so later – after 48 hours of euphoria – Barker said to Brig.-Maj. Paul Crook: 'All our transport has been sent forward and we are virtually grounded. As far as I can see the war is over for us.' The port of Le Havre had been so badly damaged by the bombing that the dock installations were not of practical value until 1 November. However, the great swan by the three armoured divisions was finished, and Operation Market Garden showed that the Boche had lots of fight left.

CHAPTER TWENTY-EIGHT

A Week in Limbo

'A Time of Great Elation'

For a few days out of action after the successful Operation Astonia, some of the Polar Bears enjoyed themselves. Lt. John Lappin, although 'demoted' after a week as a captain of the 7th Dukes, wrote:

> The lads found a portable gramophone and records, the 'Begin the Beguine' by Harry Roy and 'Beer Barrel Polka' were plugged unmercifully. Friday 15th. More good news. The CO popped in to tell me that I have got the MC, Simpson gets the MM. We were bloody lucky, that's all. Mother and Father will be pleased.

However, Pte. Walker, a stretcher-bearer, was killed and Lt. Lambert and two other men were injured by civilian looters in the wrecked town. The uncooperative attitude of the homeless civilians, although understandable, was clearly affecting the morale of the liberating troops. Lt.-Col. Wilsey withdrew the Dukes to St Martin du Manoir, and then to Gilcourt near Dieppe.

The 49th Division were now told to recognize, rest and refit outside Le Havre until the roads were clear for them to move north to the approaches of Antwerp. The 2nd Gloucesters went to the village of Notre Dame de Gavenchon, where for five days they enjoyed the hospitality of the delighted French. Two dances were held, and at the All Ranks Dance there were 800 civilian guests. The 4th Lincolns enjoyed themselves near St Aubin Rotot – in training, recreation and revelling. Lt.-Col. Peter Barclay was awarded the DSO, and Maj. Barton-Poole received the MC for the battle of Fontenay, back in June. The Hallams were stationed at La Cerlangue near St Romain. Lt.-Col. Hart Dyke and the battalion took part in a thanksgiving mass and ceremony at the war memorial, but the mayor was accused by the FFI of being a 'collaborator'. Hart Dyke wrote: 'It gave tremendous pleasure to me to hand to Tony Nicholson, Mike Lonsdale-Cooper and Doc Griffiths the ribbon of the Military Cross which they had all so richly deserved for their gallant conduct at Fontenay.'

The 1/4th KOYLI marched back for a rest at St Nicholas de la Taille. Recreation transport was run to Lillebonne, Bolbec and St Romain. 'B' Echelon had caught up, so every man could discard worn clothes for their best suit of battledress. The 'Pompadours' rested at Lillebonne. 'D' Company of the 2nd Essex, which had been disbanded through casualties, was now re-formed into a training company. Much champagne and Suze was acquired, satisfactorily marked 'Reserve' or '*Wehrmacht*'. French posters advertised a football match: '*La Lillebonnaise versus les professionelles de Essex Regiment*'. The 11th Scots Fusiliers returned to Le Mesnil and then to Bolbec to reorganize, and the seventy-seven Fusiliers who had been wounded in Normandy returned after convalescence. The Recce Regiment and the 55th Anti-tank Regiment were now stationed around Bolbec but, of the latter, Lt.-Col. Brian Gooch wrote: 'We went back to peace-time training, and fired our guns out to sea at Dieppe for practice, for it was many a month since we had fired them.'

Sgt. Bob Sheldrake remembered: 'There were singsongs in the cafés in Lillebonne and how proud I was to render '*J'attendrai*' to the delight of the locals who stuffed me with wine until it ran out of my eyes.'

On the 18th, the division moved to the Dieppe area and then drove north through the Pas de Calais into and through Belgium, carried by transport platoons formed by the 89th LAA Regiment and the 55th Anti-tank Regiment. Sheldrake continued:

As we rumbled on our way through town after town the people cheered until they hadn't the strength to even ask for cigarettes. I have noticed it many times – the tanks nose their way through a town while the civilians hide in their cellars. The infantry bearing the brunt pass through to nothing more than a sniper's bullet, but by the time the guns go through, the civilians have left their holes to cheer them on their way.

Gnr. John Mercer of the 185th Field Regiment said:

We moved into Belgium. The reception became even warmer. In one small town the column was brought to a halt for over an hour. Major Frank Lucas decided we would spend the night there. We were invited into people's houses, we were offered wine and brandy and potato soup with bread. It was all delicious and exciting. Toast followed toast and our French-speaking hosts spoke of their Royal Family and we spoke of ours. Strange to be advancing through territory that our fathers had fought over in World War I, Ypres, Poperinghe, Menin Gate. Our fathers had fought the Hun and defeated him and now their sons were doing the same. It was a time of great elation. We were chasing the Boches, we were winning the war.

Fusilier George Wilkinson:

All of the Polar Bears saw the great aerial armadas flying on their way north. Many of the planes were towing gliders, two and even three at a time. The Armada filled the skies for nearly ten minutes and the roar of the engines could be heard as an angry drone above the high noise of our carrier. We learnt later they were bound for Arnhem. We did not know of the fierce fighting that was to engulf them and how disastrous the enterprise [Market Garden], so high in expectation, was to be.

George Wilkinson of the 11th Royal Scots Fusiliers continued: 'We proceeded into Belgium at Turnhout via Brussels then to Zonderen, Maerle and eventually Oustalle.' And then the fighting started all over again.

CHAPTER TWENTY-NINE

Battles in Southern Holland – September

'Stop Firing, You Bloody Fools!'

The German LXVII Corps had been ordered to stop the allied advance, at all costs, north of Antwerp. The 11th Armoured Division had taken Antwerp and the Guards Armoured Regiment had liberated Brussels. Operation Market Garden had been three-quarters successful, with Nijmegen and the Island north now under the control of the 43rd Wessex, the Guards Armoured Regiment and the American airborne troops. The task of the 1st Corps was to clear the large rectangle some 40 miles wide and 30 miles in depth of southern Holland. The two main towns were Breda and Tilburg. By the 21st the division had moved 200 miles north to an assembly area, 10 miles south of the Antwerp–Turnhout Canal.

The Recce Regiment were now in their true element. They had moved up to Herenthout by 21 September when the Polar Bears took over from the 7th Armoured Division. Just 2 days later they liberated Herenthals, where Lt. George Bowman of 'B' Squadron was guided in by two young ladies, and men from a nearby breakers yard dragged – by horse – girders to erect a temporary bridge. They reached the Turnhout Canal on 24 September and 'B' Squadron liberated Turnhout, but all of the canal bridges had been blown.

John Barker of 'B' Squadron visited the local hospital, was given a bowl of soup by the nurses and saw a badly wounded American airman who had been shot down the day before. A little later the OC of the assault troop, who had been badly wounded on a recce of the canal, was brought in to the hospital, where he died shortly afterwards. However, the 7th Duke of Wellingtons regarded Turnhout as *their* town. In pouring rain their welcome was terrific. For 2 days, cheering, hand-clapping crowds shouting applause for 'Tommy' created a strong demand for cap badges. The RQMS was horrified – all lost owing to 'enemy action'.

The 146th and 147th brigades crossed the Albert Canal on the 22nd and 23rd. All of the bridges were, of course, blown and all barges were sunk. The bends in the canal gave the enemy enfilade fire and the flat landscape offered little cover. Of the three attempted crossings, only that of the Lincolnshires was successful. From East Ostmalle 'A' Company, under Maj.

Lt. Tom Salmon, 49th Recce, at the liberation of Turnhout, 24 September 1944. Lt Salmon was wounded along the canal three hours after this photograph was taken. He died of his wounds in the St Elizabeth Hospital. (Monty Satchell)

Sgt. Monty Satchell, 49th Recce, Dr P. Caron and seventeen-year old J. Boone (behind) at the liberation of Turnhout, 24 September 1944. (Monty Satchell)

Barlow-Poole, and 'C' Company, under Maj. E. Cook, crossed at midnight in assault boats in intense darkness and absolute silence.

In 4 hours the sappers, working in torrential rain at incredible speed, built Plum 1 and Plum 2 Bailey bridges in position opposite Ryckevorsel, and the bridges were in use just 2 hours later. The Lincolns swept their beachhead and captured more than 90 prisoners. Later that afternoon they were relieved by the Leicestershires, and they then pushed eastwards along miles of brickworks on the far side of the canal. In the process, 'A' Company were cut off and were only saved by the divisional gunners, who brought down a hail of shells to protect them.

The Hallams' attempt to cross in assault craft met point blank fire. Douglas Bell, the 'Beachmaster', was mortally wounded, and the brigadier, knowing that the Lincolns had made it across, halted the attack. The 11th Royal Scots Fusiliers 'D' Company and 'B' Company established a bridgehead near Turnhout to a depth of 500 yards, but they in turn were withdrawn, having suffered casualties.

Next the 1/4th KOYLI were given the task of taking Ryckevorsel, a large village 1½ miles north of the canal. They had concentrated at Vlimieren on the 24th and crossed the Class 9 bridge at 0645 hours, 'B' Company with two sections of carriers plus two Wasps leading. They cleared the central square, and Sgt. Andy Hardy established his mortar observation post in the church, as did the gunner FOO, Capt. Mike Hunt.

Geoff Steer of 'B' Company of the 1/4th KOYLI recalled: 'We searched some PW, we were always looking for souvenirs! In the main street – it had just started to rain – when the occupier of the first house brought out a large stone bottle of rum. So out came the mess tins. It was the real thing.' Later, Geoff was hit in the

RE bridge over the Antwerp Canal at Turnhout, September 1944. left to right: Ingram (RE), Ronny Foster (CRE), the GOC, Frank Parsons (ADC), Wilfred Tyzack. (George Barker)

leg. His section fought furiously until they ran out of ammunition, their house was surrounded and they were captured. They were taken back 4 miles to a cottage where, he remembered, a 'German officer said the war was over for us. All we would have to do is play cricket and football.' In Breda hospital 'the corridors were running in blood. You had to pick your way through the stretchers of wounded Germans, English, Canadians and French troops.'

Andy Hardy recalled: 'We had a grand view of the enemy to the north and east. There were many targets within range: the enemy seemed to be poorly trained and tended to bunch together.'

Throughout the day, counter-attacks came in from the north and east, and the KOYLI were at full stretch to contain them despite continuous DF targets being brought down. An 88 mm gun toppled the church spire, and part of 'B' Company were surrounded and taken prisoner after they had run out of ammunition. Nevertheless, 134 enemy prisoners were taken and at least another 100 were killed or wounded, against the loss of 20 from the KOYLI.

Gnr. John Mercer of 274th Battery of the 185th Field Regiment wrote home:

I was with the OP [Capt. Thompson]. At dusk our infantry with our carriers crossed over the canal and dug in a semi-circle around the bridge. At 3 am the Germans started to infiltrate into our positions under the cover of darkness. The forward section of our infantry became cut off and dawn broke to find our position completely surrounded. The nearest enemy were 200 yards away in a hedge. From 3 o'clock I sat in the carrier outside the barn manning the radio, under small arms fire, and did those Spandau bullets zip and crackle over. Two rifle grenades exploded on the roof 20 feet from the carrier. Our infantry were magnificent. They fired everything they had got. Our Captain called down a 'close target'. The rounds dropped fair and square. Out of a dozen Germans all were killed or wounded. I asked for some 'Big Boys' (tanks) over the air and they came trundling up an hour later. We took 70 prisoners and some horribly wounded casualties. All were in bad shape covered in mud and utterly fagged out.

The bridgehead was being widened and the Hallams were directed towards the Place de Mendicité, 1 mile to the east. The Lincolns moved east along the canal bank towards a large cemetery and factory. When night fell, the 2nd Essex relieved the KOYLI in Ryckevorsel, who took up positions along the road to Mendicité, a large, well-defended 'workhouse'.

Lt.-Col. G.G. Elliott of the 2nd Essex described the scene:

There was a stiff battle in progress and the KOYLI were meeting considerable opposition. 'A' on the right, 'B' on the left took over somewhat untidily after dark in the southern half of the town, with 'C' in reserve. Next morning we were heavily shelled and then counter-attacked by large numbers of infantry. The forward platoons fought back magnificently, but elements of 'B' Coy got surrounded but held on. Bullets were smacking into Bn HQ with unpleasant frequency. The SWB were said to be holding the canal bridge behind and the ground to the east and west but there was a large gap between it. Since some Canadian Sherman tanks were now across the canal I sent the LO back with an invitation to Sqn CO that he help us out with the loan of a troop of tanks. He responded with alacrity.

A young subaltern with a troop reported (26 Sept) at midday and said afterwards, 'I have had the best shooting of my career.' The identical battle took place the next day, with a second and stronger German counter-attack, with six companies totalling 500 men. Both of the leading companies took a tremendous toll in killed and wounded. Over 100 dead were counted on the battlefield and 200 prisoners were taken. Lt. A.A. Vince wrote in his book, *The Pompadours*:

> Ryckervorsel was only a small battle and probably does not appear in the history books, but it was one of our better efforts. Control was perfect on all levels, despite the terrible job, the Signals had in keeping the lines repaired. Every objective was taken as directed and the men behind the rifles and Brens rarely wasted a bullet. Our own casualties were around the 60 mark. The Bn received several decorations for this action, none more deserved than the MM to CSM Morgan of 'B' Coy.' A few days later the CO was posted to the Middle East and Lt.-Col. N.W. Finlinson DSO took over command of 2nd Essex.

Sgt. Harry Conn of 'C' Company took part in several patrols under Lt. J. Barrett towards Loenhout:

> With another man I went forward to look for my L/Cpl. Martin, found him on a slope, face down, had been shot in the head. He was dead. As we picked him up we were fired on, quickly made it back to our position. The Germans decided to attack. We opened up with all weapons available and beat off the attack – about a Platoon strength.

Conn then acted as an observation post:

> I was to tell the Artillery Officer on the radio in yards, not degrees, whether the shells were falling short, left or right and when on target. After only two rounds managed to get the Gunners on target, where they pounded the enemy positions causing mayhem. There were explosions, vehicles revving up and shouting as they pulled out.

Conn had also brought in a wounded Essex officer: 'He thanked me for what I had done, and gave me a bundle of Belgian Francs worth about £30, saying, "I wish I could have given more." '

The 2nd South Wales Borderers were guarding the bridgehead over the canal and, on the night of 25 September, 'D' Company was attacked by Germans led by a man shouting in perfect English: 'Stop firing, you bloody fools.' The platoon was overrun and another was forced to withdraw. However, 'B' Company fought a notable action, securing farmhouses and a pillbox, but in a 3½ hour battle, eventually with the help of tanks, they drove off the enemy, who left 70 prisoners and 56 dead. Everyone from the OC, Maj. Collins, to the company clerk fought back.

The next day the counter-attacks came in, but again they were driven off with heavy losses. The battalion history related: 'This defeat cracked the German defence. The Bn had fought a spirited action, perhaps the best they had ever fought and Major Collins was awarded the MC and three other members of 'B' Coy won MMs.'

However, for Spr. Bill Hudson of the 757th Field Company RE it was rather different:

> We were working as an infantry unit under Bobforce and manning a bridge over the Turhout canal, whose banks were booby trapped with trip wires attached to flares. We were at St Lenaarts and the Belgian [brigade] manned the next bridge at Brekt. Lt. Cottam took Ted

Goodman and myself on a recce patrol, rectangular in shape over the bridge into No Man's Land. By mistake a Belgian sentry fired on the patrol. I put Ted in an ambulance but he died in my arms.

In the midst of war, sometimes – thank goodness – comical situations arise. A booby-trap party of the 756th Company RE set off in the dark near St Lenaarts in two halftracks, but they missed the forward troops – not funny. They then bumped a German patrol on the road in No Man's Land – not at all funny. Their own fire brought down concentrated mortar fire from both sides, who were a bit touchy at the time. Both sides took to the roadside ditches. Two Polar Bear sappers found a German between them in their ditch. They informed him that he was surrounded and was now a prisoner. In good English he told his captors that he was proposing to desert anyway. As an afterthought he said he would be pleased to guide them back to their lines as they had obviously lost their way.

CHAPTER THIRTY

The Battle for Mendicité

Harper's Victoria Cross

The Canadians had tried but failed to take the Depot de Mendicité, between Ryckevorsel and Merxplas, a formidable barrack block – a combined prison, workhouse and lunatic asylum. With some 100 acres of farmland around it, intersected by deep ditches, the main enemy position had been reinforced by another battalion and was surrounded on three sides by a moat, 20 feet wide and 3 feet deep.

Lt.-Col. Hart Dyke described the Hallams' battle:

> Level with the moat on the south side were three modern villas. An anti-tank gun destroyed the first Recce troop tanks. 'C' and 'D' Coys advanced parallel to the road fifty yards away to avoid mortar bombs bursting in the trees. 'C' Coy played hide and seek in the woods north of the road, but 'D' reaching the farm had five men killed outright by a heavy mortar concentration. Most of the Coy – reinforcements – panicked and withdrew hastily along the road. Major Alan Boucher, the fourth Coy CO 'D' Coy since landing in Normandy remained with the old hands near the farm. John Hall, acting mortar officer, volunteered to take [the reinforcements] back again keeping well clear of the road. Lt. Toon 'A' Coy clearing the woods to the SW was killed leading his men. Further SW the Lincolns advancing along the north bank of the canal met superior enemy forces in the brickworks.

That was on the 28th. The following day, he resumed:

> We were given a squadron of tanks allocated to 'A' Coy to clear the whole wooded area west and SW of the Mendicité. Heavy casualties were inflicted on the enemy in the open woodland and 'A' coy captured a whole platoon in a workhouse cottage. To the north 'C' Coy and on the left flank 'B' Coy with their carriers were equally successful. Our artillery fire caused heavy casualties on the enemy. Elsewhere the Lincolns and Leicesters cleared the north bank of the canal and an enemy counter-attack was destroyed by our artillery. The main attack to capture the Mendicité to allow the Polish Armoured Div to thrust out to Merxplaas and thence into Holland was entrusted to 147 Brigade. The 7 Dukes and Glosters attacked from the south, Leicesters from the west. 'C' Coy, Hallams led by Lt. Judge reached the perimeter of the Mendicité but was wounded in the neck from heavy small arms and mortar fire. Corporal J.W. Harper now took control of the platoon. The enemy on the far side of the earthen defence wall were throwing grenades over the top. Throwing grenades himself Harper scaled the wall and in the face of heavy close range small arms fire personally routed the Germans directly opposing him taking four prisoners. He shot several of the remainder and brought his prisoners back over the wall. Then he led his platoon back over the wall, returned, reconnoitred the dyke and found a ford under heavy Spandau fire. He was killed directing his OC to the ford.
>
> Corporal Harper by his dauntless courage and superb self-sacrifice earned for him posthumously the highest award for valour – the Victoria Cross. On the right the Leicesters had pushed forward gallantly clearing the maze of buildings. Mike Lonsdale-Cooper with 'C'

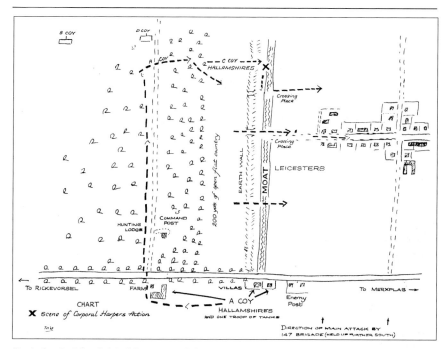

Battle for the Mendicité. (Not to scale. Diagramatic only)

Company supported them, reported very large numbers of enemy, asked for re-inforcements so I extracted 'A' Coy and the troop of tanks and sent them round to exploit the break through. Over 70 dead Germans were counted on the ground. The Boche fought stubbornly and surrounded and almost annihilated the Leicesters leading coy. As darkness fell both sides withdrew exhausted.

The Hallams also took 85 prisoners during the Mendicité battle.

At dawn on 29 September the 1st Leicesters attacked on the right (south) to capture the key roadbridge with the Hallamshires on the left. For reasons of surprise and partly for humanitarian reasons, since the prisoners and patients in the mental hospital were still in residence, the attack was to be a silent one. Throughout the cold autumn day, both battalions battled away against determined opposition. For the Leicesters, Lt. V.F.W. Bidgood won an immediate MC, as did Lt. F.A. Gaunt. Maj. A.E. Denaro was killed, and Peter Upcher, 'D' Company's CO, led the assault and earned a DSO. Sgt. Poole took his platoon across the moat, and by 1000 hours 'D' Company had reached the light railway line. Some of the enemy mingled with the patients in the barracks and made skilful use of the ditches.

There were many feats of gallantry. Pte. C.H. Woods, Cpl. W.A. Saunders, Sgt. W. Irwin and Sgt. T. Johnson all received the MM, earned in the day-long confused fighting, as did a stretcher-bearer, Pte. H.T. Gill. By

Corporal J.W. Harper VC, Hallamshires.

late evening the depot was seized, but at a cost: 70 Leicesters were killed, wounded or captured. Charles Pell wrote in *Tigers Never Sleep*:

> The mental hospital was not an easy place to capture as with its castle-like walls, the Germans found it easy to defend. The Germans had let out the inmates who were just standing around looking at us as if we were the mad ones. They were being killed left, right and centre but there was nothing we could do to help them.

CHAPTER THIRTY-ONE

Battles in Southern Holland – October

The vital bridgehead gained and consolidated, the Polish Armoured Division Shermans poured across and smashed their way through Merxplaas, in their advance towards the Dutch frontier. Early in October the Polar Bears were now held responsible for holding a long front line from Brecht along the north bank of the canal towards Poppel – a distance of 20 miles. Gen. Barker formed a series of composite task forces. The first was named Eykynforce, and consisted of the 11th Royal Scots Fusiliers with anti-tank guns, REs, Kensingtons, a 7th Duke of Wellingtons carrier platoon and part of the Belgian White Brigade. Eric Rolls was driver of a 15 cwt Bedford truck with 'D' Compamy MT section with the 11th Royal Scots Fusiliers. He recalled: 'CQMS Matherson and the Coy. storeman a Scotsman called Peter, and I, took the hot meals up in the evenings after dark to Coy HQ and the platoons would send men over to collect their rations.'

The 146th Brigade continued the advance on 3 October. The 4th Lincolns occupied Raevels and continued to Chapel St Jean, while the KOYLI, on the right, and the Hallams, on the left, tackled the village of Poppel. Heavy enemy mortaring and shelling slowed the Lincolns down, but by 1600 hours they had taken the village in return for 9 casualties. Owing to their reduced strength, 'B' Company was temporarily disbanded. Graham Roe of the Hallams recorded:

C Coy's HQ was situated behind a cottage. I passed the 18 set to Roy Carpenter. It was going dark as we advanced. I could see in the poor light that the Germans were infiltrating our lines and closing in behind us. I was acting section leader, told Ken Partner to give them a burst with his Bren and John Davidson used his Sten. We were now under intense mortar and shell fire, as well as small arms fire. Suddenly there was a blinding flash, I was struck in my left shoulder and went down. I saw Ken go down and at the same time John crumpled.

Later, L/Cpl. Saunders, a huge man, carried Roe back to the RAP in a farmhouse where his wound was patched up. Roe continued: 'Davidson sadly lost a foot but Ken died from his terrible wounds. It was the 7th October. We had lasted that long from the beach-head before the worst happened. Many of our comrades had perished even before reaching the Seine and many more had been wounded.'

With a dashing squadron of Sherman tanks from the 27th Canadian Armoured Regiment shooting at everything – farms, houses, barns and even haystacks – the Lincolns advanced on the following day for 3 miles towards Goirle. Enemy reinforcements moved south from Tilburg and the corps commander changed his plans. The Lincolns were withdrawn during darkness to Nieukirk on the Belgian–Dutch frontier. The 147th Brigade were involved in indecisive fighting in the centre of the line. The 2nd South Wales Borderers fought north of Gammel, moving on the 5th to Bock. The 7th Dukes supported the Polish Armoured Division through Merxplaas and Zondereigen. They noted that the Polish infantry always attacked in restricting great coats and that they stopped operations every time food appeared.

Gen. Barker's next composite force was named 'Bob' Force, and was formed to hold a 10 mile front from the north-west of Merxplaas to Ryckevorsel, commanded by Lt.-Col. 'Bob' Cory, CO of the 89th LAA Regiment, plus the recce regiment, two batteries of the Anti-tank Regiment and half of the Kensingtons. They acted mainly as infantry, and in their new role they carried out some excellent patrolling. Lt. 'Nick' Nicholls was now a subaltern with 'C' Troop of the 89th LAA. He remembered:

We acted as the forces light artillery, established an OP at Ryckevorsel and engaged targets S of Hoogstranten. We fired over 800 rounds all over the occupied village of Aachtel. One of our Gunner 'infantry' sections attacked a farmhouse, took prisoners but the officer who led the attack was wounded, later awarded the MC.

However, behind the lines, rest periods included visits to the bath units. Gnr. John Mercer wrote in his book, *Mike Target*:

The Polar Bears had taken over the local cinema in Turnhout. Bing Crosby in *Going My Way* was a particular favourite of George, Dennis and myself. Without passes we climbed aboard the steam train to drive the four miles to the town. The whole town was swarming with khakiclad figures wearing the insignia of the Polar Bears on their sleeves. A Belgian stopped in the street and said 'we had to get off the pavement into the streets for the Moffer (*Wehrmacht*). With your soldiers they move out of our way and get into the road. Maybe trivial to you but to me the mark of a civilised nation.

After the 294th Field Company RE had helped to build a 210 foot, triple single Bailey bridge over the Turnhout Canal, they adapted it and laid railway lines over it to run a train – the Polar Bear Special, suitably decorated with divisional and company signs – between Poppel and Turnhout. Just as it was running nicely they had to move on and leave their 'toy' behind. However, on the evening of the 6th a strong, determined enemy counter-attack came in on the 146th Brigade – the Hallams on the left at Aerle and the 4th Lincolns at Nieukirk on the right, just west of the main road north to Tilburg.

Lt.-Col. Hart Dyke described events:

Our role for the Hallams was to hold the bridge. The stream formed the international frontier. Enemy snipers were busy in the extremely thick country. At first light enemy infantry and tanks attacked at Aerle, Nieukirk and the Lincolns on our right on the main Tilburg–Poppel road. Our gunners broke up the Aerle attack, forming up inside the woods, selected for a DF target. On the right the enemy overran our forward platoon; Sgt. Newton set the first enemy tank on fire with his A/Tk gun. The remaining tanks withdrew hastily and Major Mike Halford sent a platoon of 'B' Coy to re-occupy the platoon position covering the bridge and the situation was restored. The battle had not gone so well on the Lincoln's front. Their leading company had been over-run and the Bn forced to withdraw. The enemy had no intention of giving up Tilburg without a struggle. He might even try to throw us back across the Turnhout Canal.

'B' Company and 'C' Company of the Hallams were seriously reduced in number, but they managed to bag 30 prisoners.

The Lincolns were well supported by the 273rd Battery of the 69th Field Regiment and 'B' Squadron of the 27th Canadian Armoured Regiment. At 1400 hours a counter-attack came in on the Lincolns carrier platoon and 'C' Squadron of the Recce Regiment, which were almost overrun. Capt. J.R. Ainger of 'C' Company restored the situation in a brilliant counter-attack and inflicted heavy casualties on the enemy. The next 3 hours brought heavy artillery and mortar fire, and at 1730 hours there was yet another enemy counter-attack. The imperturbable Maj. Nigel Richardson of the 69th Field Regiment brought down almost non-stop DF fire, as all through the night and in the early morning of the 7th the enemy pressure was maintained. Two platoons of 'A' Company were overrun, but again 'C' Company and the Canadian tanks drove the enemy back and restored the situation.

Throughout the 7th, machine-gun fire was poured into the Lincolns. At daybreak a company of the KOYLI came foreward to replace 'C' Company as reserve company, and in the afternoon the rest of the 1/4th KOYLI appeared, and the battered Lincolns went back to Wielde for a well-earned rest. In 4 days they had suffered 17 dead and another 70 wounded or missing, but they had accounted for 150 dead enemy and triple that number of casualties.

274/185 Field Regt RA, near Poppel, October 1944. The four Nos. 1s. Left to right: Sgt. Ronnie Owen, Sgt. Tom Davis, Sgt. Bill Roberts, L/Sgt. Eddie Gawler. (John Mercer)

274/185 Field Regt RA, near Poppel, October 1944. A group of greasy gunners. Back row, left to right: Sgt. Gawler, Sgt. Roberts, Hawksworth, Jock Marr. Front row: Orchard, Wells, 'Waggy' Weston, George Newson. Sgt. Davis (in front). (John Mercer)

On 8 October, Sgt. Bob Sheldrake of the 55th Anti-tank Regiment became a father, though he did not realize it at the time. He noted:

The four guns and THQ were in a small area in the tiny village of Aerle, overlooked by the enemy further along the road. The company of the Gloucesters whom we were supporting was dug in around and also in the farmyard. One of our guns pointed its long snout from a pigsty, another from a great pile of faggots. At first light the Boche began to stonk in earnest. It swelled and subsided and swelled again with increased fury. We played cards until George, ever resourceful, taught us to play 'cab'. A great day in my life. Stretcher-bearers collected their grim burdens and trudged back along the road to the waiting ambulances, while their mates lay black faced and still warm in death.

The next two weeks were spent in defensive positions while the 1st Corps waited for the Canadian Army to clear the Scheldt estuary. The enemy south of Tilburg were in excellent defensive positions and marshy ground would bog all of the vital tank support. Lt. A.A, Vince of the 2nd Essex wrote:

Under the new CO Lt.-Col. Finlinson DSO we held the line at Ryckevorsel to the 7th Oct – almost ten days of continuous patrolling and under constant shellfire. We were relieved by 'Bob' Force and dug in near Poppel which we held for 10 days of rain, slit trenches ankle deep in water and mud and the Boche only a few hundreds of yards away. On the 19th we concentrated in St Leonards.

Bob Faxon of the 49th Recce Regiment recalled: 'On the 18th we joined with 107 Regt RAC under command of 34 Tank Brigade, known as Clarke

Force.' Faxon spent the night of the 20th in an empty henhouse to get out of the pouring rain. 'We stunk of chicken dung', he commented.

After breakfast of tinned bacon, 'hard tack' biscuits and tea, 'A' Squadron set off in the dawn towards Wuestwezel. Faxon was the Bren gunner in the troop commander's carrier with Cpl. Tom Steel and Fred Brickel. A few hours later, Steel and Brickel were both wounded, but they later returned to their unit.

Monty visited the division on the 20th to hold an investiture. Among the many brave Polar Bears decorated were Sgt. Hall of the 217th Battery of the 55th Anti-tank Regiment, who received the DCM, Lt.-Col. Peter Barclay, CO of the 4th Lincolns, who was awarded the DSO, and Maj. Barlow-Poole, who was given the MC.

On Friday 20 October, the 1st Corps advanced with the Polish Armoured Division on the right, the 49th Division in the centre and the 4th Canadian Division on the left, directed on Breda, Roosendaal and Bergen op Zoom respectively. The axis of the Polar Bears' advance was from Wuestmalle (6 miles south-east of Ryckevorsel) through Brecht, Wurstwezel, Nieuwmoer and Essche to Roosendaal, a distance of about 20 miles. The 56th Brigade and the 147th Brigade took the lead, while the 146th concentrated in Wuestmalle. The German 15th Army deployed their 245th Division and composite forces against the Polar Bears. From the Ryckevorsel area the 56th Brigade, supported by the 9th Royal Tank Regiment's 'funnies' – flame-throwing Crocodiles and flails – set off for Stapelheide. Lt. A.A. Vince of the 2nd Essex described the battle:

> The Boche held a line in depth a couple of miles south of the small town of Loenhout on which we were directed with 2 Glosters on our right and 2 SWB ordered to put in 'worrying' efforts by clearing Brecht after stiff fighting, then moving towards Beekhoven. A direct frontal assault was ordered. Surprise and firepower provided the keystone for our success. At 0728 hrs and on 20 Oct four 25-pdrs Regiments, three Mediums and all available heavy mortars started a detailed fireplan. 'B' Coy took thirteen minutes to reach their objective but 'C' ran into trouble at the village of Stapelheide. Every hedgerow was honeycombed with weapon pits. For eight hours 'C' Coy supported by flame-throwers fought from ditch to ditch, losing 25 casualties and a whole troop of supporting tanks knocked out. Lt.-Col. Finlinson ordered 'A' Coy to join 'B' Coy and continue the advance in the centre. As darkness fell three hundred prisoners had been taken and the four mile advance into Loenhout accomplished. At first light the village was cleared by tanks and carriers. The Dutch complained that their rescuers had whipped a couple of typewriters!

The 147th Brigade were in reserve to exploit success after the breakout with Clarkeforce under Brig. Clarke commanding the 34th Tank Brigade. Maj. Upcher with 'D' Company of the 1st Leicesters rode into battle on 107 Royal Armoured Corps tanks. Also on the 20th they cut the main Antwerp–Breda road at 'Stonebridge', just north of Wuestwezel. The key bridge was seized and, guarded by the Recce Regiment, Clarkeforce moved on north-west towards Esschen, together with the 4th Canadian Armoured Division.

The following day, the 1st Leicesters were heavily counter-attacked by enemy infantry, SP guns and tanks. By midday two platoons of 'A' Company had been overrun and their anti-tank guns put out of action. Capt. V.W.J. Roussel, OC of 'A' Company, and their FOO, Lt. D. Marriott of the 388th Battery, held up the

German attacks for 3 hours, despite point-blank fire from five German SPs within 150 yards of their position. Heavy DF tasks were fired, and Roussel, twice wounded, succeeded in the smoke and confusion in withdrawing 13 of his 120 men. For his gallantry he was awarded an immediate MC.

Early in the afternoon, six German tanks, camouflaged with branches, broke through and dashed down the road at full speed firing at everything. Four were eventually knocked out by 'friendly' Churchill tanks that had just arrived, plus Sgt. Cross's PIAT. The fighting went on into the evening, when the enemy withdrew over the border into Holland, having lost 13 knocked-out tanks and SP guns, and suffered heavy casualties among both men and equipment. However, the gallant 'Tigers' suffered 111 casualties during the day, including 25 dead. Lt.-Col. F.W. Sanders, the CO, received a bar to his DSO, and the two FOOs of the 69th Field Regiment, Marriott and Frost, were both awarded the MC.

Charles Pell's *Tigers Never Sleep* gave an evocative account of the Wuerstwezel 'Stone Bridge' actions, with stories by Pell, Sgt. George Upton of the 7th platoon, who was captured, and the deeds of the 143rd Field Regiment, who fired 5,000 rounds during the day. A counter-attack by the 146th Brigade arrived in the nick of time to save divisional HQ from being overrun. Lt.-Col. Hart Dyke of the Hallams wrote:

> With considerable amazement I discovered that Div HQ was outside the perimeter which I had selected. Five 3-ton lorries belonging to the CRE were set on fire by an enemy tank. Another enemy tank approached after 'A' Coy had got into position but was driven off by Tony Nicholson who fired a rifle at the various apertures in the monster. We were ordered to

Monty presents medals to Polar Bear officers, 20 October 1944. On the left are Lt-Col Hart Dyke, CO Hallams, and Lt-Col Peter Barclay, CO 4 Lincolns. The GOC and Monty are sitting in front. (George Barker)

clear the hamlet of Steertreuvel as a platoon of RSF on our right had been overrun by tanks at Kruisberg. Sgt. Little of 'D' Coy rescued an A/Tk 6 pdr gun immobilized in a burning house, dragged it into a firing position, and knocked out an enemy SP. Little was awarded the MM for this exploit. The attack was carried out in text book manner. 'C' Coy covered by tank fire under an artillery mortar barrage. The whole enemy company holding the village were killed or captured and three 88 mm guns destroyed without loss to ourselves.

Rex Flower of the mortar platoon of the 1/4th KOYLI had gone to Antwerp on short leave with 'Slick' and Sam, hitchhiking from Turnhout and spending most of the three days eating in the ice-cream parlours: 'just like schoolboys stuffing ourselves. Nothing like that in wartime Britain.' A V-2 struck an electric tram substation, so they had to hitch another lift back to Westmalle. Flower then acquired a 'looted' Browning 7.65 mm automatic pistol.

The KOYLI were shelled in Wuestwezel on the 20th, and several of 'C' Company were wounded, including Capt. Mainprice, CSM Callard and Pte. Chris Lister. Maj. Singleton's jeep, with a tin box containing all of the Company's documents and pay records, was destroyed. The Canadian Armoured Regiment took Esschen on the next day, with Clarkeforce in the vanguard with the 7th Duke of Wellingtons and the Leicesters taking it in turn to be under command.

Sgt. Bob Sheldrake remembered:

Going in once more with the Essex, we got into the first half of Esschen and lay most of the guns to cover the ground to the north, the streets themselves running east and west. THQ we set up in a castle situated just on the edge of town, keeping Les Bullman's gun with us. There we were joined shortly afterwards by the Vickers MGs of the Kensingtons.

The sharp end can be a funny place. In the midst of one stonk, Sheldrake recalled:

the air of the barn was filled with dust and mortar, the falling debris sending up fresh clouds of dust. Through all the confusion, a few yards from me on a pile of straw an infantryman was making love to a girl with her blouse open and her head thrown back, both were grinning and chuckling. The bursting shells had no meaning for them.

In Esschen an indignant lady householder demanded in fluent English: 'Can somebody come and do something about the water downstairs. It's coming out of the tap and we can't stop it.' Tools from Sheldrake's carrier sorted out that plumbing problem. Another problem was the discovery of a wine vault: 'The 'Guv' was down there with a wine glass sampling each batch in turn.' Unfortunately, ginger-haired Sgt. 'Math' Bowers got drunk and the infantry they were supporting were not amused.

Rex Flower of the 1/4th KOYLI wrote in his diary:

23 Oct. The RE's had built a bridge, and we [the mortar platoon] went with 'D' Coy to flank patrol under heavy shell and mortar fire. A Churchill tank was stopped with a loud 'clang' right at the side of us; another Recce Honey tank was burnt out, hit by a Panzerfaust. The driver had escaped, but the crew were still in it. What was left of the poor devils. Later we were attacked by three enemy SPs. It was like Normandy again. Through the village of Shriek where 'B' Coy held a bridgehead over a stream.

25 Oct. Moved over the stream towards Esschen, just before the Dutch frontier.

26 Oct. It was a nasty little battle. Things were very lively indeed. We did a lot of firing [4.2 inch mortars] in support of 'D' Coy [who under artificial moonlight provided by searchlights had seized a group of houses 700 yards east of Esschen] and of 'A' Coy [who, starting at 0400 hours to secure a large farm and wood 400 yards north, were held up by heavy shelling]. I never forgot Esschen and never will. We also had a misfire. Doug the No. 2 put the bomb down the barrel. Nothing happened. I gave the cradle a good shake. To my intense surprise the bloody mortar fired. Boom! a ten pound bomb wooshed past my face!

Lt.-Col. Hart Dyke recalled:

We now heard with excitement and curiosity that the 1st Bn, 613 Regt of the American 104 (Timber Wolf) Division which had not yet been in action was to take over from us. They were grand fellows, took great pains to explain how very 'Green' they were and took endless trouble to learn everything they could from us. Their men arrived in vast numbers, with very little transport . . . they counted more on weight of numbers. Our Bn organization was infinitely better, more complete and less wasteful of lives . . . .. [The next day] They had gallantly advanced across the open plain like our troops on the Tugela river in the Boer War in 1899. The enemy had reserved his fire and caught the defenceless Bn in the open with everything he had. Thank God 'Bubbles' Barker always saw that our fire support was sufficient. It was contrary to our training to advance 3000 yards of open ground without the friendly cover of either smoke or darkness.

The Polar Bears' advance continued 3 days later. On the 26th, through battered Esschen, a long straggly town astride the Dutch–Belgian border, the 56th Brigade launched an attack on Nispen with the 2nd Essex leading and the 2nd Glosters to follow through. Lt. A.A. Vince wrote:

It was a perfect example of infantry-tank co-operation. The barrage opened at 0630 hours, with 'A' Company on the right and 'B' Company on the left, supported by the black-hatted crews of the tanks and Crocodiles of the 9th Royal Tank Regiment and the 1st Fife and Forfarshire Yeomanry.

Just 2 hours later both companies had completed the 2000 yard advance and were digging slits in the face of colossal enemy retaliatory shelling. Although most of the 17th Platoon became casualties, 106 representatives of the 'Master Race' were sent back.

CHAPTER THIRTY-TWO

The Battle for Roosendaal

'The Leicesters: Poor Blighters'

By 28 October, Tilbury and Breda had been captured and the Polar Bears were ordered to take Roosendaal, a large country town some 2 miles north of Nispen. The main attack was to come from the 147th Brigade from the south, the 1st Leicesters on the left and the 7th Dukes on the right, with the 4th KOYLI and the 11th Royal Scots Fusiliers to pass through and capture the town. Initially the Hallams were ordered to capture the villages to the west of Roosendaal – Vinkenbrock and Boeink.

At first, all went well with the Hallams' attack. Supported by the 9th Royal Tank Regiment's Churchill tanks and artillery barrage, 'A' Company went in with the bayonet and took Vinkenbrock, capturing a dazed and 'bomb happy' enemy company. Then 'B' Company pushed through and occupied Boeink without meeting further resistance. Lt.-Col. Hart Dyke had asked for the 9th Royal Tank Regiment troops to stay on the final objective for only 15 minutes after it was taken. Unfortunately they stayed on, and enemy 88 mm anti-tank guns picked off 10 Churchills – one after the other.

About 1,000 yards in front of Roosendaal was a stream which had been converted into a formidable anti-tank ditch, covered by well-constructed defence works. On their way north towards Roosendaal, the 1st Leicesters had had a battle at Brembosch where, on the 26th, 'B' Company forced a bridgehead over a dyke/anti-tank obstacle. Sgt. J.H. Corbett won a MM here when, wounded in the leg, he took his platoon forward in spite of heavy casualties, until the supporting tanks could get across at 1545 hours to form a bridgehead over the anti-tank ditch in front of Roosendaal. Under a huge barrage, using cover of hedges, 'D' Company, under Maj. Upcher, led, with 'B' Company under Maj. Pollard and 'C' Company under Maj. Walstell to follow through. By nightfall the Leicesters, having suffered 17 casualties, were in the town outskirts despite heavy shelling.

The Dukes from Meuwmoer had by the 24th taken Schanker. By the night of the 28/29th they were holding the line in front of the Roosendaal ditch, and they had put two platoons across but were forced to withdraw. Next, 'C' Company, under Maj. G.V. Fancourt, led the attack under sniping fire from all weapons, including SP guns. They could only crawl forward in water. 'A' Company managed to cross the main ditch, and they killed and captured many Germans, but they incurred casualties themselves through shelling, sniping and counter-attack. 'B' Company were pinned down most of the day in ditches by sniping and mortaring. 'D' Company, on the right, carried out several fine raiding patrols. Lt. John Lappin wrote:

> Friday 29th. Leicesters were attacking a strong point to cover the advance forward by the Polish Armoured. We acted as flank protection. Up at 0300, Breakfast 0330, Move 0430. 'D' Coy were 1,000 yds ahead of us. We moved up in the dark with the battle raging ahead of us. Jerry tried to reach us with mortars but missed by several hundred yards. When we came into the open in front of our objective we started to get it good and heavy from the Spandaus. The troop of Shermans came up in support and blasted away with MGs and 75 mms whilst we moved up the ditch besides them. The Boche opened up with A/Tk guns. One tank was hit several times – an unlucky shot put it out.

Lappin pulled his platoon back into a fire plantation. He continued:

> Pte. Preston was wounded in leg and arm. Godley was slightly wounded with a bullet and shell wound. Walt Horne's platoon was sitting right on the enemy's doorstep and taking everything. The Leicesters were in a very tight spot 200 yards to our left. 'D' Coy were on our right. During the afternoon the German Commander asked for a truce to evacuate wounded. A ridiculous situation for an hour. The Red Cross flag went backwards and forwards, and one just walked up and down in the open. Jerry could see where we were. We could see him. The Leicesters and 'A' Coy had a number of casualties coming out through us. Back to the battle as before. About 1500 hrs the smoke cover dropped. The Leicesters – poor blighters – they'd certainly caught it.

When the 11th Royal Scots Fusiliers and the 1/4th KOYLI passed through the Dukes and Leicesters early on the 30th, they soon cleared the town, which the enemy had evacuated, losing 80 prisoners. Lt.-Col. Hart Dyke of the Hallams recalled:

> I had to tell the brigadier that we could not effect an entry into Roosendaal from the west without a full scale set piece attack. A stretch of about 1,000 yards of completely flat ground lay between us and the wide moat and earthen ramparts of the city's defences. Under cover of an early morning mist a patrol slipped into Roosendaal the next morning to find the western outskirts and defences evacuated by the enemy. Our forward company followed in but was forestalled by our friends the KOYLI who received a rapturous reception from the populace. The city had not been damaged and the whole division was luxuriously billetted. The day after, all Divisional COs were ordered to days rest and recreation in Brussels.

Rex Flower of the 1/4th KOYLI remembered: 'We entered the town with 'D' Coy. The enemy had gone. All the people were waving, cheering. The welcome was fantastic. Orange coloured flags with the message, Orange Boven. They were frantic with joy. Boy! How they hated those Germans. We stayed with Piet a railway worker, his wife and four lovely children.'

Maj. Godfrey Harland recalled: ' 'A' Coy HQ was being royally entertained and waited on by some very good looking Dutch girls. The CO had to break up the party and tell Andrew Rutherford to move his company to less salubrious surroundings.'

CHAPTER THIRTY-THREE

Breda

The River Mark and the Taking of Willemstadt

The Lincolns now became part of several composite forces. On 23 October their CO, Lt.-Col. Peter Barclay, was in charge of a small multinational force. Two Canadian armoured regiments and a Belgian detachment, as well as the Lincolns, were christened Impforce. Their task was to keep pushing towards Breda, and so, two days later, they took Ulicoten. Next came a partition of Whiteforce (three Lincoln companies plus Lt.-Col. White's 6th Canadian Armoured Regiment) and Gorforce ('D' Company of the Lincolns under Lt.-Col. Gordon's 27th Canadian Armoured Regiment).

On the 28th, while Roosendaal was being invested, Whiteforce set off, via Baarle Nassau for Breda, some 9 miles to the north-west. For the next few days, with the Polish Armoured Division on the right under Maj.-Gen. S. Maczek and the 2nd Canadian Brigade on the left, the Lincolns had a thoroughly enjoyable 'pheasant drive', flushing out Germans in Couwelaar, Ulverhout and Mariendal. Whiteforce led, while Gorforce followed up and came through at Mariendal. The Lincolns travelled on the Sherman tanks, a 'bang' being the only warning to dismount rather quickly and prepare for action. A sweep through the Mastbosch forest met no opposition, and Breda – an important prize – was taken on the 30th when the Lincolns entered Ginnekin, a suburb. The infantry/tank cooperation was superb. The Lincolns took 200 prisoners against 11 wounded and missing since leaving Baarle Nassau. It was such a successful partnership that the Canadians tried hard to 'adopt' and keep the Lincolns.

On 2 November a ceremonial march took place in Breda, led by the Canadians, who were followed by the Lincolns. Their historian noted: 'thus ended the Bns most enjoyable and successful adventure of the war'.

Impforce was disbanded and the Lincolns returned to the fold, back in Roosendaal. Several changes of management now took place. The GSO1, Lt.-Col. Jelf, left to become CO of an anti-tank regiment. Lt.-Col. Mackay-Lewis, CO of the 185th Field Regiment, took over command of the 56th Brigade, as Brig. M.S. Ekin died on the night of 3 November. Lt.-Col. P.W.A. Butterworth DSO, CO of the Gloucesters, died from wounds received at Stampersgat. His successor was Lt.-Col. R.N. Bray DSO of the Duke of Wellington's.

Arthur McMillan, a signalman with the Gloucesters TAC HQ, wrote:

'The enemy had been firing 88 mm air bursts. The Colonel was getting a shave in the kitchen sink. There was a loud explosion, he sank to the floor. A shell had landed in the lobby of the house, mangled one chap in the doorway. A piece of shrapnel had whipped past me to hit the CO.'

The 11th Royal Scots Fusiliers, as part of Clarkeforce, moved from Uisschenheuven into Holland to take the village of Wouw and cut the main road from Roosendaal to Bergen-op-Zoom. On the 30th they attacked Brembosch with tank support, but Lt.-Col. Eykyn went on ahead to meet the advancing companies on the outskirts. He and his IO found the town to be empty, and promptly secured comfortable billets for battalion HQ before the advanced guard arrived. Pte. Eric Rolls was saddened to see a 10-year-old girl lying dead beside the road near Wouw church: 'We were all used to the horrors of war, but were never hardened to seeing women and children killed without getting a lump in the throat.'

In Brembosch, Rolls was billeted with a Dutch family of husband and wife, two aunts and a daughter: 'There was quite a rivalry between Peter and me for her attention – most charming and pretty.' A few days later she was taken away for questioning about collaboration with the Germans.

The Recce Regiment also formed part of Clarkeforce, and between 20 and 30 October they led from Ryckeversel to Kruisland, some 25 miles. Throughout the advance they led the tanks into action, often having to fight their way against stubborn opposition from enemy infantry, paratroops and SP guns. Much of the recce work had to be done on foot because of the flooded and open nature of the countryside. When 'A' Squadron swept the wood south of Nieuwmoer they took 30 prisoners – enemy who had succeeded in capturing a considerable number of the division's vehicles and men.

The sappers built seven bridges in 2 weeks on the way to Willemstadt and the Waal. They had to check miles of verges for mines, and they filled craters and culverts with 'kaput' semi-demolished houses.

Spr. Bill Hudson of the 757th Field Company of the Royal Engineers recalled: 'A strange mine had been located in Normandy, namely the French 'R' mine about 27 ins long.' Two sappers from each RE company in the division went on a day course to practice neutralizing this intricate mine. Hudson continued:

By the time we arrived at Roosendaal on 29 Oct, three of those so trained had been wounded or killed. Our Sgt. Venables and I had a wireless message to go to a map reference where a RA Sgt. had found a 'R' Mine. He [Venables] took the mine and went a few steps backwards when it exploded. We had to literally scrape him off the wall. The RA Sgt. and his driver were also killed. I came around the corner within minutes of the explosion. Orders were received later that all 'R' mines had to be pulled with a cable in case of booby trap and then exploded.

By the time Clarkeforce was disbanded on 29 October, during the fighting mainly against the 858th Panzer Grenadier Regiment, the supporting 9th Royal Tank Regiment and the 107th Royal Armoured Corps had 35 tanks knocked out, and they suffered 31 dead and 63 wounded. In turn they 'killed' 13 *Jagd* Panthers.

The Army, of course, cannot move unless codenames are given to every objective. The GSO1 was obviously a *bon viveur*. The report lines included Grapefruit, Porridge, Toast, Bacon, Haggis, Eggs, Rice, Sausage, Jam, Cutlet, Spaghetti, Bun, Doughnut, Veal, Meat, Bully, Spam and Nuts. Codewords included Breakfast, Lunch, Dinner, Supper, Marmalade, Ham, Macaroni, Bread, Butter, Biscuit, Steak, Chips, Sandwich, Cheese, Tart and Beef. *Wuerstwezel* was Cheese.

The advance towards Roosendaal was called Operation Rebound, the attack on Roosendaal was Operation Thruster and the continued advance to the Hollandsche Diep was Operation Humid.

The next objective was the river Mark, which wound its way from south to north through Breda towards Willemstadt, Moerdijk and Geertruidenberg – all firmly in German hands. The 56th Brigade were ordered to force the river Mark with the 2nd Essex at Barlaque and the 2nd Gloucesters at Stampersgat, with the 2nd South Wales Borderes to pass through and secure the bridgehead. It was to be a silent night attack with the 104th US Division making a deliberately noisy attack on the right at Stand Daarbuiten. All of the fields had been flooded by the Germans, and for the first mile there was only one obvious built-up road leading to the river Mark.

'A' Company of the 2nd Essex provided the laborious boat-carrying, launching and local protection parties. 'C' Company moved up and, a section at a time, crossed in each of the five assault boats. Soon, mortar and artillery shells poured down on 'C' Company, now across and 'A' Company protecting the far bank boating operation. Eventually 'C' Company pushed inland and found Barlaque empty. There they swung righthanded and captured an important bridge over a canal, which the Essex pioneers 'deloused' of explosives. 'B' Company and 'D' Company crossed, still in darkness, but had little success in their attack on Kade.

Before dawn the anti-tank platoon ferried two 6-pdr guns across, just in time to fend off several savage counter-attacks, Both 'B' Company and 'D' Company had a hard time, but eventually the enemy faltered and withdrew, leaving many dead and wounded on the roads and in the ditches. Lt. A.A. Vince said: 'Those who were there will forever remember the bleak, desolate and flooded country. The single, shell-swept track with the only cover a mound of turnips, the cattle that died as they swam for a little bit of dry land and the bullets that plopped in the water. . . .'

The Glosters captured their objectives and a Class 40 bridge was completed. The battle was largely over as the South Wales Borderers passed through the new bridgehead.

Willemstadt, a medieval fortress on the south bank of the Scheldt estuary, some 5 miles north of Kade, was the Polar Bears' next objective. Surrounded by flat, open countryside, it contained several thousand Dutch inhabitants, whom Gen. Barker was anxious to spare from the huge artillery and RAF bombing support. His aide-de-camp was sent in blindfolded under a flag of truce to demand surrender or, failing that, the evacuation of the local population. Leaving Roosendaal on the 3rd, the Lincolns arrived on the scene, via Kundert and Tonnecreek, to invest Willemstadt on the 7th.

The German commander refused to surrender. The Lincoln historian related:

> During the late afternoon a pathetic army of men, women and children with their necessities trudged wearily through our positions. A bombardment by our artillery did considerable damage to the town but caused few casualties to the enemy [who had escaped across the river unobserved]. 'A' and 'D' Companies advanced against torrential rain driven by a howling gale, only to find as they entered by the main gate (two moats, high twin ramparts with bastions in each corner) that the town was quite empty!

When Lt.-Col. Hart Dyke returned from leave in Brussels, the Hallams were ordered to move 20 miles east to start the advance on Willemstadt. They moved at night in teeming rain, and soon captured the small town of Fijhaart, while the KOYLI attacked on 4/5 November, eastwards along the road to Oude Stoop. The roads were straight on high embankments bordered by wide dykes. With a strength of only three companies and a recently joined platoon of ex-Anti-aircraft gunners, the colonel diverted 'A' Company on to Oude Molen and 'C' Company on to Niew Molen. Both were to mount silent attacks at dawn. 'C' Company were successful, but 'A' Company were heard, and their OC, Maj. Tony Nicholson, led his men forward armpit high in the dykes on either side of the main road.

Soon, 'A' Company ran out of ammunition and were withdrawn 300 yards to allow for an intense artillery barrage. The enemy smartly retreated, and

'A' Company, 4 Lincolns, pass a wrecked German anti-tank gun in Willemstadt. (IWM, B11802)

'C' Company were launched on Zwinglespan behind a heavy concentration of medium and divisional 25-pdrs, again successfully. However, 8 Hallams were killed and 3 officers, including the brave pioneer officer Capt. Hawkins, were wounded, as were 34 other ranks in the taking of the three small towns.

Rex Flower of the 1/4th KOYLI recorded in his diary:

> *Nov 3.* Night move across river Mark, village Old Gastel, Kaser road junction, to Oudestoof and Klundert.
>
> *Nov 4.* Attack on Oudestoof by 'D' Coy under our smokescreen. The green painted mortar smoke bombs, owing to the waterlogged ground, failed to explode. They lost 3 KIA inc Major D.H. Dunhill MC, Sgt. Healey, Pte. Hill caught by a MG firing on fixed lines. The Major a fine and brave officer, had taken us on route marches on ski-snowshoes in Iceland when we were a mountain Div.
>
> *Nov 5.* Klundert was a mass of flames. The bloody Germans had set fire to the place.

Flower's carrier, driven by Bill Sladin, contained sixty-six high-explosive mortar bombs. Flower continued: 'It was like going through a furnace, all the houses on both sides of the road were ablaze for about 200 yards. What a ride! 6 Nov. The Army Fire Service from Antwerp with 8 trailer pumps arrived to try to save burning Klundert. In five weeks we have lost 17 KIA.'

So for a few days the Polar Bears went into rest, mainly around Roosendaal, where warmth, baths, a cinema and ENSA shows were available. The Lincolns played football against the Roosendaal team, winning 5–4. Later a church parade was held in commemoration of those who had lost their lives in the campaign. Many reinforcements arrived, some only just 18 or 19 years of age. Two platoons of ex-light anti-aircraft gunners, each with its own officer, joined the 1/4th KOYLI.

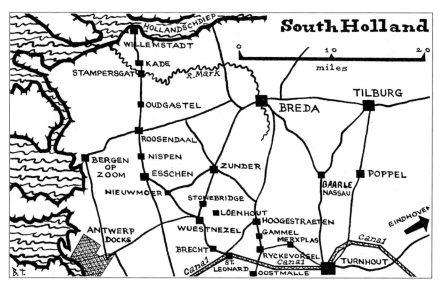

Southern Holland battleground. (Brian Thexton)

CHAPTER THIRTY-FOUR

November

Farewell to 'Bubbles' Barker

The wide Hollandsche Diep stopped further progress north. The gunners, sappers, Kensingtons and the Recce Regiment supported neighbouring units of the 51st Highland Division and the 53rd Welsh Division. The Essex, the KOYLI and the Hallams stayed in Roosendaal resting, training, drilling and playing football. RSMs and CSMs came into their own again, but the raw new reinforcements had had little time to be absorbed into the now highly professional Polar Bears. The 2nd Gloucesters spent 8 days in Oldcastel in comfortable billets among very hospitable Dutch people. Fortunately, short leave started and the lucky few went off to Ghent, Brussels or Antwerp for 48 hours of total freedom. Some of them needed a complete rest when they returned. Rex Flower visited Antwerp and recalled: 'the café Zanzibar, a girl called Jenny, a lot of 'half brothels', cognac, beer, ice-creams, black-out and V-Bombs.' On the 7th, Brig Walter Kempster, the ex-GSO1 of the 3rd British Division, took command of the 56th Infantry Brigade.

Field Marshal Montgomery now regrouped his forces ready for launching the battle of the Rhineland. The 1st Canadian Army, with 1st Corps on the left and the 2nd Canadian Corps on the right extended its front to include the salient as far as Middlelaar, 9 miles south of Nijmegen. The British Second Army faced the German bridgehead west of the River Rhine with the 30 Corps in the south, the 12th Corps in the centre and the 8th Corps in the north. The Polar Bears were now allocated to the 12th Corps, with the task of advancing on Venlo, 35 miles south of Nijmegen.

On 14 November, most divisional units moved from the Roosendaal area to Budel, a large village 26 miles west of Venlo. Only three roads of any consequence converge on Venlo, across completely flat and largely waterlogged countryside. The weather grew worse and worse, and tracks were impassable for all wheeled vehicles except for Jeeps. The 2nd Essex moved eastwards through Lille-St-Hubert and Weert, and they arrived at Panningen in the evening of the 21st. However, by then the 146th Brigade were again back in action.

The Lincolns and the 1/4th KOYLI assembled west of the Uit Canal, running across the front about 12 miles from Venlo, and by the 19th they were 3 miles across it. From Panningen through Maasbree, then Blerick and on to the left bank of the Maas opposite Venlo, were the new objectives. The Lincolns were to capture Maasbree from the west, while the KOYLI advanced to Klein Laar. The Hallams were in reserve.

During a Lincoln recce on the 17th, Maj. G.H. Newsom was killed. The Bn moved via Hamert to relieve a 51st Highland unit before advancing on the 20th to attack Maasbree. Despite mortar and SP fire, and several counter-attacks, 'C' Company led the Lincolns into the town at 0800 hours on the 22nd. Their historian recalled: 'Like troglodytes, the inhabitants emerged from their cellars with tears of joy at finding the enemy really gone.'

The KOYLI reached Op-den-Bout, south of Maasbree. Rex Flower lost three carrier platoon friends, L/Cpl. Fairhurst, John Chapman and 'Bugs' Kirk, when a large shell landed on the hut in which they were having a meal. Later on, Capt. Chapman, L/Cpl. Young, a stretcher-bearer with the MM, and Pte. Chafer of 'D' Company were caught in the open by a machine-gun and killed.

The woods east of Maasbree were strewn with anti-personnel Schu-mines, so Lt.-Col. Hart Dyke borrowed seven armoured tracked Kangaroos to take his Hallams at high speed, protected by a tank squadron and under a smoke barrage, to their new objectives. Although most of the enemy had withdrawn, the whole operation taking 'B' Company along the main road to Blerick, took just 1 hour – without any casualties. The 2nd Essex put in frontal attacks on 22 and 23 November on the villages of Kortheide and Langheide, but the enemy had withdrawn. The pioneer platoon performed yeoman service clearing mines, but 'B' Company suffered very badly from mortar and artillery fire from the Siegfried Line as they closed in on Blerick, the western suburb of Venlo.

On the 25th the Lincolns relieved the Hallamshires in front of Blerick, and for several days aggressive patrolling took place around Hout Blerick. Lt. C.J.G.White, who won the MC, and L/Sgt. Newton, who won the MM, both led daring raids, inflicting many casualties. The Recce Regiment relieved the 2nd Essex on 28 November. In one period their 3 inch mortars alone fired 1,200 bombs.

Higher command now decreed that the 15th Scottish Division would relieve the Polar Bears, who in turn would move to and through Nijmegen to relieve the 50th Tyne Tees Division, who were garrisoning the notorious Island. Arnhem, still resolutely held by the Germans, was the northern tip of the Island, 10 to 12 miles on each side of a rectangle formed by the Neder Rijn, the Waal and the Rhone. The division reverted to the command of the 1st Canadian Army.

Brig. Walter Kempster recounted:

It rained almost continuously. There were thousands of 'Schu' mines, deep bogs masquerading as roads and a few determined paratroop types in the opposition. My jeep went over a schu mine inside the Bde area which had been cleared. A review brought to light over 60 of the little beasts. On 29 Nov we planned the assault on Blerick. But 50 (N) Div were due to sail for UK on 6 Dec [to be disbanded after brilliant campaigns in North Africa, Sicily and Italy] – so no relief available. We took over from the famous 151 (Durham Light Infantry) Brigade.

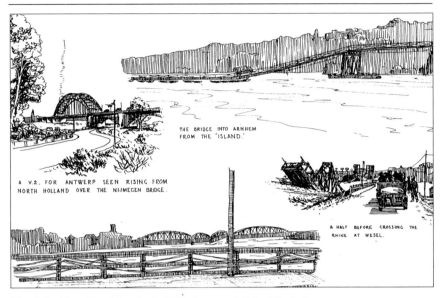

THE BRIDGE INTO ARNHEM FROM THE 'ISLAND.'

A V.2. FOR ANTWERP SEEN RISING FROM NORTH HOLLAND OVER THE NIJMEGEN BRIDGE.

A HALT BEFORE CROSSING THE RHINE AT WESEL.

Dutch 'incidents' involving the 2nd Kensingtons. (Michael Bayley)

But other changes took place. Lt.-Col. M.A.H. Butler MC took over command of the 2nd Essex. Lt. Vince, the IO, described his eccentricity: He 'wore an old jeep drivers' coat which he lost on average twice a week. He lost many other things. His cigarette case was always empty, his consumption of map chinagraph pencils was prodigious – but he never lost a battle.

Maj. C.D. Hamilton assumed command of the 7th Dukes as Lt.-Col. J.H.O. Wilsey took temporary command of the 56th Brigade. Brig. Desmond Gordon DSO took over command of the 146th Brigade from Brig. Johnnie Walker, who took over the 151st Brigade of the 50th Division. The CO of the 1/4th KOYLI, Lt.-Col. 'Mouse' Harrison Topham, was invalided home sick. His successor was Lt.-Col. Tony Arengo Jones of the Gloucesters, who promptly blew himself up on a 75 grenade, and he in turn was succeeded by Lt.-Col. Maurice Jenkins. The 185th Field Regiment RA was disbanded. Gnr. John Mercer wrote:

> The Colonel (Mackay Lewis), 'Charlie Handlebars' called us altogether, battery by battery. He told us he had been awarded the OBE. 'I have sad news for you. This regiment of which I am so proud is to be disbanded.' 'A feeling of dread came over everyone in our regiment. Dismay at the break up of the warm camaraderie and pride in our mob.

Some became infantrymen, but George, Jenkins and Mercer joined the Desert Rats. On 1 December the 74th Northumbrian Field Regiment RA, who had supported the 50th Division in all of its campaigns, now joined the Polar Bears, under its CO Lt.-Col. H.W. Harris DSO. However, the most important change was the promotion of the GOC, 'Bubbles' Barker, to command the 8th Corps, who was succeeded by Maj.-Gen. G.H.A. MacMillan CBE, DSO, MC. This was the General's farewell message:

It is a great personal regret to me that I have to say goodbye to the Div with which I have been connected for so long. My only hope and ambition has been to help the Div through the campaign with flying colours and I had hoped to see it through to the end. The record of the Div is a fine one. It has done magnificently ever since the initiation at Cristot and Fontenay. The battle of Rauray was the first milestone in the defeat of the Boche in Normandy. Then came the difficult advance forward to the Seine over numerous rivers – a splendid feat by the Infantry and the Sappers. Next was the outstanding success at Le Havre, followed by the classic advance towards Tilburg and later to Roosendaal and Willemstadt. This is a series of great achievements in which the Div was so ably assisted by the various Armed Bds which support it. The Div has taken prisoners, 200 officers 6,300 men captured at Le Havre.

First class commanders and troops and efficient staff officers all imbued with a high Div spirit. What more can a Div Cmdr ask for? All comes so easily under such conditions I cannot fully express the pride it has given me to command such a splendid Div and therefore what sorrow it is for me to leave. No one could have received more loyal support than I have. The machine has gone so smoothly because all the different units – infantry, artillery, antitank, recce, RE, MG Bn – I can see no flaw. The LAA Regt both in the normal role and as part of Bobforce has done sterling work. The co-operation in battle of all these has been of the fullest and the friendliest. It has been one party. Then comes the never ending work of Div Sigs without whose efficient work no success is possible in battle. How well all have been served by the admin units – RASC, RAMC ORD, REME and without exception, is well known and is a reflection of the state of efficiency of the Div. We have been guided across France, Belgium and the others by the Provost Coy and how well our Postal Unit has looked after our moral welfare. Never a hitch anywhere at any time. The machine works by itself as only a team permeated with the team spirit can do. The Polar Bear whose butchery was so kindly mentioned by 'Lord Haw Haw' is a mark of distinction which we can all be proud to wear. It did not have its mouth opened without reason as the Boche has duly found. Under your new GOC, Maj.-Gen. Macmillan, you will have many more successes. I shall look forward to seeing you all again in Berlin.

The General had written in his diary, and in letters to his wife:

23 Sep. It's splendid to be up again and cracking. I had a most interesting run up through the old, old country – Abbeville, St Pol, Bethune, Armentiéres, Wytsches to St Eloi where I was wounded in '15. Turcoing, and stayed the night close to my old billet. Most of the pill boxes which I had constructed remain. On Thursday I came up the same road as in '40 through Brussels. Belgium is so much cleaner and the concrete road a pleasant contrast to the pavé of N. France. The whole country here a kitchen garden, apples, pears, grapes, plums and peaches.

27 Sep. We have a bridgehead across the Antwerp–Turnhout canal. Not bad. Since Div march from Dieppe area, on Thurs 21st, we had completed two bridges over Albert canal by early am 24th and had a bridge over the Turnhout canal by 6 am 25th. We took 10 offrs and 508 men prisoner and killed and wounded quite a packet. I must say I consider we are now complete professionals. Everything works like well oiled machinery. I have a Canadian Armoured Regt with me and their CO made the unsolicited remark after being 24 hrs with us, that he had never enjoyed working with any formation so much!

28 Sep. These somewhat piecemeal battles with a fluid enemy are far more tiring for me than a good deliberate party like the Le Havre battle.

8 Oct. One of my battalions [the Lincolns] had the devil of a battle with very obstinate Boche from mid-day on 6th to late yesterday morning. Some 600 or so tried to infiltrate around them through the woods by day and night and they fought them off. We 'stonked' the Boche with everything we had and two counter attacks were put in to relieve troops who had been surrounded. They must have killed some 200 or more. Our casualties very light in comparison.

21 Oct. Monty came, in v.g. form. After presenting the medals he addressed the problems of the 21 Army Group ie himself, with never a word about the Div or how well the chaps had done. He is completely self centred in that respect: very refreshing to talk to. He bought some cases of cigarettes and Bovril. We have got in front of the Canooks who had half the distance to go. They just don't know how to put their troops into battle to my mind.

23 Oct. Frank Parsons [the aide-de-camp] and I were nearly shot up by a Boche SP gun driving back in my jeep from Esschen. Two shots went through the trees behind us. In the shelling yesterday I had a piece through my caravan which missed my [Polar] bear by a foot. The German infantry is poor stuff but they are backed up by some good SP gunners and a few tank chaps.

26 Oct. [Monty sent the GOC a letter, indicating that he was being recommended to command an Army corps.] I have told him I don't in the least want a Corps and would much prefer to stay and see the Div through the party. The Div is my only interest. A Corps is so impersonal. However, I told Monty I was delighted that he had considered me fit for promotion. I am so afraid I might be pushed off to India or some bloody place with no interest like this.

27 Oct. Dick Jelf [the GSO1] is leaving me and going to command a SP Anti Tank Regt after 17 months – quite long enough. A. Welby-Everard, Lincolns, is taking his place. Seems a good chap.

31 Oct. Roosendaal not much of a place, bombed by US A.F. early in the year. My chaps resting before finishing off the party in the Maas estuary. We have crossed 20 miles in 10 days and had to fight every inch of it.

4 Nov. I hate this country [Holland]. All the houses are built in a ribbon along the raised roadways and the Boche gets into them and so we have to shell them knowing full well that civilians are there too and there is nowhere else for them to go. We can only deploy on a very narrow front. The Canadians have had a perfectly b—y job at Walcheren Island and on the mainland south of it.

7 Nov. We got into Willemstad last night. The Boche pulled out their remnant by sea. It was a damnable place to take on. I sent Frank [Parsons] with a white flag to the commander to argue with him to let the civilians come out and sent transport up to meet them. I am now going to join [Lt.-Gen.] Neil Ritchie. I prefer Neil to [Lt.-Gen. Brian] Jorrocks.

18 Nov. Have got my chaps under cover. Some civilians have complained they have NOT been given any British soldiers to put up!

19 Nov. The war seems to be going quite well on all fronts. I fear the Yanks do it with undue casualties. They simply don't know how to use their artillery. I can switch my guns onto any point in a moment. *24 Nov.* 'Bimbo' Dempsey looked in a few days ago. Told me he looked on our Rauray battle as the turning point of the Normandy Campaign – the start of the Boche collapse there.

26 Nov. To my Bde HQ in a 'Weasel', a delightful little American broad tracker vehicle.

28 Nov. Saw Monty, 'Bimbo' and Neil today – all very charming and seemed pleased at my appointment [to command the 8th Corps].

CHAPTER THIRTY-FIVE

On the Island, December

'A Fearsome Sight'

During the ill-fated Operation Market Garden in September, Gen. Horrocks' 30th Corps and the American airborne divisions had fought their way – usually on one beleaguered centreline – to Nijmegen and 12 miles north to the outskirts of Arnhem. The 43rd Wessex Wyvern Division put a doomed battalion across the Neder Rijn to link up with the gallant 1st Airborne Division, but in vain. When the Polar Bears were tasked with the garrisoning of the Island, the fields, dykes, hamlets and cottages were cluttered with the debris of war. Only two brigades were needed – not two whole divisions – because of the flooded areas. Recce parties went off on the 30th, and when the 1/4th KOYLI arrived in Nijmegen on 1 December, they found the 147th Brigade on the right flank around Haalderen and Bemmel, 2 miles north of the Waal, and the 56th Brigade around Elst, 3 miles north-west on the main road to Arnhem. The KOYLI moved to Ressen, 1 mile west of Bemmel, while the Lincolns and the Hallams remained in Nijmegen for a well-earned rest. The Lincolns settled into a large school for two weeks of training before going into divisional reserve (Ressen) between the rivers Waal and Lek. Football matches were played against the 185th Heavy Battery and the 69th Field Regiment RA, and a 3 mile fitness run was held.

Rex Flower of the 1/4th KOYLI recalled:

We passed over the Grave bridge, captured by American 'Paras' of 82 US Airborne Div, and then over the famous Nijmegen bridge captured by Guards Armoured Division and the US 'Paras'. We veered to the right on the other side, passing the wrecked 88 mm gun, to the straggling village of Ressen. It was water, water everywhere and it got worse before it got better. We shared the Island with the enemy. I expect he hated it as much as we did. The platoon was in an empty house. The enemy shelled the area at night. There was mud everywhere off the small roads. It was going to be a wet, cold and later, icy and snowy winter. The river was in flood. It has huge banks and the water was well above the level of the surrounding countryside. A fearsome sight. It became impossible to have trenches; as soon as a hole was dug it filled with water. Houses around Elst were used as strong points. The enemy blew the river banks on the 2nd and flooding ensued.

Patrolling was very difficult, sometimes impossible. On 4 December the enemy made a determined attack on the 7th Dukes at Halderen. Maj. Hamilton had just attended a brigade conference for Operation Noah, an emergency evacuation plan. He noted: 'The Boche had blown several gaps

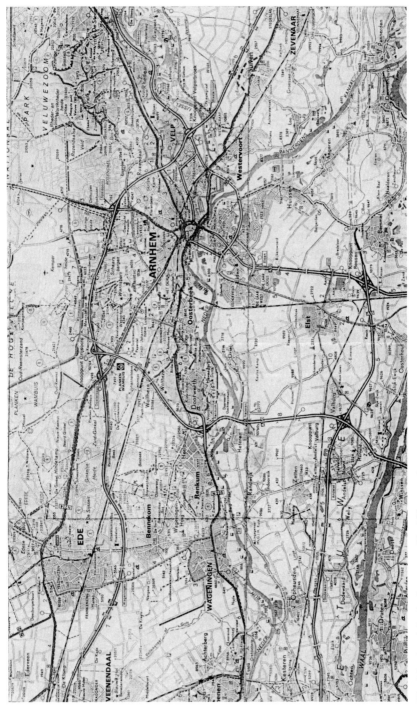

The Island and the Arnhem area. (Fred Hoseason)

in the bund (river banks) in the NW of the Island and rushing Rhine flood water had already overwhelmed some defensive posts without warning. We expected every distant rumble to be followed by a tidal wave.'

Three companies of the German 16th Parachute Regiment attacked the Dukes at 0315 hours with heavy Spandau and mortar fire, and they swept through the forward positions. Chaotic close-quarter fighting went on all night. The Polar Bear field regiments brought down shattering DF targets. Many casualties were inflicted on the enemy, many diving into nearby ponds, where they drowned. Bazookas were fired at the houses held by the Dukes in Haalderen. By 1100 hours on the 5th, of the assaulting parachute company strength of 161 men, 110 were taken prisoner and 50, including the company commander, were killed. Heavy casualties were also inflicted by the divisional artillery on the two rear parachute companies. The 7th Dukes' own casualties were only 31. It was a notable victory.

Lt. K. Evans was awarded the MC and Pte. Stimpson, who kept his Bren gun in action for 4 hours, after being wounded, received the MM. As Maj. Hamilton recalled: 'It was a soldiers' battle – even the cooks joined in.'

Maj. A.L. Rowell commanded 'D' Company of the 11th Royal Scots Fusiliers, who were in a counter-attack role supporting the Dukes and helped in the final phase, clearing part of Haalderen and capturing 77 prisoners for the loss of 3 casualties. The Fusiliers took over for ten days to relieve the Dukes, and they in turn were relieved by the 1st Leicesters on the

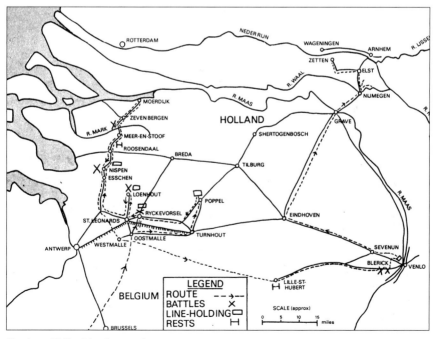

Southern Holland battleground.

'Coq au vin tonight.' Sgt. Monty Satchell, 49th Recce, the Island, Christmas 1944. (Monty Satchell)

2 Troop, 49th Recce, Nijmegen, Christmas 1944. (Monty Satchell)

16th, moving back to Bemmel. A mixed divisional force constantly guarded the main bridge over the River Waal. The majority of defensive positions on the Island were based on buildings which were turned into pillboxes with sandbags, wood, earth and wire. Battalions held wide frontages and in many positions companies could only be visited at night as all approaches were under enemy observation from the high ground around Arnhem. Gumboots were essential footwear, and rum issue was ordered daily. Despite enemy shelling, the GOC's orders were that the northern sector of the Island – No Man's Land – must be dominated by patrols going straight down a road with a deep ditch with freezing water on either side. Brig. Kempster said:

On 6 Dec at 1730 an explosion was noted on the banks of the Neder-rijn and in 48 hours only about 1/3rd of original bridgehead was habitable. 51st Highland Division on our left had to evacuate two Bridges, leaving one behind at Andelst. On 16 Dec 56 Bde took over with one Sqn 49 Recce Regt, became responsible for 20,000 metres of front. Patrolling very active on both sides, often in assault boat or canoe, part wading, part on foot.

The brigade in reserve had an easier time. Rex Flower wrote in his diary: '*8 Dec*. Back in Nijmegen, billeted with Mrs Klaason, made us welcome. We slept on the floor upstairs.' Flower played the harmonica: 'I had a small Bandmaster and they would get us to teach them wartime tunes and songs. It was nice and homely and that of course was what we were missing.' He went to the café Eindos and danced the evening away. Flower continued:

13 Dec. We tracked down a pig in a deserted farm, shot it, put it in the mortar carrier, covered it with sacks. I sat on it as we passed the MPs. We let the 'civvies' have it. Well it was better than the poor thing starving to death, wasn't it?

14 Dec. To the Winter Gardens to hear the band of the Coldstream Guards. I love to hear a military band.

19 Dec. My 26th birthday, sixth in the army.

20 Dec. Xmas dinner in Winter Gardens in two sittings, a band played the whole time. A great dinner and the officers waited on us, as is the tradition.

22 Dec. Over the bridge to take over from 1 Leicesters at Haalderen. No mortar pits or slits. Breastworks or sangers had been built up with each sods, sandbags, anything handy. We were issued with leather jerkins and 'wellies' which were a godsend in the cold and wet. Plenty of buzz-bombs coming over. No means of heating. Used 'Bengazi' burners in the day for cooking.

Brig. Kempster recalled: 'Severe frost on 23rd and icebound until 21 Jan – patrols under ice conditions were hellish as 'cat-ice' formed, thus the softest footed man sounded like a Squadron of cavalry galloping over a tin bridge.'

The Hallamshires received reinforcements from the broken-up 50th Division. The original 'A' Company of the Hallams under Maj. Mackillop now became 'D' Company Hallams. Cinemas and ENSA parties were now available, despite the shelling of Nijmegen by long-range enemy guns. The headmaster of the large Catholic School which billeted many Polar Bear units also provided suitable partners for evening dances. Firm friendships were made with Dutch families which endured for many years. The NAAFI provided absolutely first class Christmas dinners with every possible trimming.

Winston Churchill told us the truth!

"We can't win the war unless we shall have finished it before the leaves of autumn fall."

Like the waves of a flood lashed by a storm the A.E.F. swept over France. Everything seemed to go according to plan. Nevertheless Mr. Churchill uttered these ominous words:

"I know of terrible things", he said at a time when the newspapers were triumphant and your generals promised an early end of the war.

Now things have turned out as Winston predicted. The Germans having been concentrated within and behind the Siegfried Line for many months have commenced their attack, which you must face now. Weakened by those deadly and senseless battles near Aix-la-Chapelle the Allies are now confronted with the German onrush. Allied Headquarters have to tackle a difficult problem.

The casualties suffered by the American units of the Allied Forces till the beginning of the German offensive amounted to 500 000 men. 30 000 prisoners were brought in during the first week of the offensive. The losses in dead and wounded are by far greater and careful estimates put them down at 150 000 to 180 000 men. As happened before the Americans intended to show off once more by marching up to Berlin on their own in order that their folks at home might celebrate them as the great victors. Now we have broken through their lines and are fighting deep inside Belgium. Instead of working with you in good fellowship they got into a tight corner by their desire to show off. Now you are expected to help them in their efforts to get out of their troubles. You'll certainly realize this when you think of the units transferred from your own sector in order to be sacrificed in this endeavour. Boys, I really feel sorry for you! But you have to resign to your fate and bear in mind that you are at war!

If you should meet the Americans who show off for the merest trifle happening in the USA don't forget to express them your thanks in a suitable manner.

A German propaganda leaflet. (Fred Hoseason)

Brockforce, commanded by Lt.-Col. D.V.G. Brock of the 2nd Kensingtons, was the name of the special force to defend the vital Nijmegen main bridge. The companies' marksmen fired joyously on pieces of wood, wreckage, hen coops and anything that might harbour an explosive. Their historian related how, over Christmas, 'Lord Haw Haw' and his female counterpart, 'Mary of Arnhem', broadcast that the hated Polar Bear Butchers (derived from the battle of Rauray) would be annihilated during the festive season.

'D' Company became the mortar company, with four platoons of 4.2 inch mortars with Lloyds carriers. Their trailers were most unreliable. They had a huge supply of UK training ammunition which also was not very reliable. They were deployed on the divisional front under their OC Maj. R. Bare, along with the 12th, 13th, 14th and 15th platoons. An Air OP fed targets over to the 14th platoon. When the observation post wireless went 'kaput', the Kensingtons spelled out messages in the snow with mortar boxes, courtesy of Capt. Nichols and Lt. W. Stoltenhoff. This worked well, but rather slowly.

CHAPTER THIRTY-SIX

On the Island, January

'Booby Traps and Midget Submarines'

The dramatic German counter-attack in the Ardennes came, and by early January it went back from where it had come. This was thanks to American bull-dog tenacity, to the RAF and USAAF who eventually had a series of field days, and helped by Gen. Montgomery's emergency back-up forces rushed down to hold the Namur front. Lt. Brian Lott of the 55th Anti-tank Regiment was a liaison officer at the 147th Brigade HQ in a large house in Nijmegen which belonged to the margerine family, the Van der Bergs. He remembered: 'I saw the maps marked-up for the German thrust in the Ardennes. No hint of panic or concern.' Sgt. Bob Sheldrake noted:

> Von Runstedt's offensive threw the whole front into a fluid state and all available divisions were drawn off. Every man put into the line. Leaving our A/Tk guns under a Battery guard in the school yard, we went on to the Island to take up our job as infantrymen taking over from a platoon of 2 Essex. The village of Elst was surrounded by water. THQ and two detachments were in a farmhouse with Math's section out in front astride the railway line. We could only reach them by boat and my nightly pilgrimage to them with rations and water was an eerie business.

One patrol found a deserted dry farm with a large number of pigs. A Polar Bear fighting patrol surprised the Germans in the act of killing the pigs. When the ice froze hard, rations were delivered on improvised sleds, and some Polar Bears went skating. Sentries had many duties, which included taking the bearings of the V–2 rocket-launching sites rising vertically from the ground on the way to Antwerp, London and the south-east of England.

In Nijmegen, Sgt. Bob Sheldrake was billeted with a baker's family in Heutstraat. He recalled: 'At night behind drawn curtains, while bursts of Ack Ack followed lone raiders across the darkened sky, we would sit in the parlour with the Wilhems family drinking their weak tea, laughing and talking with them in a strange language – a cross between German, Dutch, English and deaf and dumb alphabet.'

Lt. A.A. Vince of the 2nd Essex said:

> With a three mile stretch of 'sea' in front and the bulk of the Bn surrounded by water, we used Dukws, amphibious Jeeps, Weasels and assault boats both to get food up to the forward Coys and also for patrol work. Snipers and patrols of varying strengths occupied the upper floors of flooded farm buildings well in front of our main defence line and gave us early warning of any

Ken West (far left) and fusiliers of 11 RSF, Christmas 1944. (Ken West)

4th Lincolns flood patrol, Nijmegen area. (IWM, B15001)

aggressive enemy intentions. Patrol clashes were frequent and many 'naval' engagements were fought in flimsy canvas assault boats. Victory usually went to the side that fired first.

The enemy held the villages of Elden, Huissen and Angeren. Both sides laid mines and booby-trapped unoccupied houses. The average tour of duty was 4 weeks in the line and 2 weeks of rest in Nijmegen. Lt. A.A. Vince wrote: 'Our Mr Botting and the boys of the [Regimental] band joined us and gave us many a pleasant evening.'

The Hallams had a number of adventures. Their New Year saw around a hundred shells and machine-gun fire landing on 'B' Company's cabbage patch without causing any casualties. The next evening they were infiltrated by thirty enemy into an orchard between 'B' Company and 'C' Company, so Lt.-Col. Hart Dyke called down a DF target. A flock of sheep had been the cause of the alarm. Many attempts were made to capture a prisoner for identification purposes. Lt. Simmil, Lt. Smalley and Lt. Gallagher went out, separately, on patrols in heavy snowfalls in snow suits – but no prisoners were captured. On the 14th, Lt. Godlee's attack on two houses failed and the whole Hallamshire patrol was captured.

George Wilkinson recalled: 'One of the 11 RSF's duties (part of Brockforce) was to guard the bridge and shoot at random any suspicious objects floating downstream. At night two searchlights shone down the river. These were very effective and known to us as Monty's Moonlight.'

Maj. Edwin Bowring's 143th Field Regiment had their FOOs out all the time in Bemmel, Haalderen, Elst, Valberg and Zetten, with the gun positions on either side of the river Waal, although the flooding of gunpits was a great discomfort.

On 13 January there was much anxiety for Brockforce. The wreckage lying in the river at the railway bridge was shattered by an explosion at 3 a.m. It was an attack by three midget submarines. One beached on the north bank of the river Waal and the crew were killed by shelling. Another was hit by artillery fire and blew up, and the third was heavily engaged, turned round, dived and disappeared. They carried mines or torpedoes, and also large floating logs with mines lashed to them – 12 ft long and 2 ft in diameter. Although hit by 40 mm shells, the logs did not blow up and the mines had to be defused. Nevertheless, it was a brave effort by the Boche frogmen. The defenders were now christened HMS Brockforce.

Spr. Bill Hudson of the 757th Field Company RE remembered:

The three RE Field Coys took their turns to operate the 'Woolwich Ferry' across the Waal. It was a Class 9 close support raft running to a scheduled timetable. Lt. Oglesby was our 'Skipper'. The main channel was fairly narrow, but about one third of the strip on either side was made over flooded fields and farmland with houses, barns, fence poles protruding out of the water. Our many other jobs included laying booby traps for 2nd Essex, and anti-personnel mines for 2 Glosters, demolishing a footbridge at Weterings canal, dismantling 50 ft Bailey bridge at Slijk-Ewijk, and constructing hot baths unit.

Stan Faulconbridge of the Recce Regiment said:

We had the most westerly position on the Island, quite isolated. The scout troops took up a perimeter position, while Sqn HQ and the Mortar Section were stationed at the rear. We had 2 inch mortars lined up on fixed lines for covering fire to any of the Troops. The Dutch SS unit were our immediate opponents. We (the Mortar Section) manned a trench dug just below the top of the Dyke giving a view of the roadway. There were two of us complete with Bren gun, 2 inch mortar with flares, Sten guns, pistols and a box of grenades. It was an eerie position as we were in a deserted village. Several goats seemed to be feeding themselves, occupied an empty garage. They came pit a pattering down the road about two o'clock in the morning. A number of chickens, who laid a pile of eggs in a house loft, were visited by our patrols.

Towards the end of January the divisional boxing championships were held in Nijmegen in the crowded Wintergardens. Pte. Panter of 'C' Company was bantam weight champion and Pte. Udall of 'B' Company was runner-up in the welterweights.

The Battle at Zetten

'C' Company of the 1st Leicesters were holding part of Zetten, a medium-sized village on the Island, 6 miles north-west of Nijmegen. 'C' Company occupied nine houses at one end, and the Germans held the other end of Zetten. Company HQ had two houses and were linked to each platoon by wireless and line. The gunner FOO and mortar platoon fire controller were both based at company HQ. Raids and counter-raids were frequent.

Early in the morning of the 18th, a much heavier attack was put in by the 3rd Battalion of the 7th Parachute Regiment, who had crossed the Neder Rijn on

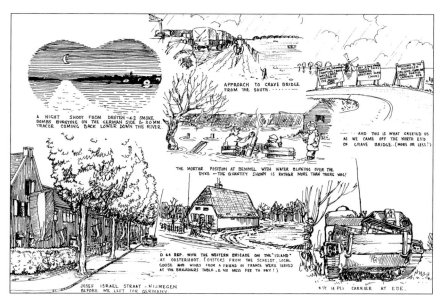

Winter on the Island with the 2nd Kensingtons. (Michael Bayley)

the night of the 17th, supported by bazooka and Spandau fire. Maj. G.P. Brown deployed his Wasp carriers. Lt. A.P. Gardiner was awarded an immediate MC as his platoon were attacked on three sides and L/Cpl. Basil Light earned the MM in bitter house-to-house fighting. The battle raged all day on the 18th as 'D' Company came up to help with a troop of Canadian tanks.

At nightfall, two platoons of the 2nd Glosters also arrived, and they were counter-attacked at 1815 hours on the 19th. Lt. Bidgood's platoon of 'D' Company of the Leicesters was cut off and, in confused fighting, Cpl. H. Mansfield won an immediate DCM for his conspicuous bravery. Most of the 19th was quiet apart from intermittent shelling. At nightfall, 'A' and 'B' Company of the Leicesters and two companies of the Glosters relieved the battered survivors. The Leicesters suffered 60 casualties in the 2 days of battle, but they accounted for 150 enemy killed, wounded and captured.

However, the Boche kept on attacking and the GOC sent in most of the 56th Brigade to stem the tide. It was now estimated that twelve companies of paratroopers were determined to get through to Nijmegen bridge via Zetten. During the 20/21st, 'B' Company of the Kensingtons fired 300,000 mortar bombs in support.

On the 20th the 2nd South Wales Borderers and the 2nd Essex were ordered to recapture the whole town of Zetten, supported by two troops of Canadian Armed Regiment tanks. The main objective for the Welshmen was the capture of the fortified 'castle', a stone-built building surrounded by a moat, at Hemmen. To everyone's surprise, no less than

2nd Essex move into Zetten. (R.E. Gough)

120 enemy emerged – at teatime on the 21st – from the ruins and surrendered to a bewildered but proud South Wales Borderers platoon. Máj. Gillespie had the bright idea of using mortar smoke bombs to set the 'castle' alight.

During the 2 days of fighting, the Welshmen suffered 46 casualties but they captured 208 prisoners. The battle was fought in blinding snow and bitter cold, and several cases of frost bite were reported.

On the right flank the 2nd Essex had an equally difficult battle. They were now commanded by Lt.-Col. M.A.H. Butler DSO, MC, who referred to all ranks of men as 'Prunes'. On his first recce in the Zetten affray he had 'Gone to have a Jimmy dekko at the Prunes'. Lt. A.A. Vince recalled:

'A' Coy ran into the toughest opposition and fighting developed from house to house, room to room and then hand to hand. One Sherman tank took twelve Bazooka hits and still kept firing its guns. Two company commanders were wounded. At first light next morning, 21 Jan, all the remaining houses and farm buildings were cleared and the few remaining Boche fled across the Wettering Canal to the hamlet of Indoornik which was immediately flattened by Typhoons, artillery and mortars. 2 Essex casualties over the whole action were 62.

During the Zetten battle the Polar Bears suffered 220 casualties, but they took 400 prisoners and accounted for another 300 killed or wounded.

CHAPTER THIRTY-SEVEN

On the Island, February

'The Nijmegen Home Guard'

The winter frost went on until 6 February, and the huge 2nd Army offensive to clear the River Maas and River Rhine started 2 days later. Most units disliked the eastern sector around Haalderen. Lt. A.A. Vince of the 2nd Essex recalled:

> We agreed that it was the worst sector to look after. On the right ran the river Waal well above ground level and contained by a 'bund'. The only road was under small arms fire and approach had to be made by the 'Jeep' track made out of rubble from the destroyed houses. Whether the ground was frozen or feet deep in black mud, it was impossible to dig and one had to fight from the ruins of buildings and from cellars. Not a house remained whole and almost every room was fortified with sandbags and chests filled with dirt. In the small slits where windows used to be, there was a weapon of some kind with the safety catch permanently at fire and a finger always on the trigger. The few houses not defended were mined and the unwary patrol from either side, rarely left such a building in one piece. Contact with the enemy was as little as 100 yards. The whole Bn area could be, and was, swept by Spandaus and other weapons. The little clusters of wrecked buildings earned their own names such as 'Rotten Row', 'Sniper's Alley' and 'Spandau Joe the Third'.

The Hallams were on the western part of the front, taking over from the 11th Royal Scots Fusiliers the defence of the villages of Andelst and Zetten. Two companies held Zetten with a good gunner and mortar observation post in the church tower. The remaining company, with battalion HQ and support company with a troop of Canadian tanks held, Andelst, 3 miles south. When the flood rose after the thaw, maintenance and visits to forward companies could only be carried out by amphibious vehicles, such as DUKWs, Weasels and storm boats. Lt.-Col. Hart Dyke described his front line:

> Staring from right to left along the Wettering canal were the isolated farms of Het Slop and De Taart, then Talitha Kumi on the far bank of the river, on the main road Zetten – Indornik – Randwijk. On the left was Hemmen, where there was a castle, two houses and a demolished bridge. The Hallams put out strong patrols on 10th Feb across the Wettering. The Polar Bears were ordered to patrol even more offensively to simulate a coming divisional advance, to mislead the enemy and thus drawing off reinforcements from the main 2nd Army battles in the Rhineland and west of the Siegfried Line. Brigadier Gordon ordered the Hallams to occupy the De Hoeven farm, 6,000 yards ahead from Zetten. The Dutch SS troops in front knew their patch only too well and the Hallams had several disasters. One section's assault boat was blown up on a mine causing ten casualties, mostly fatal. Another platoon, 29 strong, of 'B' Coy was trapped and all its members killed, wounded or taken prisoner inc Sgts Newman and Potter. On 11th March the 2 SWB relieved the Hallams.

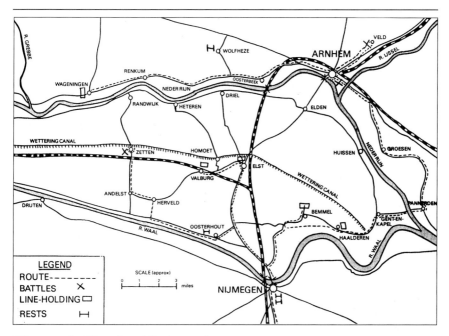

Nijmegen – the 'Home Guard 'battleground.

The Scots Fusiliers also had a patrol ambushed across the Wettering at De Taart. Their historian wrote:

Two sections from 'B' Coy were sent to help. Fusiliers Lorimer and Millar knocked hell out of the buildings with PIATs. Corp Halliday MM with some of his men crossed the plank bridge and lifted out of the water, the numbed members of the Support Coy under the very noses of the enemy. Fusilier Wilkins was taken prisoner but rescued the next day.

Lt.-Col. C.D. Hamilton, CO of the 7th Dukes, recalled:

The 'I' staff headed by Capt. 'Wrecker' Tris Bax published the first issue of the 'Yorkshire Pud' – a digest of world and Bn news, with cartoons which, through snow or battle, has come out every day since. At the end of February we had another six-day break off the Island at Druten where a taxi service of V–1 bombs overhead made a rest period more harrassing than usual. I wonder if GHQ realize that in a 'rest' period as they are so charmingly called, one works twice as hard. We now discovered that 220 days of the 250 since D-Day had been spent in the line. We have taken more Boche prisoners than we had lost in casualties and since D-Day had travelled almost 700 miles. We were still to be the Nijmegen Home Guard. . . .

The South Wales Borderers' band played in several concerts in Nijmegen. Their 'rest' period was a succession of church parades, CO's parades, dances and officer parties.

Rex Flower of the 1/4th KOYLI had just returned from Brussels leave, where he experienced

in civilian billets in rue de l'Armée, food in the Café Metropole, visited the Monty '21' Club near the Palais de Justice, cognac, tea and buns, posh cafés, sightseeing, visited the Congress

Corporal Barnett's fighting patrol on the Island. (IWM, B15008. Property of Lt-Col G. Barker Harland MC)

Corporal Edwards' recce patrol on the Island. (IWM, B15009. Property of Lt-Col G. Barker Harland MC)

column, tomb of the unknown warrior. The Grand Place is a beautiful medieval square – the Cathedral – the Mannekin Pis 'weeing in the gutter', ubiquitous trams.

On his return, Monty visited the Polar Bears on the 17th. Flower continued: 'We all lined the road, paraded in companies and platoons; he inspected us, then stood on his jeep, motioned us all around him, gave us a pep talk. He took the trouble to talk to his men. He was a great soldier.' On 15 February, Lt.-Col. Arengo-Jones, Maj. A.M. Parker and Lt. S.K. Taylor (the pioneer officer) were all wounded when removing some '75' grenades across a road.

Lt.-Col. M.B. Jenkins took over command, but Maj. Douglas Wardleworth was wounded visiting the 218th Anti-tank Battery in Nijmegen when a V–1 bomb hit their officers' mess. Maj. Godfrey Harland, OC of 'A' Company, set up Operation Lark to occupy a hamlet south of Dreil. Starting from Operation Raven, another hamlet halfway to Operation Lark, a fighting patrol under CSM Bert Chadwick MM and Sgt. Harry Wood occupied Operation Lark for 8 days, 2 miles in front of the KOYLI lines. A German standing patrol of eleven men was taken prisoner. Every night supplies came up, quietly, by boat, and Lt. Clarkson, the FOO of the 69th Field Regiment, attended with great glee to the Boche-occupied houses round about.

Lt.-Col. Peter Barclay left the 4th Lincolns to command the 1st Battalion Royal Norfolks in the 3rd British (Ironsides) Division and Lt.-Col. P.R.

German CQMS taking tea round to the Polar Bears? (Lt-Col. Godfrey Barker Harland)

Ashburner arrived to take over. Boat patrols were soon organized, and Sgt. Stevens of 'C' Company and L/Sgt. Hibberd of 'B' Company distinguished themselves.

Around Druten the 55th Anti-tank Regiment practised their new role. Their 17-pdr guns (and gunners) were taught by Maj. Jaine, the RA rep with the 49th Recce Regiment, how to fire indirect targets. The commander of 'D' Troop claimed that his guns could shoot to cause a factory chimney to fall in any chosen direction. On 23 February the Loyal Suffolk Hussars left Nijmegen for Ewijk and took their last look across the Island to the Arnhem heights. Lt. 'Nick' Nichols of the 89th LAA Regiment remembered: 'We were given a German fuel dump as a target. Our tracer shells started a magnificent fire. The Germans promptly mortared us, but having SP guns we could pull out quickly. In February we laagered our guns and adopted our infantry role. One night a sinister sound of a tracked vehicle could be heard in front.' Lt. 'Nick' Nichols led a patrol with PIAT to destroy it. It was a wind pump with a loose ratchet.

CHAPTER THIRTY-EIGHT

On the Island, March

'The Thaw Brought Dead German Bodies'

Four months had gone by garrisoning the Island. The Polar Bears were not required to take part in the ferocious fighting around Goch, Cleves, the clearing of the Reichswald and the cracking of the Siegfried Line. On 1 March the 56th Brigade sent recce parties to both towns to relieve the 53rd Welsh Division, but the move was cancelled.

Fusilier Ken West, a signaller with 'A' Company of the Royal Scots Fusiliers, in his book, *An' it's Called a Tam-o'-Shanter*, had a number of anecdotes. Part of his diet included cheese and marmalade sandwiches, which, toasted over a charcoal and cow muck fire, produced a flavour beyond description. He (and others) listened to Glenn Miller on the American Forces network: 'The song 'American Patrol' would come over the airwaves and instantly we would hear the machine-gunners firing in time to the music. Brrup, ti, brrup, ti, brrup, brrup and so on right through the song.'

Ossie, their cook, a swarthy Geordie of about 30, had devised a special jerrycan cooker. His porridge, bangers, and powdered-egg omelettes and apple tarts were regarded with much favour. They saw a screaming whining plane over Bemmel. 'We could see the sleek silver belly of its fuselage. 'It got no bloody propeller an' it's arsehole's on fire,' was one inspired comment. It was not a V–1, not a V–2 but a brand new ME 262, the first operational jet plane in the world.

In their Pastorie (church) the Scots Fusiliers repaired the smashed organ with tape and chewing-gum. Ben Brenner, a peacetime cinema organist, played 'Bells Across the Meadow', 'Silent Night' and 'The First Noel'. At the Wintergardens, most big American films were shown, including Bing Crosby and Bob Hope in the 'Road' series. Laurence Olivier in *Henry V* was also very popular.

When Capt. Murray MC reported a party of 57 enemy passing through an orchard and the brigade stood to, he was afterwards nicknamed 'Heinz'. There were no beans and no enemy, but certainly 57 trees and possibly a goat or two. When the great thaw came, 20 dead Germans and 3 dead British soldiers were discovered buried deep under the snow.

Every night the Polar Bears listened on the radio to 'Mary of Arnhem', who had a nice cultured voice with a friendly approach. Radio Hilversum gave the war news as seen through German eyes, often mentioning British towns (pubs and dance halls) damaged by their V–1 and V–2 bombs. Instead of graffiti,

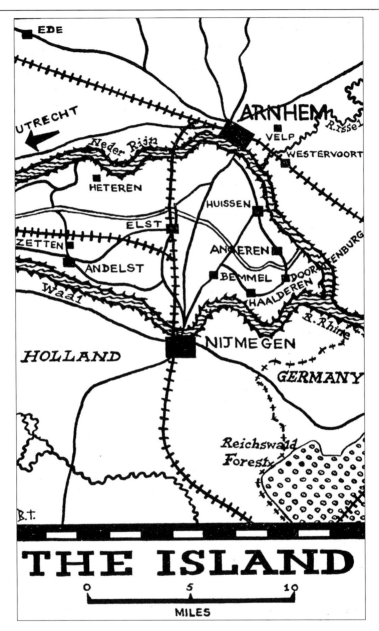

The Island. (Brian Thexton)

AT THE O.P. A VISITING BRASS HAT SAW A WALKING
GERMAN SOLDIER & ASKED IF WE COULD KILL HIM —
CALCULATIONS WERE MADE — BOMBS FIRED — & 60 SECONDS
RUNNING COMMENTARY OF THE SCENE & HIS MOVEMENTS
WAS RELAID OVER THE RADIO — THE FIRST 2 ROUNDS
MORTAR FIRE HIT HIM — THE SECOND KILLED HIM.

A SECTION SHOOT FROM A FARM YARD NORTH OF BEMMEL (AN INFANTRY BN HQ.) WE — 15 PL. —
WERE NOT WELCOME GUESTS BUT IT WAS THE ONLY LAND OUT OF WATER NEAR ENOUGH.

CAPT DICK THORNHILL WHO WAS AT THE O.P.

2nd Kensingtons in action on the Island. (Michael Bayley)

the Polar Bears produced crayon or charcoal posters. One was: 'The Island Follies – General Rawlins' Internationally famous Circus with its performing Polar Bears. Crocodiles, Alligators, Weasels, Buffaloes, Kangaroos and Capt. Saunt [whose patrol went in the bag] and his famous Tigers.'

On 19 March 'D' Company of the fusiliers in four assault landing craft staged a daring dawn river Waal assault, 1,200 yards behind the enemy lines. They caused 36 casualties and took 10 prisoners for the loss of 11 fusiliers. The OC, Maj. A.L. Rowell, was awarded the DSO for this naval exploit. Lucky Rex Flower got 'Blighty' leave on the 21st, drew back pay, leave pass, ration book and coupons, and via Osterwyk to Calais arrived home on the 23rd, the day the Anglo-Saxon armies dropped across and stormed the river Rhine.

The 2nd South Wales Borderers returned to Zetten on the 11th and found in the grounds of the castle – the floods having vanished – 'a satisfactory number of Boche corpses'. 'A' Company carried out a night raid on Randwijk and bottled up the defectors in the village church. Then, on the 25th, the battalion moved to the eastern sector at Bemmel.

The 4th Lincolns took a company of Belgian fusiliers under their wing, and on the 12th they were relieved by the Essex and moved to Oosterhout. Here a divisional cross-country run took place, which was won by Cpl. Barnett.

Soon plans were being made for the final irrevocable clearance of the Island.

CHAPTER THIRTY-NINE

April –
Operation Destroyer

The Taking of Arnhem – 'You Have Come Back'

The original plan was for the 147th Brigade to clear the south-east corner of the Island by breaking out of the bridgehead at Haalderen and clearing due east as far as the river. The 146th Brigade would continue the advance northwards through the 147th Brigade's bridgehead between Hevendorp and Oosterbeek. Finally the 56th Brigade would take Arnhem.

At 0600 hours on 2 April, the 7th Dukes set off to capture Haalderen under a huge barrage from five field regiments, four mediums, two heavy, two HAA and a mattress of 240 rockets, Crocodiles, flails, tanks and a call on the RAF. By 0825 hours all objectives had been taken. Lt. Lyons, with the leading platoon, winkled out 20 Boche in 'C' Company's attack down the Langestraat, although 'D' Company had been held up by well-defended houses. At 1000 hours the Royal Scots Fusiliers secured the flank and reached their objectives, despite cratered and mined roads. When later that day the Leicesters reached the Neder Rijn, Capt. Colin Kent, dressed in his astrakhan-trimmed jeep jacket and armed with a walking-stick, strode with complete confidence to the nearest house, knocked on the door – very polite the Leicesters were – and shouted *'Kommen sie hier'*. Out tumbled seven Germans, with their hands above their heads.

The KOYLI effected a bridgehead over the Wetering Canal and cleared Zand. A mile or so to the east the 4th Lincolns seized Angeren, led by Maj. C.E. Corben's 'A' Company, Maj. J.O. Flint's 'B' Company then pushed ahead 3 miles to Huissen, but they were attacked by the RAF on the way and suffered casualties. By 2140 hours, 'C' Company had taken Huissen and probed forward to the river Rhine.

Maj.-Gen. S.B. Rawlins, the new GOC, was pleased with the progress and sent complimentary messages. Maj.-Gen. G.H.A. McMillan left to take command of the 51st Highland Division when their commander, Maj.-Gen. T.G. Rennie, was killed in action at the River Rhine crossing battle.

Lt.-Col. Hart Dyke had left his Hallams in February for promotion on the Burma front and was succeeded by Michael Halford. At first light on the 3rd, the Hallams took Rijkers Waard and 'D' Company fought their way up the

A 2nd Kensington carrier on the Island. (Michael Bayley)

Autobahn as far as Kranenburg. Their supporting flails were held up by mud or mines but, undeterred, 'D' Company reached the Neder Rijn. Capt. Robinson was blown up by a Schu-mine, while Lt. Morris and six other men wounded by machine-gun fire. 'C' Company leap-frogged past 'A' Company, occupied Elden and took 23 prisoners. The enemy withdrew across the river at nightfall. Lt. Farmer led a patrol across the river, so the Hallams were the first Polar Bears to cross the river Seine, to cross the Dutch frontier and now to cross the Neder Rijn. The 4th Lincolns crossed the river Rhine near Loovier, and 'D' Company patrols penetrated as far as the river Ijssel and had a good view of Arnhem. By the 5th the whole of the Island was, at long last, in British hands. The Recce Regiment immediately went out on an exercise, 'to attain our old standard of the Clarkforce and Blerick battles' in readiness for some more geniune armoured car work across the river Rhine.

Operation Quick Anger

Although patrols had probed the outer defences across the river on the 3rd and 4th, the next major operation planned with the 1st Canadian Division was to take place on the eastern flank. The west was overlooked by commanding heights and the crossing would have been difficult and expensive in lives. The tower of the Saxen Weimar barracks had a particularly good view.

On 8 April it was decided that the attack would take place east of Arnhem near Westervoort, 24 hours after the landing of the Canadians

1/4th KOYLI advance on Arnhem. (Lt.-Col. G. Barker Harland MC)

near Wilp. 'C' Squadron of the Recce Regiment nipped across the river Rhine at Emmerick to look at the west bank of the Neder Rijn and the river Ijssel. The logistic problems were immense. Troops were on the move everywhere, and tanks, trucks, carriers and jeeps congested the centre lines.

The Polar Bears moved over a period of several days to the Westervoort area, via the Neder Rijn or via Emmerick. The KOYLI moved on the 10th to Zevenaar. The 56th Brigade were to make the night crossing on the 12th, with the Glosters leading to form a bridgehead over the river Ijssel with the 2nd South Wales Borderers and the 2nd Essex following up and advancing into Arnhem.

During the day, Typhoons flew violent raids on all of the German positions. The artillery barrage started at 2040 hours with a 2 hour Pepperpot programme. At 2240 hours on a cold, clear night, aided by searchlights, all four Gloster rifle companies set off. Unfortunately, Sod's Law was working overtime.

The sapper charges that were set to explode the 'bund' riverbank in front of 'A' Company and 'C' Company did not detonate. 'B' Company had trouble with their assault-craft engines. 'D' Company went ahead into violent opposition but took the 'Spit', which was their objective. In the centre, 'A' Company and 'C' Company manhandled three of their craft over the 'bund', crowded into them and sailed across to capture an old Dutch fort and a silk

2nd Battalion, the Essex Regiment, Arnhem, April 1945. (Harry Conn)

factory that the Germans had fortified. 'B' Company got over a bit late, but took their brickworks objective. Capt. R.V. Cartwright of 'A' Company captured 60 fully armed 'Master Race' cowering in the inner cells of Scheisprong Fort, almost single-handed. The Glosters suffered 32 casualties, but by 0300 hours the South Wales Borderers and the 2nd Essex had passed through according to plan. Lt. A.A. Vince of the 2nd Essex recalled:

> We raced westwards through the heart of the town, but on the high ground surrounding Arnhem, the Boche had masses of artillery and mortars, so little difficulty dropping his shells in the correct places. Captain Peter Butler died of his wounds, one of a number of casualties. We took 145 prisoners, the remainder fled westwards leaving incendiaries to fire the town. We saw the evidence of the tragedy of Sept 44, the broken guns and equipment, the little shallow slits the Airborne had dug in a few seconds and from which they had fought for days. We saw the little white crosses in corners of Dutch gardens, often with an inscription such as '31 Unknown British Soldiers'. On top of the cross would be a weather-stained Red Beret placed there by the Germans as a tribute to the cream of fighting men.

Pte. H. Fensome of the 13th Platoon 2nd Essex, a 19-year-old reinforcement, went into his first major attack well briefed by Sgt. Conn, his platoon sergeant – a veteran of D-Day. He remembered:

We crossed in Buffalo assault boats, landed in the factory area and came under heavy shelling from 88s, Rockets and mortar fire. Some of our section got caught in the open. When the barrage stopped Sgt. Conn and Corporal Frank Hudspeth went on a Recce and found Hoppy Hopton, Olly Oliver and Paddy McCulloch – all unharmed. We then moved into Arnhem clearing the area around the Railway Station and up a street near the Museum. We took eight prisoners in one building. Amongst them was a blonde woman who we thought was 'Mary of Arnhem', the radio broadcaster. They were taken away to the POW cage. During one advance Lt. Willis banged on the turret of a Sherman tank with his Sten gun, asking for covering fire. I observed Billy Bebber towing a toy brass cannon taken from the Museum, for a souvenir.

Later on, in Velp a young Dutch nurse invited the young 'Pompadours' into 'her' hospital to talk to the wounded civilians who wanted to meet their liberators. Fensome continued: 'We had a wonderful time. The nurses made a fuss of us, pictures were taken.'

However, 2 hours later the youngsters had to march 10 miles to catch up with the battalion for that misdemeanour. 'We got 8 days which meant on patrol every night and more than our share of guard duties!'

By nightfall the 2nd South Wales Borderers were firmly into the centre of the town, most of it badly shattered, and they claimed to be the first battalion into Arnhem. The following morning the sappers bridged the river with prefab. Bailey pontoons and the 146th Brigade passed through into Arnhem. Lt.-Col. Hart Dyke wrote:

Friday 13th was a most satisfactory day for the Hallams, with three objectives captured. Next morning the advance continued with 'A' Coy and tanks overcoming all opposition. In it Lt. Davies was killed and 12 ORs wounded. This brought our total losses up to 158 killed and 689 all ranks wounded or a little more than the total strength of the Bn when it arrived in Normandy eleven months before.

Maj. Godfrey Harland of the KOYLI recalled:

At first light with the aid of some Canadian tanks we attacked some German positions in the grounds of Sonsbeek hospital. It was to be our last company attack in NW Europe. The company was digging in, having taken the objective, when the customary German counter attack by shell and mortar fire arrived, landing on a section of the right hand platoon. Three were killed and two were wounded. Sad to lose those three splendid young soldiers, Geordie Alcock, M. Durham and F. Lees who had fought so many battles with the company only to lose their lives so late in the war.

The 4th Lincolns had an all-day battle to clear the huge ENKA factory occupied by the 346th Engineers Battalion and the 46th Festungs Machine-gun Battalion. Tanks, armoured bulldozers, AVRES and flame-throwers were needed. The place was so vast that more Germans kept appearing from all sides to replace those already killed. Eventually, 234 prisoners were rounded up and as many were killed in the fierce fighting. The Lincolns suffered 53 casualties, including Lt. Burns, Lt. Paulger and Lt. Hill. The 147th Brigade moved from the Island to join the rest of the division on the night of the 13th. The 7th Dukes passed through the South Wales Borderers towards the railway station. Lt.-Col. Hamilton, their colonel, wrote:

2nd Battalion, the Essex Regiment, Arnhem, April 1945. (Harry Conn)

Hugh Le Messurier appeared leading my 'rear' 'B' Coy as 'A' Coy's route had been blocked by the detonation of the enemy MG Bn ammunition truck. The Sappers started to clear a gap under the bridge for the rest of the Bn. Soon my party were lost in a maze of streets. The company commanders treated every new horror as a great joke. By dawn the bottleneck of roads, Arnhem station and the first high ground was ours. The next day – the 14th – the Dukes joined in a Brigade movement to secure all the high ground. The Boche reaction was confusing. He plastered our area unmercifully for half an hour killing brave CSM Fellows of 'A' Coy. At dusk a company of [German] infantry supported by three French Renault tanks tried to re-occupy the cross roads. Prisoners said they had no idea we were there. 'D' Coy made short work of the complete outfit. The following day – the 15th – Gerald Fancourt's 'C' Coy occupied Arnhem Zoo. Fancourt was soon on the air offering the Brigadier a live Polar Bear to replace the wooden one on his caravan!

The Leicesters had come down the river all the way from Nijmegen to Arnhem using the 36th LCAs of the 552nd Flotilla, got to the top of the Westervoortsedijt near the harbour and dug in near the Elisabeth Hospital in the western suburbs.

The civilian population of Arnhem had been evacuated in late September with the exception of policemen, firemen and the Landstorm Nederland of the 83rd (Dutch) 55th Regiment. The latter were dug in around the Schelmseweg–Kempenbergerweg crossroads and gave the Dukes some trouble.

The Canadians and Gen. Rawlins were keeping up maximum pressure. To the east, Bronbeck and then Velp were soon taken. On the night of 15/16 April, helped by Fife and Forfar flails, the 56th Brigade led again. The 2nd Essex attacked on the north side of Velp, taking 100 prisoners. The 2nd South Wales Borderers forced their way into the residential area. The Glosters captured the Meteor factory on the Yssel and took 50 prisoners. The Lincolns passed through towards De Steeg, and Rheden was reached by midday on the 16th.

The leading tanks and companies of the South Wales Borderers were amazed to be greeted in Velp by a delirious and overwhelming crowd of civilians, with

French-built German tanks, knocked out by 7th DOW 'D' Company outside Arnhem, April 1945.

CO 7th Battalion giving out orders to the representative of GOC 6th Parachute DOW Division, who surrendered to the Battalion.

Fred Hoseason, HQ Coy, 4th
Lincolns, 1945. (Fred Hoseason)

1st Battalion Leicesters preparing to sail down the Rhine for the attack on Arnhem. (Charles
Pell)

ONE OF 13 PL MORTARS.
SMOKE SCREEN COVERING VELP PUT UP BY
13 & 14 PL DURING THE CAPTURE OF ARNHEM.
MORTARS ACTUALLY RED HOT & ONLY MUZZEL SMOKING.

ONE OF 14 PL MORTARS
LEAN TO PIG STYES WHERE
SGT. ..... 'FOUND' A LONELY
PIG WHEN WE HAD PORK FOR LUNCH.

HON OP. IN HOUSE OR FAR BUND OF DYKE
300' OFF — WE MORTARED IT LATER.

R.A. O.P. SHOT UP IN FRONT
OR BARN THAT IS BURNING UP

PART OF THE 30, 3 TON
LORRY LOADS OF 4.2" MORTR
HE & SMOKE HIT BY 88 mm
& SET ON FIRE

2nd Kensingtons' mortars in action at Velp. (Michael Bayley)

swarms of excited children, all waving flags, throwing flowers and shouting 'good boy, Tommy'. It was truly an amazing and exhilarating experience, so great was the relief of the Dutch to be freed from their oppressors.

The left flank of the 146th Brigade was protected by the Recce Regiment. Maj. Gooch wrote in their history: 'We had a field day comparable with our best in France (operating from Terlet) taking 143 prisoners, killing many others and clearing the whole flank of the Division.' The Hallams and the KOYLI had advanced on Rozendaal, captured it with the Ontario Regiment Shermans and thundered on via Beekbergen, Zijpenberg and Postbank to De Steeg. The Hallams 'B' Company on tanks moved on to Dieren and Laag Soeren, where they linked up with other Canadian troops. By the end of 16 April, Operation Quick Anger was over, and Arnhem had been taken at a cost of 62 killed and 134 wounded. More than 1,600 Germans had been made prisoner and double that number had been put out of action.

Robert Dunnett, a journalist, visited Arnhem on the 17th. He wrote:

> I drove in from the south past powerful German forts and redoubts which had been shelled and bombed and burnt out by thousands of our rockets firing hundreds at a time. The town was a deserted, burning shell. Fires were blazing. Machine-guns chattered from the high ground north of the town. There were craters everywhere. White tapes through the minefields. A British soldier who'd lost a foot on a schu-mine. Two other soldiers being buried. Engineers making demolitions. Bulldozers shaking their heads in roaring anger. A Martian ant-hill – a bedlam of men at war. Tanks and Bren carriers dashing through to the next battle. All the noisy, clanking machines and paraphernalia of war.
> A lone Dutchman, the first civilian we had encountered, came slowly down a long street. He shook hands. 'You have come back,' he said quietly. Just that. The British had come back, as they always do.

Operation Dutch Cleanser

'Singing "Tipperary"'

The 147th Brigade now received orders to launch an attack on Ede, 10 miles north-west of Arnhem. The 146th Brigade, together with the South Wales Borderers and the 2nd Essex, had concentrated around Arnhem and the KOYLI remained in Rozendaal. Rex Flower recalled:

> Billeted with local schoolmaster and family. Four days clearing up jobs. Found a sanitorium, many of the patients had been killed or wounded. Found a mass grave, miserable and brooding. We did not dally. We moved to Wolfeze woods, scores and scores of Airborne gliders, some wrecked, most undamaged.

Ede was held by 300 Dutch SS troops of the 83rd SS Grenadier Regiment, part of the 34th SS Division. They were a motley unit of renegades, but their fighting spirit and fanticism had already been proven. On the afternoon of the 16th the Royal Scots Fusiliers led, together with tanks of the Canadian Calgary Regiment. Progress was slow due to defended German roadblocks with anti-tank guns. The following morning, under a thick smokescreen, the advance continued until halted by the Simon Stevin barracks defences. A heavy artillery bombardment of the barracks at midday also unfortunately caused damage to Ede town centre. Now Wasp flame-throwers of the Royal Scots Fusiliers set the barracks alight. 'B' Company and 'C' Company advanced on the railway station where they quenched their thirst, among an elated crowd in the *Stationsweg*.

Fusilier Ken West remembered: 'We were in the beautiful Veluwe district north of Arnhem. Thick woods of silver birch, oak and beech, a haven for wild life.' He had watched his leading platoon run shouting and screaming up the road and out of sight. On top of a very small hill the fusiliers were dancing around and singing 'I'm the King of the Castle' until Maj. Weir, Webley piston in hand, appeared. 'It's not a damned Sunday School outing – bloody fools,' he said.

Pte. Bob Day of the 1st Leicesters recalls:

> In woods outside the town of Arnhem which the retreating Germans shelled heavily as we marched in single file through the streets, our Coy was mistaken by other British troops for the enemy. There followed a rocket barrage, the ferocity of which defies description. When the shrieking and blasts of those devilish weapons came to a merciful end, a young officer's arm was left hanging from the shoulder by a shred. I gave the Bren gunner a gentle nudge (I was his

1/4th KOYLI mortar platoon, Velp, near Arnhem, 1945. (Rex Flower)

No. 1 Detachment mortars, 1/4th KOYLI, Velp, near Arnhem, 1945. (Rex Flower)

No. 2). He fell to one side limply. He was dead. A piece of shrapnel had penetrated his spine killing him instantly. When darkness came we buried him in the dell with a makeshift wooden cross.

On the 17th the 2nd Essex returned to Arnhem, embarked on LCAs and LCMs and sailed down the river to Renkum. Lt. A.A. Vince recalled:

We disembarked in this completely razed village and marched into Wageningen again without opposition. Here Lt.-Col. Butler DSO left us to return to command a Bn of his own Regiment. Lt.-Col. E.S. Scott MBE took command. Between our own positions and those of the enemy ran the floodable valley of the river Grebbe and once more the battle became static with extensive patrolling by both sides in which the enemy suffered far more heavily than we did.

Fusilier Ken West watched rocket-firing 'Tiffies' screaming down on the Ede barracks, and 'C' Squadron of the Recce Regiment pushed ahead in front of the 11th Royal Scots Fusiliers to Lunteren. West noted: 'Newspaper reporters and Canadian news-reel men were out in force to record the scenes for posterity. It was rather nice to be the centre of attention. Teenage girls ran to place garlands of laurel around our necks as we marched along singing the old Boer's trekking song which had become a favourite of ours.'

The Burgomaster assumed that the fusiliers were Canadians. West continued: 'We had to inform him that we were indeed British.' 'If you were English you would be singing "Tipperary".' 'So we sang "Tipperary" again and again and again.'

The Leicesters had advanced to Ede-South, following the railway line much of the way. On the large Ginkel Heath near Ede the 7th Dukes found

1/4 KOYLI enter Utrecht.
Maj. Godfrey Harland, OC 'A'
Company is helped by eight
children and a dog! (Lt.-Col.
G. Barker Harland MC)

1/4th KOYLI officers at De Steeg, north of Arnhem. Left to right: Maj. Harland (OC 'A' Company), Maj. Singleton ('C' Company), Maj. Barlow Poole (Bn 2i/c), Maj. Whitworth ('D' Company), Maj. Carter (FOO 69 Field Regt RA), Lt. Firth (Intelligence Officer). (L:t-Col G. Barker Harland MC)

much airborne equipment and parachutes from the September landings. Lt.-Col. Hamilton recalled:

> There was no respite. At 5 o'clock we followed the RSF out of Arnhem along the great autobahn leading west to Rotterdam: by mid-day Ede was captured and, mounted on tanks, 'C' Coy pushed south six miles to the Rhine, thus taking 56 Brigade's objective! Their Brigadier gave me a cool reception at Wageningen that night! The Boche had gone back five miles to the Grebbe line and our startling advance was halted while negotiations opened for the passage of food convoys through the Boche line for the starving people of NW Holland.

Operation Dutch Cleanser was a full-scale offensive by the Canadian Army to force a wedge from the Arnhem area to the Zeider Zee to cut off 120,000 German forces. On the evening of the 17th a halt was called. It was now decided that the 1st Canadian Corps would advance no further into north-west Holland in an effort to prevent the enemy flooding the whole countryside west of Utrecht. However, aspects of war continued. Rex Flower of the 1/4th KOYLI wrote on 21 April:

> Assault pioneer platoon lifting German Teller mines, hundreds of them – but their own Pioneer officer Lt. J.C. Crabree, driver Pte. J.W. Dean were both killed when their vehicle struck a mine. The last casualties of the war. A Truce arranged. Seyss Inquart the Nazi CO threatened if the advance continued he would open the sea dykes and flood the countryside. This threat was taken seriously by our Army Commander. No movement whatsoever during the day on pain of court-marshal. But 'A' Coy killed, wounded and captured part of a German patrol as they tried to get into the Coy position. The Germans broke the truce, we didn't. They had no chance.

On the 22nd the South Wales Borderers left to join the 53rd Welsh Division for the last fortnight of fighting in north-west Germany. It was a pleasant surprise for the 4th Lincolns at Wolfheze when their regimental band unexpectedly arrived from Lincoln and played at concerts and church parades. On the 26th the battalion marched to Lunteren, played in by the band as Brig. Gordon took the salute. Three days earlier the 1st Leicesters had their last bitter little battle at Renswoude where against German–Dutch SS troops Sgt. R.C. Evans and Pte. Trevor Williams earned immediate MMs for gallantry.

CHAPTER FORTY-ONE

Round-up

The Liberation of Utrecht and Amsterdam

For a week, food convoys poured through the Polar Bear lines, and through the still heavily armed German troops on the River Grebbe truce lines. Lt. Brian Lott of the 55th Anti-tank Regiment returned from leave to rejoin his unit at Ede. He recalled:

> We were involved in a 'humane' role helping to feed the Dutch who in the towns and particularly Amsterdam, were starving. I was given a platoon of trucks and we moved to Bilthoven. The trucks travelled to Utrecht each day where food was being flown in by the RAF. We distributed the food from Bilthoven. The people were very grateful. Once I took a motor cycle and rode into Amsterdam. It was incredibly quiet and a terrible smell of death hung over the city. I did not see any Germans. I think I may have liberated Amsterdam on my own!

On 3 May much activity was noticed in the small shattered town of Wageningen. The Kensingtons saw many staff cars in the square outside a small hotel and an imposing array of red tabs. There was a BBC mobile recording van there as well. Gen. von Blaskowitz, GOC of the German army in Holland, his face a grey mask of defeat, had just signed the unconditional surrender. The Lincolns noticed Lt.-Gen. Bedell Smith of SHAEF, Prince Bernhardt of Holland, the GOC of the 1st Canadian Corps and also, for the opposition, Seyss-Inquart.

Just 2 days later, Maj. S. Jacobson MC, second in command of the Recce Regiment, was sent to the HQ of an SS battalion beyond Utrecht to negotiate their surrender. He recalled:

> I went off in my jeep with Pte. Hall my driver, a Dutch Resistance interpreter (with a Sten) and a German SS officer as guide. It was a queer drive through an area not yet occupied by Allied troops. The villages seemed deserted except for armed German sentries. But as we drove through curtains were drawn aside, windows flung open, flags put out . . .. The SS Colonel and Adjutant had obviously just bathed, shaved and put on their best uniforms. I was in rather tired battle dress.

When the capitulation papers were signed, he continued:

> We were faced by an amazing sight. Piled high with flowers, the jeep was hemmed in on every side by men, women and children, all perfectly quiet. But when I came out with the bit of paper in my hand, something snapped. They cheered, laughed and cried. I made a speech. It was funny, exciting, deeply moving. The war was over.

On the evening of the 4th came news that all German troops in north-west Germany, Denmark and western Holland had surrendered unconditionally, to take effect from 0800 hours on the 5th. On the 6th, Maj.-Gen. Rawlins met the commander of the German 88th Corps to arrange the occupation of north-west Holland and the disarming and concentration of the enemy. All units took part that day in thanksgiving church parades, and there were double rum issues that night.

Lt.-Col. C.D. Hamilton of the 7th Dukes recalled:

> The plan was for the 49th Division to disarm the three divisions holding the Grebbe Line based on Hilversum and Utrecht, while the following day the Canadian 1st Division went on to the Hague and Rotterdam to put the coastal divisions behind the wire of their own defences. 'Our customers' were our old opponents of 4th December, the 6th German Parachute Division who had found us in the way when they tried to take the Nijmegen bridge.

A new brigade of division artillery was formed with most of their guns laagered behind the lines. They concentrated at Doorn to start supervising the notorious 34th Landsturn Nederland SS Division. The Kensingtons formed part of this 'new' brigade and rounded up, their historian wrote: 'the avowed Nazi SS and all foreign Fascist volunteers, notorious in occupied Holland for their brutality. We received a rapturous welcome by the inhabitants of Doorn when the SS officers were evicted from the best houses.' On 10 May the Kensingtons disarmed the 84th SS Regiment of 77 officers and 1,415 men from other ranks. Then 2 days later, Operation Pied Piper took place to comb the area for German deserters and Dutch Nazis, as a result of which 53 arrests were made.

On 7 May the Recce Regiment in Otterloo led the advance into western Holland. 'A' Squadron was directed on Utrecht, 'B' Squadron on Hilversum and Amsterdam and 'C' Squadron on Baarn and Amersfoort. The Germans fulfilled their surrender conditions with correctness. The only impediment was the civilians. The vehicles could only just get through the enthusiastic crowds.

'B' Squadron of the Recce Regiment were at Otterloo, and on the morning of the 7th two troops were detailed to proceed to Amsterdam: No. 1 troop (two heavy and two light recce cars) under Lt. George Bowman MC and No. 4 troop (six Bren gun carriers) under Lt. John Rafferty. Tpr. Percy Habershon was the gunner operator in a heavy armoured car commanded by Sgt. 'Dai' Davies, the driver of which was L/Cpl. Seagrove. Percy Habershon recalls:

> The route was via Hilversum and once we started moving through the villages the reception was tremendous. National flags and Orange banners were hanging from all the buildings. At one of the bridges on the outskirts of Amsterdam, we were met by a Dutch Resistance officer [Lt. Tony van Renterghem], the liaison officer of the local Resistance group. He led us through the suburbs into Dam Square in front of the Old Royal Palace. Several thousand people had turned out but eventually two Heavy Armoured Cars managed to get to the main doors of the palace where Lt. G. Bowman posted a notice regarding the surrender. The situation was becoming very volatile. There were fully armed German soldiers on the streets and Resistance fighters brandishing Sten guns were appearing. We then moved to a building some distance away at the side of a canal, the HQ of the German occupational forces. Lt. Bowman and Lt. Van Renterghem went inside. We were near a local hospital and a large crowd of nurses descended on us. Being twenty years old I lost interest in military matters

Left to right; Tpr. Lee, Tpr. Ken Kensley, Tpr. Percy Habershon, Lt. George Bowman MC, Tpr. Ken Pollard, L/Corporal Alf Seagrove, Corporal Bill Sheldon, Sgt. Fred Millam. (Percy Habershon)

until we were rescued from a fate worse than death by Lt. Bowman who told us we were to move to a RV outside the city. What a shame!

Leonard Marsland Gander, a journalist for the *Daily Telegraph*, was also there wearing a British uniform and red beret. He remembered:

The Dam Square was a wild sea of celebration within a ring of sullen, German troops. We clawed our way through with difficulty, dispensing cigarettes, more in demand then food. After we left, the scene erupted. Attempts were made to disarm a German officer. German marines in the De Groote Club fired into the crowd and at least 20 civilians were killed. Scattered fighting broke out until the Dutch Resistance leader arranged a truce. Our small troop was reinforced and a column of 10 armoured cars returned to the centre of Amsterdam.

It is clear that the Polar Bears liberated the city.
Lt. Tony Van Renterghem, a Resistance leader, said:

25,000 Dutch civilians had already died of hunger and thousands more were on the point of dying, particularly newborn babies and the very old. We were down to a diet of 330 calories a day, down from 1200 calories in the summer of 1944. Even the German army in Amsterdam was down to 1000 calories a day. The SS and Gestapo (unlike the *Wehrmacht* who were ready to surrender) still executed large numbers of the Resistance, Jews and hostages before the arrival of the Polar Bears. There was no electricity, gas, fuel of any kind. The sewage system had stopped pumping. There was no soap, no hot water. Meanwhile the Resistance was trying to feed 70,000 people who had gone 'underground' such as Jews in hiding, or like myself, people who had been condemned to death, but were hiding. They had to stock up food for some 10,000 Resistance fighters who were called up to fight a guerilla war as soon as the Allies were near enough, and ordered us to attack the Germans from the back. Even more important was the protection of dykes and canal locks which the

Tony Van Renterghem, Chief of Staff, South Amsterdam Resistance District, April 1945.

fanatical SS wanted to blow up to flood and destroy Holland. Three hundred bridges were down, not one single bus, streetcar, or electric train was left in Holland. I was chief of staff of the South Amsterdam Resistance District. My main task at liberation was to prevent any fighting in my district between the trigger-happy Resistance and die-hard German Army or SS, until a large enough Allied Force was present. On May 3rd the German Command finally allowed the Allied Air Force to drop food near the big cities, but collection and distribution without vehicles would take at least two weeks. Lt. Bowman, out of radio contact, was advised by the Resistance CO when the shooting in Dam Square started, to withdraw to the town outskirts. Back at the bridge he called in reinforcements and later Major H. Taite joined him there with the main force a little later. At City Hall Major Taite met the German CO Lt. Kolonel Schroeder, a 'good' German who had long co-operated with the Resistance. The main Canadian force arrived the next day, May 8th, to take over military control of Amsterdam.

At noon on the 7th the 4th Lincolns set off for Utrecht. Debussing on the outskirts of town, they marched in, headed by the regimental band amid scenes of indescribable enthusiasm. The vehicles almost disappeared under the numbers of people who swarmed over them. Those who were too ill or too weak from hunger to stand were wheeled out into the streets to join in the cheering and celebrations. Armed German troops looked on apathetically and were completely ignored by both Dutch and British. Battalion HQ was in the Hotel Terminus. In the evening a band concert played the Dutch National Anthem, 'Wilhelmus', followed by 'God Save the King'. The next day, a Sunday, a thanksgiving service was held and on the 9th the battalion moved to Maarssen, 6 miles away, to disarm the German

'A' Sqn, 49th Recce Regt, arriving in the Dam Square, Utrecht, 7 May 2945. (Monty Satchell)

Aspects of war in Holland. (Michael Bayley)

Assault troop, 'A' Sqn, 49th Recce Regt (BAOR). (Bob Faxon)

troops. The battalion pioneer officer, Lt. Daykin, arranged for the enemy working parties to blow up all dangerous ammunition.

Lt.-Col. C.D. Hamilton of the 7th Dukes recalled:

> The German Paras first passed completely equipped through our 'sausage machine'. They dumped personal small arms, binoculars and watches in one house with 'A' Coy, then passed on to the open fields where their larger weapons, steel helmets, anti-gas kit and all the other multitudinous impedimenta of the division was stacked. For two days roads were blocked by hundreds of horse-drawn carts, the platoon trucks of one of the crack German divisions. Afterwards the Germans marched into a large wood where we guarded them for a week as they made themselves fit for their long march back to prison camps in Northern Germany. I had one exhausting day inspecting every unit of two enemy brigade groups.

The 1/4th KOYLI left Ede at 1300 hours on the 7th. Rex Flower recorded:

> The whole Bn in troop carriers along the road to Utrecht, as we came to the outskirts, everyone was out. There were thousands lining the streets. The convoy had to slow down. The people were absolutely going mad! They were absolutely going mad! They were ecstatic! It was definitely our best welcome of all. First we had children jumping on the vehicles, then a few young ladies. (We were not complaining.) It was fiesta time in the staid city of Utrecht. Poor semi-starving children clustered round the cookhouse. Everyone gave up part of their meals; the cooks gave them all leftovers. Doug, Jim and I were plied with drinks all day.

The Hallams also 'fought' their way into Utrecht. The column was a splendid sight. Tulips bloomed in every rifle barrel, while hundreds of girls walked arm in arm with the allied soldiers as they eventually marched in triumph through the town. The 1st Leicesters moved to Hilversum, where they also started to disarm the *Wehrmacht*. There was a certain grim satisfaction in doing so, and a carnival atmosphere in the town every

The Polar Bear monument
on the Kade, Roosendaal,
Holland. (Bill Hudson)

49th Division memorial, Utrecht, Holland. (Bill Hudson)

evening. The 2nd Glosters were given the pleasant duty of disarming the 346th Infantry Division at Amersfort, 12 miles from Utrecht. As that division had opposed the 56th Sphinx Brigade in Normandy, throughout their advance to Stampersgat and again at Arnhem, the regimental historian ended by saying: 'It was altogether a very satisfactory arrangement!'

By 12 May, all German divisional troops were disarmed and concentrated. HQ, signals and administrative companies of the German 88th Corps were disarmed by the Recce Regiment on the 13/14th.

There were several victory services. One took place in Utrecht Cathedral on Sunday 13 May with the Burgomaster and Lt.-Gen. C. Foulkes CBE, DSO, GOC of the Canadian 1st Corps, present. However, the main victory parade took place in the Hague on the 21st before Queen Wilhelmina, Prince Bernhardt and Gen. Crerar. Each Polar Bear battalion produced 100–200 men under their RSM. They had a heavy infantry drill practice the day before. Lt.-Col. D.A.D. Eykin's orders to his 11th Royal Scots Fusiliers included:

Each company will provide ten men of not less than five feet ten inches in height. Decorated men will be given preference. Medals will be worn. Best battledress will be worn, boots will be highly polished. Brasses will be highly polished. Webbing, belts and gaiters will be blancoed. Caps T-O-S (Tam-o'-Shanters) will be worn.

Nothing Changes

During the parade, Fusilier Ken West remembered the faces he would not see again: 'the faces of Pottsy, Little Monty Montague, young Bill's and Lt. Wilson our first Canloan officer, Corporal Donaldson, Paddy Inglishby and his mate, Patterson three times wounded.'

Rex Flower of the 1/4th KOYLI recalled 'The Victory Parade took place in pouring rain – our best uniforms were soaking wet – a right washout in more ways than one! We said goodbye to our gallant Canadians in arms.'

Envoi

Lt.-Col. Hart Dyke DSO summarized the achievement of the allies:

The war in Europe was at an end. The training in Scotland and Suffolk; the tough days in Normandy; the breakthrough; the long weary months of patrols in floods and ice and snow on the Island; the sacrifice of the dead and the suffering of the wounded had received their just reward. The victory at Arnhem and the great reception at Utrecht were a fitting climax to such a campaign, not lightly won. What was more important, the liberation of Europe from the Nazi yoke had been completed.

In eleven months of tough unrelenting struggle, the Polar Bears suffered nearly 11,000 casualties, including 1,642 killed in action and 7,750 wounded. The 2nd Gloucesters lost 718, the 2nd Essex 804, the Hallamshires 847, the 11th Royal Scots Fusiliers 797 and the 1/4th Koyli 986. During the campaign the 7th Lincolns suffered 203 dead. In Normandy the 6th Duke of Wellingtons suffered 369 casualties and the Tyneside Scottish 101 dead.

Gen. 'Bubbles' Barker wrote: 'My fortune was to command the Polar Bears whose achievements were made possible by its great efficiency at all levels, its high morale and the marvellous team work . . .. It was a splendid fighting machine.'

It seems appropriate to end the story of the Polar Bears with a poem, 'Assembly Area', from Capt. Lewis Keeble MC of the 1/4th KOYLI, which was composed while he and his men were waiting in slit-trenches before moving to the start line for the attack on Tessel Wood:

> Across the pitted freshness of the dewy field
> The raucous cordite drifts disturbedly
> And hides the frantic-sweating gunners
> At their ugly play.
>
> The dawn is shuddering with rutting cries of hate
> And far above the black lace trees
> The slender moon hangs grey.
>
> I walk apart towards the shattered farm
> And look with clear and tender eyes across the past;
> The frost of autumn and the gas-warmed office smell.
> Far roses of a Summer dawn and Sussex bluebells' mist.

All that remained of 120 men of 1st Leicesters, 'A' Company, before being sent to Egypt, *c.* August 1945. (Charles Pell)

The barrage gasps and holds its
Fierce inferno blast, a moment's pause in which I hear
Across the fondling waves delight a song of city towers,
A faded wisp of melody which tells
Of fragrance and a fragile bridge of love
Made sturdy in a moment's charity and joy.

Then as the talons of the rising sun search
Lovingly towards the sea the fury breaks again;
The soldiers rise with deadened feet and plod across
The sprawling wheat.

Oh death, my friend, my ever-present brother of the dusk
Be kind and if this day you need my company
And draw me ever from the welcome of the sun
Be kind and leave remembrance within my mind.

Bibliography

Barclay, Brig. C.N., *History 6th and 7th Bns Duke of Wellington's Regiment*
Bowring, Maj. E.R.H., *History 143 (Kent Yeomanry) Field Regiment RA*
Brett, G.A., *History of South Wales Borderers*
Crook, Brig. Paul, *Came the Dawn*
Daniell, D.S., *Story of the Glosters*
Dyke, Brig. T. Hart, *Normandy to Arnhem: History of the Hallamshires*
Ellenberger, G.F., *History 1/4 Bn Kings Own Yorkshire Light Infantry*
Gates, L.C., and Griffin, I.A.A., *History 10th Foot: Lincolnshires Regt*
Gooch, Lt.-Col. Brian, *Loyal Suffolk Hussars: 55 Anti/Tank Regt RA*
Harland, Lt.-Col. Godfrey Barker, *Battlefield Tour*
Harland, Lt.-Col. Godfrey Barker, *War History of 1/4th Bn KOYLI*
Hughes, Lt.-Col. F.K., *Short History of 49th West Riding and Midland Infantry Division*
Jacobson, Maj. S., and Cannon, Maj. R.J., *History 2nd Bn Kensington (Princess Louise) Regt*
Kemp, Col. J.C., *History of Royal Scots Fusiliers*
Lindsay, T. Martin, *History of Sherwood Rangers Yeomanry*
Mercer, John, *Mike Target: 185 Field Regt RA*
Pell, Charles Raymond, *Tigers Never Sleep: 1st Leicester Regt*
Rissik, David, *10th and 11th Bn Durham Light Infantry History*
Underhill, Brig. W.E., *History of Royal Leicestershire Regt*
Vince, Capt. A.A., *The Pompadours, History 2nd Bn, The Essex Regt*
West, Kenneth, *An' it's Called a Tam-o'-Shanter: 11th Bn RSF*
Whitehead, Capt. A.P., *Harder than Hammers: History of Tyneside Scottish*
Willis, Leonard, *None Had Lances, History 24th Lancers*

Unpublished Journals, Letters and Notes

W. Ashby, 'Operation Martlet: battles of Fontenay and Rauray'
Barker, Lt.-Gen. Sir Evelyn, CB, DSO, MC, diary and correspondence
Conn, H.M., notes on 2nd Battalion Essex Regiment
Cowie, Gordon, Tyneside Scottish at Fontenay and Rauray
Day, R.H., notes on the 1st Battalion the Leicestershire Regiment
Dinnin, Maj. R.N., notes on the 10th Battalion the Durham Light Infantry

Elliott, Lt.-Col. G.G., campaign notes on the 2nd Battalion the Essex Regiment

Flower, Horace Rex, 'An Infantryman's Saga', 1/4th Battalion KOYLI

Hamilton, Lt.-Col. C.D., DSO, journal 7th Battalion DWR

Lappin, Capt. John, MC, campaign journal 7th Battalion DWR Regiment

Longfield, John R., journal 1/4th Battalion KOYLI

Lott, Brian, notes on the 55th Anti-tank Regiment RA

Marsden, George, notes on the 7th DWR campaigns

Newsum, Capt. R.A., notes on the 4th Lincolnshires

Nicholls, H.J., journal 89/The Buffs LAA Regiment

Oakley, Jack, diary 2nd (Princess Louise's) Kensingtons

Richardson, Maj. N.W., MC, journal 69th Field Regiment RA

Roe, Graham, notes on the Hallamshires' campaign

Sheldrake, R.D., 'The uphill road', 55 Anti-tank Regiment RA

Steer, Geoff, notes on the 1/4th Battalion of the KOYLI

Van Renterghem, A., notes on the Dutch Resistance movement: liberation Amsterdam

Wilkinson, George, notes on the 11th Battalion the Royal Scots Fusiliers

Appendix

Order of Battle

49th (West Riding) Infantry Division

September 1939 A First Line Territorial Army Infantry Division.

April   1940 On 5 April the Division ceased to function.

June   1940 Division reconstituted in the United Kingdom on 10 June.

26 April   1942 The Division again reconstituted in the United Kingdom as an Infantry Division.

GOC

3 September	1939	Maj.-Gen. P.J. Mackesey	
10 June	1940	Maj.-Gen. H.O. Curtis	
12 April	1943	Brig. N.P. Procter	(acting)
30 April	1943	Maj.-Gen. E.H. Barker	
30 November	1944	Maj.-Gen. G.H.A. MacMillan	
27 January	1945	Brig. R.H. Senior	(acting)
6 February	1945	Maj.-Gen. G.H.A. MacMillan	
24 March	1945	Brig. R.H. Senior	(acting)
28 March	1945	Maj.-Gen. S.B. Rawlins	
18 April	1945	Brig. E.N. Crosse	(acting)
27 Apriol	1945	Maj.-Gen. S.B. Rawlins	
23 August	1945	Brig. H. Wood	(acting)

Divisional Troops

RAC

49 Recce Regt   1.1.44–31.8.45

RE

Fd Coys

228	3.9.39–30.9.39
229	3.9.39–4.4.40
294	26.4.42–31.8.45
756	26.4.42–31.8.45
757	26.4.42–31.8.45

Fd Pk Coys

231	3.9.39–4.4.40
289	26.4.42–31.8.45

Br Pl

23	1.10.43–31.8.45

Sigs

49 Div	3.9.39–4.4.40
	10.6.40–23.6.40
	26.4.42–31.8.45

RA

Fd Regts

69	3.9.39–23.6.40
	9.9.42–31.8.45
70	3.9.39–8.6.40
71	3.9.39–8.6.40
79	8.6.40–23.6.40
80	8.6.40–23.6.40
143	26.4.42–31.8.45
178	15.5.42–28.12.42
185	24.12.42–29.11.44
74	30.11.44–31.8.45

Atk Regts

58	3.9.39–23.6.40
88	17.6.42–24.7.43
55	26.7.43–31.8.45

LAA Regts

118	7.5.42–12.8.42
89	29.12.42–31.8.45

Inf

MG Bn

2 Kensingtons	28.2.44–31.8.34

Recce

49 Regt	5.9.42–31.12.43

Sp Bn

2 Kensingtons	7.6.43–27.2.44

146th Infantry Brigade

September 1939 A First Line Territorial Army Infantry Brigade.

Commander

2 September	1939	Brig. C.G. Phillips	
12 April	1940	Lt.-Col. R.W. Newton	(acting)
17 April	1940	Brig. C.G. Phillips	
10 March	1941	Lt.-Col. C.G. Robins	(acting)
31 March	1941	Brig. N.P. Procter	
11 April	1943	Lt.-Col. R.L. de Brisay	(acting)
1 May	1943	Brig. N.P. Procter	
20 January	1944	Brig. A. Dunlop	
19 June	1944	Brig. J.F. Walker	
6 December	1944	Brig. D.S. Gordon	
25 July	1945	Lt.-Col. M.B. Jenkins	(acting)
3 August	1945	Brig. D.S. Gordon	

Units

4 Lincolns	3.9.39–19.8.42
	9.9.42–20.10.44
	31.10.44–31.8.45
1/4 KOYLI	3.9.39–31.8.45
Hallams	3.9.39–31.8.45

147th Infantry Brigade

September	1939	A First Line Territorial Army Infantry Brigade	
3 September	1939	Brig. L.D. Daly	
28 February	1940	Brig. G. Lammie	
26 May	1941	Lt.-Col. H.Mc.L. Morrison	(acting)
9 June	1941	Brig. K.a.T. McLennan	
3 December	1941	Lt.-Col. J.H.C. Lawlor	(acting)
27 December	1941	Brig. E.R. Mahony	
4 July	1944	Brig. H. Wood	
25 January	1945	Lt.-Col. F.W. Sanders	(acting)
7 February	1945	Brig. H. Wood	
19 July	1945	Lt.-Col. D.A.d. Eykyn	(acting)
12 August	1945	Lt.-Col. A.I. Novis	(acting)
19 August	1945	Brig. H. Wood	
23 August	1945	Lt.-Col. C.d. Hamilton	(acting)

Units

1/5 W Yorks	3.9.39–7.9.42
1/6 DWR	3.9.39–27.1.43
1/6 DWR	28.1.43–6.7.44
1/7 DWR	3.9.39–27.1.43
1/7 DWR	28.1.43–31.8.45
147 Inf Bde Atk Coy	20.3.40–1.8.41
11 RSF	8.9.42–31.8.45
1 Leicesters	6.7.44–31.8.45

70th Infantry Brigade

September	1939	A second Line Territorial Army Infantry Brigade, duplicate of 151st Infantry Brigade.
27 June	1940	Designated 70th Independent Infantry Brigade.
16 September	1940	Ceased to be an Independent Infantry Brigade
19 October	1944	Disbanded in NW Europe.

Commander

3 September	1939	Brig. P. Kirkup	
26 September	1941	Lt.-Col. C.D. Marley	(acting)
22 October	1941	Brig. P. Kirkup	
24 July	1942	Brig. P.P. King	
20 January	1944	Brig. E.C. Cooke-Collis	

Units

10 DLI	3.9.39–11.9.40
	25.10.40–19.12.41
	9.1.42–18.10.44
11 DLI	3.9.39–18.10.44
12 DLI	3.9.39–31.1.40
1 Tyne Scots	1.2.40–18.10.44

56th Infantry Brigade

15 Feburary   1944   Headquarters formed in the United Kingdom. (1)

Commanders

27 February	1944	Brig. E.C. Pepper	
4 July	1944	Brig. M.S. Ekin (killed 4.11.44)	
4 November	1944	Lt.-Col. M. Lewis	(acting)
9 November	1944	Brig. W.F.H. Kempster	
3 December	1944	Lt.-Col. T.H. Wilsey	(acting)
9 December	1944	Brig. W.F.H. Kempster	
20 January	1945	Lt.-Col. R.H.C. Bray	(acting)
23 January	1945	Brig. R.H. Senior	
27 January	1945	Lt.-Col. R.H.C. Bray	(acting)
6 February	1945	Brig. R.H. Senior	
14 August	1945	Brig. K.G. Exham	

Units

2 SWB	2.3.44–25.4.45
	14.6.45–31.8.45
2 Glosters	2.3.44–31.8.45
2 Essex	2.3.44–31.8.45
7 RWF	28.4.45–13.6.45

Index